THE COURTLY LOVE TRADITION

BERNARD O'DONOGHUE

Literature
in context

Manchester
University Press

BARNES & NOBLE BOOKS
TOTOWA, NEW JERSEY

First published 1982
by Manchester University Press
Oxford Road, Manchester M13 9PL

British Library Cataloguing in Publication Data

O'Donoghue, Bernard
    The courtly love tradition. – (Literature in
    context; 5)
    1. Courtly love in literature
    I. Title   II. Series
    809'.93354   PN682.C6

    ISBN 0–7190–0887–5
    ISBN 0–7190–0910–3 Pbk

Published in the USA 1982
by Barnes & Noble Books
81 Adams Drive
Totowa, New Jersey, 07512
ISBN 0–389–20347–5 (cased)
ISBN 0–389–20348–3 (paperback)

Photoset in Times by
Northern Phototypesetting Co., Bolton

Printed and bound in Great Britain by
Biddles Ltd, Guildford and King's Lynn

Contents

Latin literature

Poetry outside the main European tradition

The troubadours

The northern French tradition

The Minnesänger

The Stilnovisti

General editor's preface

One of the basic problems in reading literature is that of establishing a context for it. In the end the context of any work is infinite and unknowable. But if we approach the problem more simple-mindedly (and ignore questions posed by biography) we can say that a work's context is to a large extent definable by the ideas — theological, philosophical, political, and so on — current in the period in which it was written, and by the literary forms and genres that a period fosters and prefers. It is the ultimate aim of this series to try to help the student of English literature place works of all periods in their various contexts by providing volumes containing annotated selections of important background texts on the assumption that it is through contact with original texts only that true understanding may develop. Some of the volumes will be wide-ranging within a given period, containing a variety of texts (some in full, some extracts) illustrating dominant ideas and themes or forms; others will be more specialised, offering background material to the ideas and forms embodied in individual works of a particular author or concentrating on one or two thematic obsessions of a period. Although the emphasis is on English literature, much of the background material adduced will be of European origin. This will be presented in translation and, in appropriate cases (usually verse), the original will be printed with a translation on the facing page. The series should thus be of use to students pursuing comparative literature courses as well as interdisciplinary courses involving literature. In each volume there will be a substantial introduction, explanatory headnotes to the texts, and a bibliography of suggested further reading.

Douglas Brooks-Davies

Preface

The object of this book is to provide readers of English with a fairly broad sample of the love poetry that comes under the heading of courtly love, to provide a background for English works which drew on that tradition. Most of the texts come between the mid twelfth and mid thirteenth centuries, from the great period of courtly love writing and early enough to form a tradition of forms and ideas that the later medieval writers in English could draw on. Some earlier works that are thought to have influenced or to be related to the poetry of the main period are also represented. The purpose is to present those works as an end in themselves, as well as to enable readers to assess the conventionalism, originality or deliberateness in the use of courtly love elements by English writers: to judge, for instance, the significance of the inconclusive ending of *The Parlement of Fowles*, or the attitude to married love in *The Kingis Quair*, or the deliberateness of the courtly setting of the bedroom scenes in *Sir Gawain and the Green Knight*. The English work most often linked with courtly love writings is *Troilus and Criseyde*, as a glance at the Bibliography here shows. Chrétien, the troubadours and their schools can help towards an understanding of the situation of Chaucer's lovers. But the book is primarily aimed at widening the conception of courtly love which is often introduced in English criticism without any very precise outline of what it was. The poetry that illustrates it, in Latin, Provençal, French and German, has great virtues.

I am indebted to many people for help in preparing the book: to Keith Hanley, Roger Holdsworth, Nick Havely and Alan Hollinghurst for information and advice of various kinds, and to Alan Robinson for considerable help with German. I have received invaluable expert help from Peter Dronke, Malcolm Pasley, Olive Sayce, Ursula Dronke and Alan Press. I am very grateful to the librarians of the Bodleian and Taylorian Libraries, to Jasper Scovil, the Librarian of Magdalen College, and to Pauline Adams, the Librarian of Somerville, who gave me free range of Somerville's extensive collection of medieval books. John Banks of Manchester University Press helped me beyond the call of duty. Above all, I am indebted to my wife Heather for help with Norse, proof-reading and, in particular, for her share in divine activity in creating time for the work.

Magdalen College, Oxford   *Bernard O'Donoghue*

Introduction

1. THE USE OF THE TERM 'COURTLY LOVE'

The term 'courtly love' is not admired nowadays, and the justification for its use at all has been questioned, most famously by D. W. Robertson and E. Talbot Donaldson.[1] Such scepticism is understandable in view of the frequency and imprecision with which the phrase has been used, and of the way that discussion of this area of medieval literature has turned away from the poetry itself to concentrate entirely on its 'meaning' and heritage. In 1930, Cross and Nitze already refer to 'the quagmire of the irrelevant' in which the scholarly discussion of the troubadours is 'entangled'.[2] The intention of this anthology is to be guided by the spirit of Dronke's flourish in the last sentence of the first chapter of his admirable book, *Medieval Latin and the Rise of European Love-Lyric*: 'it is a garden in which roots can seldom be disentangled, and in which it is far more important to watch the growth of the flowers'.[3] The growth metaphor in these quotations (mixed in the first, sustained in the second) is significant of the concern with influences and origins of the students of courtly love. In this florilegium, theoretical considerations are subordinated, and the endeavour has been as much as possible to present in their own right the writings of the high period of medieval love literature, from 1100 to 1300 but concentrated in the quarter-centuries before and after 1200. This concentration is only qualified by the essential inclusion of some earlier Latin and Arabic texts, without which the view that this literature was absolutely original in the eleventh and twelfth centuries would have to be left unconsidered. There is no intention to add another theory about meaning or origins to the many, contradictory ones fully outlined in Boase's book[4] on the subject.

First, however, the justification for the use of the term 'courtly love' must be emphasised. The love poetry in this book does have important consistent features. If one looks at the lyric poetry being written in Provençal, Northern French and German at the end of the twelfth century, it is unquestionable that the three schools do have qualities in common. What is more, some of these definable qualities are shared with Italian poetry in the following century, and with poems in Latin and Norse, for instance. Many of the features of love as celebrated in these short poems are also paralleled in the weighty romances of the same period and have some relation to the theoretical discussion of love by the contemporary Andreas. Even if there is reason to question C. S. Lewis's placing of the absolute origin of the phenomenon in Languedoc at the end of the eleventh century (Lewis says that 'everyone knows' that it happened 'quite suddenly' then)[5] and to accept in general Dronke's argument that the covert and religious love of Lewis's definition can be found in all ages, that is not to say that this kind of love poetry was not more concentrated in that period than in most. Courtly love was the prevailing literary topic in this period. As a parallel one might say that the fact that marriage is mentioned in writings of all ages does not mean that it is not a more pronounced theme in the eighteenth- and nineteenth-century novel than in other literary periods. We must not lose sight of what is particular about these love poems, and it becomes immediately evident when they are read in any number. The ideas concerning love behind the poems of Bernart de Ventadorn and Heinrich von Morungen, and in Chrétien's *Lancelot*, for example, are the best material for an anatomy of courtly love. They are also the best context for a reading of medieval English love poetry.

A second qualifying and clarifying point must be made, about the relation between courtly love and 'love in general'. J. S. P. Tatlock, in a rather confused introduction to his assessment of 'the People in Chaucer's *Troilus*',[6] says that 'a fundamental modern error has been identifying the expressed romantic love with what is at present habitually called 'courtly love' ' (p. 88). He goes on to say that it is necessary to distinguish (though he is not going to do so) courtly love, 'a rather silly outgrowth', from 'the mid-medieval romantic love or any supra-sensual love' (p. 88). This is not a possible distinction, and it is not one that Dante would have understood, even if it were clear what exactly is meant by 'mid-medieval romantic love'. Any definition of courtly love will show it to be bound up with romantic and supra-sensual love, as is immediately obvious from a reading of the troubadours.

The explanation for this false distinction has already been given by Donaldson[7] and others. There are two very significant traditions of courtly love writings from the 1180s onwards, even if their similarities make them logically inextricable. On the one hand, there is the tradition from Ovid (though it is not his only manner), to Andreas, to one aspect of Jean de Meun's part of the *Roman de la Rose*, which is concerned, often in a humorous way, with procedure in love between the sexes. On the other there is the religion of love, perhaps verging on blasphemy in theory (at least according to Denomy)[8] but in practice often metamorphosing into love of God. This tradition which has elements of St Augustine's view of secular literature[9] and some Neoplatonism in it, is most clearly seen in the later twelfth-century troubadours and in the Italian writers of the *dolce stil nuovo*. (If the Stilnovisti are thought not to be poets of the troubadour school of love, it should be remembered that the phrase 'the new style', to refer to the crypto-religious poetry which developed from the troubadours, was invented by the Provençal troubadour Montanhagol.)

The distinction between these two traditions, from Andreas and from the troubadours, cannot be made by saying that the former is courtly love and the latter is not. Indeed, it would be less inaccurate to say that the courtly love of the troubadours is strictly, by definition, the second. But both schools – practical advice for lovers, and the anatomising of love – were active from the beginning.

2. HISTORY OF THE LITERATURE

An historical survey of the writings we are concerned with can conveniently begin at the turn of the eleventh–twelfth century, where Lewis places the origin of courtly love. One suspects that the explanation for Lewis's view is that this is the period when vernacular writings of a popular kind are first found in any volume. Elements of love literature of a similar kind are found in many cultures before that, as Dronke has abundantly demonstrated and as the classical Latin and Arabic texts included here suggest. One might, for example, adduce pieces of Old English literature such as 'Wulf and Eadwacer' or 'The Wife's Lament' as parallels to the love-longing from a distance with religious echoes which is often at the heart of the situation in courtly love. But in twelfth-century Provençal, we find in Guilhem IX poetry of a sophistication and sureness which implies an established tradition, and which is clearly related to the poets that follow. By the late twelfth century, courtly love poems are plentifully found in Provençal, Northern French, German and Latin, all emanating, it is usually thought, from a centre in the Midi. We can trace a series of influences; we know that Bernart de Ventadorn came from the south to the northern French court of Eleanor of Aquitaine, and we know too that the first Italian troubadours, such as Sordello, learnt the language of Provence in order to know and copy its literature.

Though we cannot always trace the lines of influence in detail, it is certain that the great courtly writings in lyric poetry and romance were widely spread by the last quarter of the twelfth century, not very much later than the first surviving Provençal sources. Speed of transmission is a striking feature of twelfth-century literature, and evidence of the keen energy with which literature was approached. The spread of Arthurian literature, an important impulse in the development of the courtly tradition, is a notable case in point. Geoffrey of Monmouth's *Historia Regum Britanniae* was finished about 1136 and used as the basis of his Anglo-Norman verse *Roman de Brut* by Wace in 1155 (and Wace himself was not the first translator of Geoffrey). By the end of the century Wace had been an influence on Chrétien's Arthurian writing and the source, in part, for Laȝamon's English version. The spread of the Tristan legend, which is at the centre of much courtly writing, lyric as well as romance, was even more dramatic. Although Gottfried von Strassburg's German *Tristan* is dated 1210, the version by Thomas is roughly contemporary with Chrétien's lost version (and with Bernart de Ventadorn and Raimbaut d'Aurenga who mention Tristan). Thomas's Anglo-Norman version is dated about 1160, but that is only one of Bédier's five types of the story. If there is a single archetype for them all, as Bédier suggests, this would place the legend back in the first half of the century, amongst the earliest troubadours. We do not know, of course, what the language of that ur-version was; if it was Northern French, then the courtly influences of Provençal and Northern French would be a mutual one. (It is believed that Dante, when he places Tristan in the Second Circle of *Inferno*, takes his knowledge of him not from the thirteenth-century Italian version of the legend but from one of the twelfth-century Northern French ones.) But, whatever the lines of influence in detail, the courtly tradition was active in several countries by the end of the century. As well as the romance-writers and troubadours mentioned above, the songs of Chrétien and Blondel come from this period, as do those of the first courtly *Minnesänger*.

Broad similarities of theme, terminology, form and situation can be traced in all these streams of twelfth-century lyric love poetry, as can be seen from the introductions to each of the sections of medieval poems in this book. The lover sings the song; he is the lady's inferior and her adoring votive; his love inspires and refines him; above all, he is totally possessed by love, and all he does is in response to it. In nearly all cases it seems that the poet is more concerned with his feelings and the form he gives to his expression of them than with the object of his love in herself. A terminology is evolved in each language, to translate precisely the expressions that are being copied. This language requires words for 'love-service', 'joy' and 'tale-bearer', and for kinds of poem: 'morning-poem', 'argument-poem' and 'elegy' for example. (The lack of corresponding terms in medieval English indicates that there was no tradition of this kind of poetry in English of the period.)[10] Many of the poems are concerned with the miseries of loving from afar and the resolution of them, a problem often related to the Crusades in that period (though paralleled in Arabic and Norse Skaldic poetry too). They are very often set within a religious framework; those with an explicit sexual dénouement are exceptional, although the earlier troubadour poems of *amars*, such as most of those of Guillaume IX, were more overtly sensual. In all languages the form of the poetry is of the first importance; often, as Valency says,[11] the fixed love-situation seems to be only a vehicle for the brilliance of the form which was the poem's real *raison d'être*.

The great love romances of the twelfth century are concerned with the same matters, spread over a wider canvas. Tristan is the classic figure, as his occurrence within lyrics as well as full-scale romances testifies. (Indeed De Rougemont has even suggested that the gloom of the lover and the death-imagery of the courtly love lyric are entirely attributable to the influence of the Tristan legend.) The many Tristan versions, and Chrétien's *Lancelot*, are central of the definition of courtly love, and it is clear that the same notions (possession by love, service in love, joy, secrecy and tale-bearers) are as important there as in the lyrics.

After 1200, the development of courtly love literature follows a similar pattern throughout Europe. It is a pattern into which Italian literature fits, even though it was well into the thirteenth century before Italian literature inspired by courtly traditions began to appear. After 1200 the courtly lyric developed in three different ways, to be seen in various degrees in Provençal, French and German. Firstly, some poets develop the form of the poetry and the abstraction of the ideas within it to a very high degree of refinement. This was already the case with the later twelfth-century troubadours, but the development is very marked in the later *Minnesänger* like Hartmann von Aue and even more so in the practitioners of the *meistergesang* where inspiration in content seems to have been entirely forgone in favour of concern with form and subtlety of expression. A second tradition concentrated on the religious terminology of courtly poetry which had been inherent in it since the early troubadours, particularly Marcabru. This tradition is much in evidence in later Provençal poets such as Montanhagol. Like the development towards over-formalism, this tendency was marked by loss of inspiration and vigour, except in Italy where, partly perhaps because the whole tradition was new but more because it was taken up by great writers, intellectual vigour informed a new school which was a combination of these two.

The third direction which lyric poetry took in the thirteenth century was a movement altogether opposite to these two, towards a naturalistic kind of poem, related often only by deliberate contrast to the courtly love lyric. This is most obvious in Neidhard and the German *dorfspoesie* but it is also evidenced in later French poetry. This tradition moves outside the courtly world altogether, but the importance of its connexion with it is obvious from the *Roman de la Rose* which is the clearest example of the development of a 'bourgeois' (to use the term favoured by many critics from Gaston Paris to Muscatine) love-poetry out of courtly love. The first of the two elements in the tradition of courtly love poetry mentioned above, that descended from Ovid and Andreas rather than the troubadours, was the principal influence here. But the split became very wide in the late thirteenth century, as we can be seen if we reflect on the difference between Jean de Meun's *La Vielle* (the Duenna) and Cavalcanti's contemporary poem 'Donna me prega'. Except in Italy, the bourgeois became the vigorous mainstream.

The first major figure in the thirteenth-century development was Guillaume de Lorris (his part of the *Roman de la Rose* dates from 1225–30). His writing is a mixture of the courtly spirit and the new, commonsensical, 'bourgeois' view of love. The sceptical spirit, which is more marked in the continuation of Jean de Meun and tends to be associated with his name, is already in evidence in Reason's speech in Guillaume 2971ff. Although this great work draws on many traditions (traced by E. Langlois in *Origines et Sources du Roman de la Rose*, Paris 1890), its principal inspiration was, as C. S. Lewis showed, the courtly love affair which it allegorised in detail. Lewis with brilliant insight says that it was the 'realistic account of imaginative passion' in Chrétien which interested Guillaume de Lorris (*The Allegory of Love*, p. 115). The situation on which the poem is founded is the approaching of a beloved by the suppliant poet of courtly love. Once again, the lady is hardly actualised at all; since she is described only as a desirable rosebud, she is less real even than the evanescent object of the troubadour's addresses. What is more, there is now little concentration on the poet's state of mind either. The personifications which present the argument (Reason, Largesse, Jealousy or, on the lady's side, Bel Acueil and Danger) are all part of a universalised, social drama. But this social drama uses the themes of courtly love in its framework: love-service, the God of Love attacking the heart of the poet, the lover's entire subjugation by love, the tale-bearer and the argument about procedure in love.

On all this, and even more on the second part of the poem, the concern about practical procedure in love-affairs evidenced by Andreas is a very significant influence. His *De Arte Honeste Amandi (The Art of Loving Honourably)*, thought to have been written in the 1180s at the court of Marie de Champagne, is a codification of procedure in love, prompted no doubt by the refined debates about how to plead in love by the troubadours, but bringing in as an authority and as a model for the book's structure the cool and sceptical works of Ovid, the *Ars Amatoria* and the *Remedia Amoris*. It is important to stress that the range of love emotion in Andreas is negligible, and that the troubadours and twelfth-century romance writers were vastly more passionate in their view of love. Besides, though Andreas was a major influence both on Guillaume de Lorris and, even more, on Jean de Meun, the continuator of the *Roman de la Rose* in 1275–80, he was not the only influence on later writers though he has tended to be the principal expositor for the modern critics of courtly love. The effect of the modern exaggeration of his influence has been to turn courtly love into the sterile, artificial code of procedures that medieval writers had to depart from before they could display any intensity or seriousness. Of course a code of procedure in love *is* given by the god of love in Guillaume de Lorris and it is alluded to by *La Vielle* in Jean de Meun. But it forms a very small part of the work of the two writers of the *Roman*. It could be argued too that the 'bourgeois' element in the *Roman de la Rose* was more a symptom of the stage that the development of the courtly tradition had reached than simply a new phenomenon in France. But what is indisputable is that the influence of Ovid and Andreas on the much-copied *Roman* meant that it was difficult afterwards for courtly poetry ever to concentrate without irony on the refinement of the courtly feeling.

For the influence of the *Roman de la Rose* on subsequent European literature was of course immense. It is the one work without which fourteenth-century literature cannot be understood, and the principal influence on the major popular literary form of the Middle Ages and Renaissance, the romance. It influences the form even of literary works which are not primarily concerned with courtly love, such as the *Divina Commedia* (in which, of course, the ideas of the later, rarefied courtly poetry are also very important) and *Piers Plowman* whose loosely-connected structure owes much to Jean de Meun. No major English work of secular literature, certainly, in the fourteenth and fifteenth centuries can be realistically considered without constant reference to it. There is a paradox in its purveying of courtly love ideas, however: on the one hand it changes their emphasis by giving much greater weight to the Ovidian, procedural side of the courtly tradition; on the other hand, because it *was* founded upon this tradition and because its influence was huge, courtly love ideas extended far wider than they otherwise might have done. If it had been left to the late, religious troubadours, the *meistergesang* or the *dorfspoesie*, the influence of courtly love would have been dead by 1250. Its influence was not always good: the vapid charm of the lyrics of the school of Machaut and Deschamps, and the often rather spiritless narrative of their *dits amoureux*, as well as the narrowness of the 'Flower and Leaf' dialectic, are constricted by the setting of the *Roman*; and the encyclopoedic wanderings of Jean de Meun (even if they are explained in terms of rhetoric, as by Gunn)[12] have to answer for some of the directionlessness of the vagarious learning of some of Chaucer (the *Hous of Fame*, in particular) and Gower, and of their fifteenth-century followers such as Lydgate and Hawes. But the flowering of literature in the late fourteenth century in England (Burrow's 'Ricardian Poetry') owes a great deal to the *Roman*, directly and indirectly. Indeed Burrow's insistence on the lack of an established literary tradition in the middle of the fourteenth century in England might be qualified in the light of the *Roman*'s very general influence.[13]

But, as far as courtly love according to its narrower definition is concerned, the tradition reaches the end of its active development in Jean de Meun. Some minor new departures can be seen, even in English in such works as Thomas Usk's *Testament of Love* (before 1388) or *The Kingis Quair* (1423);[14] but these works are long after the period of general courtly debate. Though it remains extremely important as an influence on romance and lyric poetry up to the sixteenth century, its last and most rarefied appearance as a dialectical code is in the stilnovisti, at the end of the thirteenth century. The corpus to be studied for its influence on late medieval English writers is complete by 1300.

3. 'THE BACKGROUND OF IDEAS'

In the course of the present century in particular, though to some extent in earlier criticism too, the significance of the ideas of courtly love literature has been said to extend far beyond its immediate, ostensible content of procedure in love, composition of love poetry and the morality of love. Perhaps because of the extraordinariness which Lewis ascribed to the emergence of the phenomenon ('Compared with this revolution the Renaissance is a mere ripple on the surface of literature')[15] and the apparent narrowness of its original provenance, very close attention has been paid to the social and ideological context that produced the troubadours. Much of the findings of this search has been incorporated into the 'meaning' of courtly love, as the answer to the obsessive critical question of the first half of this century, 'what is it about?'. To look for the precise meaning of a literary tradition might seem a strange pursuit, but strikingly exact answers to this question have often been found.

Most of these definitions have concentrated, at least to some extent, on the practices of the people amongst whom the troubadours emerged, the Albigensians of the Midi. The most remarkable case of this identification of a code of love with a religious view at first glance not identical with it was Denis de Rougemont's *Passion and Society*[16] which speaks of 'the myth of Courtly Love' (in the religious sense of 'myth', not to suggest, like Donaldson, that it did not exist) and its becoming 'a religion in the full sense of the word' (p. 130). The dualism of the Manichean beliefs of the Cathars regarding the physical side of humanity as insignificant, was said to account for the extreme rarefication of the sublimated love of the troubadours and their followers, and the status of the *perfecti* (the leaders of the Cathar sects who had transcended the limitations of the human in their religious development)[17] was cited to explain the psychology of the metamorphosis of secular love into divine. There is no doubt that it is useful and informative to examine the beliefs and customs of the society that produced the troubadours and their poetry. But the argument that the organisation of that society accounts for the theories of love propounded by the Provençal poets is not convincing because the poetry seems to be sufficiently explained by reference to other schools of love poetry (Ovid, the Arabs, the romances), without recourse to any historical factors other than the feudal relationship, universally prevailing in Europe, between master and servant which this poetry used as an abiding metaphor.

Without attempting to refer exhaustively to all the theories about the origins and psychology of courtly love, some other theories of religious parallel and influence should be mentioned. First, a good deal of attention has been given to the possible influence of the devotional theology of St Bernard, which Southern outlines as 'the Cistercian programme', with its emphasis on 'progress from carnal to spiritual love'.[18] No doubt there is some affinity between this kind of mystical theology and the semi-mystical love-making of the contemporary troubadours of the twelfth century; but Gilson argues on chronological grounds that it is more likely that courtly love influences Mariolatry and Bernardine devotion than the other way around.[19] This argument about the relative influences of the religious and the secular is of course a recurrent one in medieval literature, most familiar in English in the vexed taxonomy of the lyric. As Boase says, before mentioning the importance of *amor de lonh* in both areas, 'it would indeed be surprising if certain general analogies could not be found between religious and literary movements during this period' (p. 85). It can be added, moreover, that much of the psychological paralleling here is also evidenced in the Arabic *The Dove's Neck-Ring* (*c.* 1022), so no simple theory of influence, one way or the other, can have full authority.

One final, important view of courtly love from the vantage-point of contemporary religion must be noted: that it is a pseudo-religion of an explicitly anti-Christian, heretical kind. This view was substantially developed by A. J. Denomy in a series of learned, deeply-researched articles published mostly in *Medieval Studies* between 1944 and 1953, and presented in lucid summary in his book *The Heresy of Courtly Love* in 1947.[20] Denomy's argument, in brief, is that, whereas most of the traditional features of courtly love are to be found in the classics, medieval Latin and Arabic (description of nature in the opening; personification of love as a god; love as sickness; fear of loss of beloved, of unworthiness of her or of displeasing her; capriciousness of beloved; need of secrecy; the danger of talebearers, and so on), there are three new features in the love of the troubadours: first, the ennobling nature of human love; second, the elevation of the beloved to a position superior to the lover; third, love as ever-unsatisfied, ever-increasing desire. Denomy says these three characteristics can be found neither in any of the literatures mentioned nor in Albigensianism, but only in Arabic philosophy (not Arabic poetry). According to this theory, this noble view of love is heretical precisely because it has an idealistic basis. So the spiritual love of troubadours such as Marcabru, with its emphasis on the noble love *amors* by contrast with the ignoble *amars*, is just as heretical (and perhaps more dangerously so because it offers an alternative, conflicting ethic) as the false love of such troubadours as Guilhem IX.

All of these views of courtly love as some kind of surrogate religion are significant because they raise a question which is a recurrent issue in the criticism of medieval literature. Why does the secular use of religious elements in this literature (and the religious use of secular elements) avoid, for the most part, the charge of blasphemy? How can secular love literature share a terminology with writing in praise of the Mother of God? If courtly love was heretical, why does it influence so profoundly the language of religious as well as of secular literature for several centuries? (Condemnations of its more extreme manifestations, such as Tempier's proscription of Andreas in 1277, were surprisingly rare.) The answer must be that, in spite of the strictures against casting pearls before swine, the use of religious parallels and terminology was thought to elevate its context in secular literature without prejudice to its religious source. Besides, the earnestness (at least ostensible) of the pursuit of virtue in the courtly lover meant that his behaviour was not incompatible with Christian morality. A considerable number of the troubadours took religious orders at the end of their probation in self-perfecting love song. A virtuous love affair ought to be a figure of the love of man for God. Dante's elevation of the scene of the love action to make it identical with love of God is a new departure, a 'new life'; but a process of love that was primarily concerned with increasing the refinement and worthiness of the soul was not incompatible with the soul's search for God. The two could therefore share terminology, and it is not patently absurd to look at this code of love from the point of view of contemporary religion.

The various interpretations of courtly love in the light of its social, religious and political contexts are treated with immense thoroughness in Boase's *The Origin and Meaning of Courtly Love*. To a reading of courtly love texts as love literature, which remains their primary level and is the approach to them that this book hopes to facilitate, the intricacies of their origins is of secondary importance, interesting as it may be. There is a great deal of material of this secondary kind, as the bibliography here hints, and it has tended to stifle an awareness of the literature itself.

4. APPLICATION TO LATER MEDIEVAL LITERATURE

It is unquestionable when one looks at the history of courtly love writings that they have a major influence on the development of European literature, and this influence has never been doubted. But, returning to the opening paragraph of this introduction, the usefulness of an understanding of the assumptions and themes of this literature in reading medieval literature has been questioned. D. W. Robertson says that the concept of courtly love is a positive hindrance to reading.[21] Looking at courtly love from the point of view of religion only (the vantage point from which he always surveys medieval literature), Robertson argues that the great texts of courtly love, Andreas, Chrétien's *Lancelot* and the *Roman de la Rose*, are ironic and humorous. He claims that courtly love has reality only in nineteenth- and twentieth-century scholarship, and was not a 'code' in the Middle Ages. But his scepticism extends further; 'both the god of love and the 'gently nurtured' as they are alluded to by Professor Kittredge clearly belong to the realm of romantic and Victorian fiction, and have nothing to do with the Middle Ages' (p. 7). There is so much evidence that contraverts this in Arabic, the *Roman de la Rose*, the troubadours and elsewhere (the question precisely whether love is the proper preserve of the 'gently nurtured' is constantly debated, and the god of love makes many appearances in the medieval texts) that it is not easy to see quite what Robertson can mean. There are two further objections to Robertson's view: first, his sample is too limited and should surely, by any reckoning, at least consider the troubadours; second, there is a body of love literature which can conveniently be taken together with common conceptual elements in it. If it has been wrongly defined, then the definition should be corrected; but it does exist.

But many others have shared Robertson's doubts, if not always on the same grounds. Most of the sceptics (I have already mentioned

Tatlock) are unconvinced by Lewis's requirement of Adultery for the definition of this love. H. A. Kelly[22] is doubtful about the formulation of courtly love in general, and is particularly hostile to Lewis's specification of Adultery as an essential element. He is mostly concerned to deny the importance of this view of love in Chaucer, pointing out, for instance, that Andreas was unknown in England. It is clear that Chaucer's view of love was not formed by theoretical reading in the textbooks of courtly love, so direct knowledge of Andreas in England is hardly an issue. Chaucer encounters the phenomenon indirectly through French and Italian writers (most of whom were themselves, like Boccaccio, at one remove at least from the formulating of the twelfth- and thirteenth-century writers).

What appears at first to be the most formidable attack is Talbot Donaldson's 'The Myth of Courtly Love'. In the event, what Donaldson objects to is again Lewis's excessive reliance on Andreas, whom Lewis seems to read rather too seriously, and Lewis's emphasis on 'Adultery' as a definitive factor. Donaldson indeed expresses great enthusiasm for 'sublimation' as a feature of courtly love at the end of his article. No doubt he is right to call into question Adultery and Lewis's reliance on Andreas (although he is unjust to Andreas in failing to notice his declaration that the love he is writing about in *De Amore* is not married love which he says is different and not necessarity inferior, showing a recognition of the distinction between the two loves).[23] Donaldson's impatience with the too general use of 'courtly love' as a facile critical category, like Robertson's characterisation of it as a 'treasured academic platitude,' is sympathetic; after all, it is a similar starting point to Dronke's. But what Donaldson does not make clear when he treats courtly love as a myth is that, if the term were abolished, a large body of European literature from different countries and in different languages but with striking common features would be without a name.

Something must be said then, if the admissability of the term is claimed, about the usefulness of applying this conceptual knowledge, inferred from texts such as those in this book, in approaching subsequent medieval literature. Some cases of this application in English are readily to hand, regarding courtly love either as an influence or as an aid to the interpretation of texts. G. L. Brook, in the introduction to his edition of *The Harley Lyrics*,[24] shows how several of the features of courtly love poetry are to be found in them, adding that in general these features are held in common more with the Northern French practice than with the intellectualism of the troubadours. In fact the English lyrics, with their more pronounced and observant interest in the beloved lady, are dissimilar in substance to the courtly lyric although they do borrow some details. T. A. Kirby[25] in *Chaucer's Troilus: a Study in Courtly Love* offers a good brief history of courtly love literature (though he anticipates at the end the likely objection to the absence of discussion of the *Roman de la Rose*, the *Minnesang* and the *trouvère* lyric: p. 87) and then examines *Il Filostrato* and *Troilus and Criseyde* in the light of it. He agrees with C. S. Lewis[26] that the ending of Chaucer's poem is inevitable, being implicit throughout the poem in Chaucer's attitude to the artificial side of the courtly code (what Lewis calls 'the cynical Latin gallantries' of Boccaccio). It might be felt that Kirby keeps too closely to the letter of courtly love, and that he fails to bear in mind his own caveat: 'after all, there seems to be no good reason for trying to attribute everything to courtly love" (p. 93). Examples of studies that take courtly love as a given body of concepts in criticism of later literature (many of them as influential as W. G. Dodd's *Courtly Love in Chaucer and Gower*)[27] can easily be listed. They can all be read with more confidence if the poems on which this conceptual framework is based are kept in mind.

The influence of this literature on Medieval and Renaissance English literature is no less important for being purveyed indirectly through French and Italian. Boccaccio and Petrarch are better understood in the light of it; many of the ideas associated with Petrarchanism[28] are developed from it, and much of *Decameron* is pastiche of courtly love. Accordingly, the great body of literature that draws on these two writers is drawing on their sources. It is sensible to look at the woodenness of Troilus or Criseyde's circumspection as part of a courtly situation. But the influence is more pervasive than that; it affects, as Dronke shows,[29] the area which is usually divided off as 'popular'. For example, familiarity with the lyric tradition of the troubadours affects one's reading of an apparently ingenuous poem like 'Foweles in the frith'.[30] The contrast of the nature opening with the poet's love melancholy is not surprising, perhaps, and universal enough to make a consideration of its sources unnecessary. But it is the standard structure of the Provençal spring lyric, extending back to classical literature. It is not so much that courtly love influences everything that follows, as that it is the central poetic tradition of the Middle Ages. Echoes of it can be heard in all medieval poetry, learned and popular.

5. THE TEXTS INCLUDED

In selecting the texts for this anthology, the main concern has been to represent the principal texts in several languages in the high period of courtly love writing, from the first troubadours to the German poets of about 1220. The high period corresponds with surprising consistency to the German *Blütezeit*. It seemed inevitable to include some Ovid and Arabic as Background, and the *Roman de la Rose* as the most important later influence. The Stilnovisti are half a century later, but they represent the culmination of the tradition's refinement. In them and Jean de Meun the debate about love is still progressing. Other texts might well have been added, both as parallels to what is already here and as offering different aspects of love literature. Rather surprisingly, there are several Norse parallels (as Dronke points out): there are some striking 'amor de lonh' verses in *Eyrbyggja saga*, for example where Bjǫrn laments: 'Hlin of the sea's fire, who spreads woven material on to a wide bed, would not be happy about my situation if she knew that I was lying alone, frozen with the cold, in a stone cave',[31] hinting at a link between the poetry of courtly love and the elegiac tradition of Old English literature (this would not be too far-fetched, in the light of the tradition of medieval Latin). In the verses included in the saga of *Bjǫrn Hitdoelakappi*, the poet pauses to remark that he is composing good verse,[32] just as the Arabic poets do. The tenth-century Skaldic strophes of Kormakr and Hallfrethr, preserved in thirteenth-century sagas, have been noted by Dronke, who quotes Sveinsson's description of Kormakr as 'the forerunner of the southern troubadours'.[33] More could perhaps have been made of the traditions of love casuistry, perhaps by including some of the cases and pronouncements in Ermengaud (*c*. 1300).[34] But the range of themes and the extent of their provenance is well shown by Dronke. Here it seems better to present the high period in some depth, rather than to offer a smattering of six hundred years.

As a general rule I have given the short lyrics in parallel texts and longer extracts only in translation. At the price of consistency in the book's method, I have thought it necessary to sketch in the development of texts between the anthologised pieces. This interrupts the poetic excerpts, but it is essential if their meaning is to be brought out. The resulting, imperfect compromise seems the best way of presenting a wide range of texts, as well as some sense of the shape of particular works as a whole. The excerpts are numbered sequentially through the whole book; this too causes some inconsistency in method, in that I have headed each of the selected passages from *Amores, Ars Amatoria* and *The Dove's Neck-Ring* as separate items while including all the excerpts from *Lancelot*, for example, or Jean de Meun under a single heading. This is because each of the Arabic excerpts, for instance, has been chosen as representing a single *idea* which it is useful to be able to cross-refer to directly. Jean de Meun and *Lancelot* are represented more as total, argued poems.

For easy reference, the technical terms of courtly love, in the various languages, are explained in the glossary at the end of the book, in those cases where they are not explained at the point where they occur in the text.

6. TRANSLATIONS

The translations are new, except when their source is indicated. The intention has been to give a bare, literal translation for the shorter poems where the original is given too; in those cases the translation is meant to direct attention to, and explain, the original, and my versions have no claim to literary merit. They are simply aids to understanding, at the farthest possible remove from what Robert Lowell calls 'Imitations'. The numbers of the notes (which are at the end of each section) are given in the translations, not the originals, to be consistent with the texts which are only represented in translation.

NOTES

1   D. W. Robertson, 'The Concept of Courtly Love as an Impediment to the Understanding of Medieval Texts', in *The Meaning of Courtly Love* ed. F. X. Newman (University of New York Press 1968), pp. 1–18 and reprinted in his *Essays in Medieval Culture* (Princeton, NJ 1980). E. T. Donaldson, 'The Myth of Courtly Love', *Ventures: Magazine of the Yale Graduate School* v (1965); reprinted in *Speaking of Chaucer* (Athlone Press 1970), pp. 154–63.

2   T. P. Cross and W. A. Nitze, *Lancelot and Guenevere* (University of Chicago Press 1930, p. 91).

3   P. Dronke, *Medieval Latin and the Rise of European Love-Lyric* (Oxford University Press, 1965), I, p. 56.

4   Roger Boase, *The Origin and Meaning of Courtly Love: a critical study of European Scholarship* (Manchester University Press 1977).

5   *The Allegory of Love* (Oxford University Press 1936), p. 2.

6   *P.M.L.A.* 56 (1941), pp. 85–104.

7   *Speaking of Chaucer*, pp. 158–9.

8   A. J. Denomy, *The Heresy of Courtly Love* (New York 1947).

9   See, for example, 'St Augustine and Humanism' by J.-B. Reeves O.P. in *A Monument to St Augustine* (London 1930), particularly pp. 131ff.

10   The famous passage from the *Ancrene wisse* (*c.* 1230) containing the chivalric metaphor for the love of Christ for mankind uses a higher proportion of French vocabulary than is normal in that work. See edition of Ms. Corpus Christi College Cambridge 402 by J. R. R. Tolkien (E.E.T.S. 249, Oxford University Press 1962), pp. 198–9. French works here are *saluz, beaubelez, sucurs, deboneirte*.

11   M. Valency, *In Praise of Love* (New York 1958), p. 123.

12   A. M. F. Gunn, *The Mirror of Love: a Reinterpretation of 'The Romance of the Rose'* (Lubbock, Texas 1952), pp. 65ff, and *passim*.

13   J. A. Burrow, *Ricardian Poetry* (London 1971), pp. 2–4.

14   See *The Allegory of Love*, pp. 234–7, for Lewis's view that *The Kingis Quair* is 'the first modern book of love'.

15   *Op cit.*, p. 4.

16   Translation by M. Belgion (London 1940) of *L'Amour et L'Occident* (Paris 1939).

17   The social structures and beliefs of the Cathars have become more familiar since the publication of E. Le Roy Ladurie's *Montaillou* (Paris 1978; English trans. B. Bray, Scolar Press, London 1978).

18   R. W. Southern, *The Making of the Middle Ages* (Hutchinson, London 1953), pp. 219ff.

19   See *La Théologie Mystique de Saint Bernard* (Paris 1934), appendice IV 'Saint Bernard et L'Amour Courtois' (pp. 193–215), especially p. 215 where Gilson concludes that the two phenomena were independent, although St Bernard may have contributed to the decline

of *Amour Courtois* and Cistercian monasticism may have drawn on its terminology.

20   See items by Denomy in Bibliography here.

21   *Op cit.* in note 1 above.

22   *Love and Marriage in the Age of Chaucer* (Cornell University Press, New York 1975), pp. 36ff., etc.

23   See Book II, ix (*The Art of Courtly Love*, trans. of J. J. Parry, New York 1941, p. 171), included amongst excerpts from Andreas in Latin section here.

24   Manchester University Press 1956; pp. 8–14 in 4th edition, 1968.

25   Louisiana State University Press, N.T. 1940.

26   'What Chaucer really did to *Il Filostrato*' (*Essays and Studies* XVII, 1932, pp. 56–75).

27   Boston 1913. See too J. F. Kiteley, 'The *De Arte Honeste Amandi* of Andreas Capellanus and the concept of courtesy in Sir Gawain and the Green Knight' (*Anglia* 79 (1961), pp. 7–16).

28   Or 'Petrarchism'; cf Leonard Forster, *The Icy Fire: Five Studies in European Petrarchism* (Cambridge 1969), particularly first three Studies.

29   *Op. cit.*, vol. I, chapter 1, 'The Unity of Popular and Courtly Love-Lyric'.

30   See Carleton Brown, *English Lyrics of the XIIIth Century* (Oxford University Press 1932), No. 8, p. 14.

31   *Eyrbyggja saga*, verse 29, chapter 40.

32   *Bjarnar saga Hitdoelakappa*, the first verse of the saga, in chapter 4.

33   Dronke, *op. cit.*, p. 40

34   Matfré Ermengaud (*c.* 1250–1322), *Le Breviari d'Amor*. Ed. G. Azais (Béziers 1802), 2 vols.

Latin literature

The writers in this section are united principally by their use of the Latin language, since they are obviously far removed from each other in period and literary tradition. The Latin poets of the *Carmina Burana* and from other medieval manuscripts are broadly (and in some cases closely) contemporary with the other writings in this book, as well as having many forms and conventional ideas in common with them. Andreas is contemporary with Chrétien and the troubadours, and not accidentally so; indeed since much of his book *De Arte Honeste Amandi* is a handbook of procedure in love, prompted by the love-situation in the courtly lyrics, it might seem more natural to include him in the French section. But he is profoundly different from the troubadours and Chrétien in the spirit and form of what he writes. He is connected with Ovid not only by the language he writes in, but also in his capacity as a sardonic theoretician of love.

So this section could be subdivided into the Latin lyrics, on the one hand, and Ovid and Andreas, 1200 years apart though they are, on the other. Ovid is included for two reasons: first, he influenced Andreas and Jean de Meun, and is traditionally regarded as the inspiration for the aspects of courtly love which are concerned with practical procedure in lovemaking; second, he stands in the same relation to the pre-decadent Latin elegists, Tibullus and Propertius, as Andreas does to the love poetry of the troubadours. In the same way that a rhetorician deduces from literary practice the devices that can be used to emotional effect, so Ovid outlines the prayers and declarations that have been used to good effect in love and love poetry. It was this derivativeness in him that led Postgate and other nineteenth-century commentators to deny Ovid 'any of the qualities of the poet',[1] although this judgement would not, of course, command assent nowadays. Ovid, then, as well as being an influence, provides an enlightening parallel for the twelfth century. One might argue that, just as he would not be taken as a typical Latin elegist, Andreas (who was not a poet even in form) should not be cited as the principal exemplar of courtly love poetry. But that is precisely what has happened in much courtly love criticism, particularly since C. S. Lewis.

That is why Tibullus and Propertius are briefly represented here, although they have no direct influence on the Middle Ages (the pre-Ovidian elegists were a rediscovery of Petrarch and the Renaissance) and they do not bear a striking resemblance in form or conventional idiom to the twelfth-century poets. But without them it is not possible to get into perspective the ironies of the *Ars Amatoria* and the *Remedia Amoris*, with their references respectively to Propertius's falling in love with Cynthia, and his attempts to get over his love for her which were so liable to relapse. That perspective, in turn, is enlightening for the relationship of Andreas to the lyric poets. The passion of Propertius's poems to Cynthia and of his Arethusa poems in Book 4 of the *Carmina*, like the earnest intimacy of Tibullus's Delia poems, prompt the calculating humour of Ovid in the same way that Chrétien's *Lancelot* and the troubadours' heart-searching suggest the casuistic handbook of Andreas for the entertainment of the court of Marie de Champagne.

This important point is hinted at by J. P. Sullivan in his *Propertius* (Cambridge University Press 1976). He says 'when the troubadours 'misunderstood Ovid' (referring to *The Allegory of Love*, p. 7) they were returning to the sentiments and attitudes of the earlier Roman love poets' (p.88). He concludes that 'we must be wary of approaching Roman love elegy backwards through Ovid' (p. 90); we must similarly be wary of approaching courtly love poetry 'backwards' through Andreas, rather than through the lyric poetry itself. Even if Andreas has his *raison d'être* in that poetry, the poetry is not at all fully represented by him. This argument is important as a corrective to Lewis's view that 'the courtly tradition' recommended seriously what was ironic in Ovid (Lewis does not, in fact, say that the troubadours themselves misunderstood Ovid); only Andreas recommends it, and he does so in the same spirit of irony.

Ovid and Andreas, then, as theoreticians only and not practitioners of love, are in a different category from the other poetry in this book. (Not that a theory of love was not of immense moment to the poets from the first troubadours to the Stilnovisti; but invariably the theorist poet was also an exponent of love, at least ostensibly.) But the medieval Latin Lyrics included here are quite central to the courtly tradition. Helen Waddell, even if her translations seem rather distant from the spirit of the originals, performed an enormous service to English readers in bringing these lyrics to general attention in a popular form in *The Wandering Scholars* (London 1927) and *Mediaeval Latin Lyrics* (London 1929). The service of Peter Dronke, in showing these poems to belong fully to the mainstream of living European poetry, is hardly less. Helen Waddell, in her note to '*Levis Exsurgit Zephyrus*" (*Mediaeval Latin Lyrics*, p. 333), make a comparison with the *Minnesang*; Dronke, commenting on the Regensburg poems, shows them to have a terminology parallel to the Provençal: *virtus* for *virtu*; *probitas* for *valensa, proeza; garruli* for *lauzenjadors (losengeours).*[2] The tendency to regard medieval Latin literature as scholastic and cloistered, removed from the 'popular' and the everyday, has declined, but it still seems to be regarded as a special case, in isolation from vernacular literature. These poems are polished and literary, certainly, and it is perhaps their strict form that makes them continue to be regarded as foreign to the vernacular. But nothing could be formally more strict than the troubadour songs, and these Latin poems often have a universal appeal and availability far greater than the difficult, intellectualising poems of the troubadours.

Other similarities, further to those from Waddell and Dronke mentioned in the last paragraph, can be noted. Most striking is the contemporaneity with the great period of the courtly lyric of the most famous manuscript, the Benedictbeuern Carmina Burana. Helen

Waddell dates various poems in this manuscript 1177, 1187 and 1189,[3] observing that the handwriting of the manuscript is thirteenth-century, but its contents place it in the twelfth and early thirteenth centuries. The forms shared with the Provençal and later European lyrics stamp them as poems of the same genre. The *alba* (Waddell p. 138: XXIII here) with its watchman; the repeated contrasts between the joy of spring and the lover's gloom; the madness of the lover ('the ox behind the plough' in Waddell p. 228, line 12 (XXVI here) reminds us of Arnaut Daniel's hunting the hare on oxback in LII here); and the divinity of love appealed to for mercy ('Help me!', Waddell pp. 246–8: XXVIII here): all are familiar as the staples of courtly poetry. Indeed the early date of this tenth-century *alba* (the structure and theme of which are very reminiscent of the great medieval aubades such as LXXXII here, Wolfram's '*Sine klawen*', even if the poem is not explicitly linked with love) tempts one to suggest these Latin poems as an important influence on the writers of the courtly lyric. It has traditionally been argued that the Latin Lyric could not have influenced the courtly tradition because the troubadours were not learned enough to know Latin literature and all courtly love writings descended from them. But this objection disappears if we accept Dronke's view that the ideas of courtly love literature are, to some extent at least, perennial. The troubadours, the writers of Latin Lyric and perhaps the northern French poets too are all writing in an established tradition of love-poetry. It should not be thought surprising, especially since Curtius's *European Literature and the Latin Middle Ages*,[4] that a major influence on the love writings of the Middle Ages in Provence and elsewhere was the great body of Latin literature from the classical period to the time of those writings.

TIBULLUS
(*c*. 43–18 B.C.)

I

Pace tua pereant arcus pereantque sagittae,   105
   Phoebe, modo in terris erret inermis Amor,
Ars bona: sed postquam sumpsit sibi tela Cupido,
   Heu heu quam multis ars dedit ista malum!
Et mihi praecipue. Iaceo cum saucius annum,
   Et faveo morbo, cum iuvat ipse dolor,   110
Usque cano Nemesim, sine qua versus mihi nullus
   Verba potest iustos aut reperire pedes. . . .

                    (II, 5, 105–12)[5]

II

Castra Macer sequitur: tenero quid fiet Amori?
   Sit comes et collo fortiter arma gerat?
Et seu longa virum terrae via seu vaga ducent
   Aequora, cum telis ad latus ire volet?
Ure, puer, quaeso, tua qui ferus otia liquit,   5
   Atque iterum erronem sub tua signa voca.
Quod si militibus parces, erit hic quoque miles,
   Ipse levem galea qui sibi portet aquam.
Castra peto, valeatque Venus valeantque puellae:
   Et mihi sunt vires, et mihi facta tuba est.   10
Magna loquor, sed magnifice mihi magna locuto
   Excutiunt clausae fortia verba fores.
Iuravi quotiens rediturum ad limina numquam!
   Cum bene iuravi, pes tamen ipse redit.
Acer Amor, fractas utinam tua tela sagittas,   15
   Si licet, extinctas aspiciamque faces!
Tu miserum torques, tu me mihi dira precari
   Cogis, et insana mente nefanda loqui.

                    (II, 6, 1–18)

I

O Phoebus, by your leave, let bows and arrows perish if only love can wander through the lands unarmed. Art is good; but after Cupid took arms for himself, alas, to how many people has this art brought evil. To me in particular: since I have lain stricken for a year and encourage my indisposition – indeed the pain is pleasing. All the time I sing of my Nemesis, without which no verse of mine can find again words or right rhythm.

II

Macer[6] goes to war; what will happen to tender love? Will he be a comrade and bear arms bravely at his neck? Whether lands or wandering oceans lead the hero on his long way, will he want to go at his side in arms? Burn,[7] boy, I beseech you, the untamed man who leaves your leisured life and summon again the deserter to your standard. But if you are kind to soldiers, I[8] too will be a soldier and carry in my helmet quick-running water for me. I am off to war; farewell, Venus and girls. I too have strength, and the trumpet is sounded for me too. I say great things, but the doors bolted behind me banish my great, brave words of glorious speech. How often I have sworn that I would never return to her threshold. When I have sworn well, yet the foot makes its own way back.[9] Cruel love, let me see, if it is allowed, your weapons, your arrows broken, your torches quenched. You rack me in my misery; you make me pray for awful things on myself and speak impiously from a deranged mind.

PROPERTIUS
(died *c*. 15 B.C.)

III

Sic mihi te referas levis, ut non altera nostro
    Limine formosos intulit ulla pedes.
Quamvis multa tibi dolor hic meus aspera debet,
    Non ita saeva tamen venerit ira mea,
Ut tibi sim merito semper furor, et tua flendo   15
    Lumina deiectis turpia sint lacrimis.
An tua quod peperit nobis iniuria curas,
    Quae solum tacitis cognita sunt foribus?
Omnia consuevi timidus perferre superbae   25
    Iussa, neque arguto fata dolore queri,
Pro quo divini fontes et frigida rupes
    Et datur inculto tramite dura quies;
Et quodcumque meae possunt narrare querelae,
    Cogor ad argutas dicere solus aves.   30
Sed qualiscumque es, resonent mihi 'Cynthia' silvae,
    Nec deserta tuo nomine saxa vacent.

        (I, 18, 11–16 and 23–32)

IV

Non ego nunc tristes vereor, mea Cynthia, Manes,
    Nec moror extremo debita fata rogo:
Sed ne forte tuo careat mihi funus amore,
    Hic timor est ipsis durior exequiis.
Non adeo leviter nostris puer haesit ocellis,   5
    Ut meus oblito pulvis amore vacet.

        (I, 19, 1–6)

III

That you might bring yourself back to me, mercurial girl! I swear that no other woman has brought her beautiful feet over my threshold. Although this sorrow of mine owes you many harsh turns, yet my anger will not become so fierce that I should be to you always, as you deserve, a fury and your eyes become ugly by weeping with tears poured down . . .

Or is it the case that your injury towards me has given birth to miseries which are known only to silent doorways? I have grown used to bearing all the orders of this proud one tamely and to not complaining in piercing sorrow: in return for which I am given inhuman springs and the cold rock and hard rest on an untrodden bypath.[10] And whatever my complaints can tell, I must tell it alone to the clear-toned birds. But, whatever you are like, the woods will re-echo 'Cynthia' to me, and the deserted rocks will not be empty of your name.

IV

I do not fear now the sad shadows, my Cynthia, nor do I delay the debt to fate at the final funeral-pyre. But the fear lest perhaps my death should not be attended by your love: this is harder than the funeral itself. Not so lightly has the boy[11] pierced my eyes that my dust should lie alone, love forgotten.

V

Quandocumque igitur nostros mors claudet ocellos,
  Accipe quae serves funeris acta mei.
Nec mea tunc longa spatietur imagine pompa,
  Nec tuba sit fati vana querella mei,   20
Nec mihi tunc fulcro sternatur lectus eburno,
  Nec sit in Attalico mors mea nixa toro;
Desit odoriferis ordo mihi lancibus; adsint
  Plebei parvae funeris exequiae.
Sat mea sat magna est si tres sint pompa libelli,   25
  Quos ego Persephonae maxima dona feram.
Tu vero nudum pectus lacerata sequeris,
  Nec fueris nomen lassa vocare meum,
Osculaque in gelidis pones suprema labellis,
  Cum dabitur Syrio munere plenus onyx.   30
Deinde, ubi suppositus cinerem me fecerit ardor,
  Accipiat manes parvula testa meos,
Et sit in exiguo laurus superaddita busto,
  Quae tegat extincti funeris umbra locum.
Et duo sint versus: 'Qui nunc iacet horrida pulvis,   35
  Unius hic quondam servus amoris erat.'
Nec minus haec nostri notescret fama sepulcri,
  Quam fuerant Phthii busta cruenta viri.

(II, 13, 17–38)

V

Whenever, then, death will close my eyes, listen to what procedure you must follow at my funeral. Let my cortege not then stretch out in a long display, nor a trumpet be the empty complainer of my fate, nor a bier then be spread for me on an ivory base, nor my body be rested on a cushion of Attalus.[12] May the row of incensed dishes be absent, and only the small funeral rites of a common man be there. It is enough for me if there are three[13] books as a display, which I will bear as the greatest gift to Persephone. But you, all tortured, will follow with bare breast, nor will you be weary of calling my name, and you will place on my cold lips the last kisses when the onyx casket full of the gift of Syria[14] will be given. Then, when the glow placed below will make me ashes, let a poor jar receive my remains, and let a bay-tree be placed over my poor burial-plot as a shade to cover the place of my dead body. And let there be two verses: 'He who now lies as loathsome dust was once the servant of love alone'. No less will this reputation of my grave become known than the bloody tombs of the hero of Phthia.

OVID
(43 B.C. – A.D. 17)
From *Ars Amatoria*

Ars Amatoria is divided into three books: the first advises men on how to choose and win a lady; the second gives advice on how to keep her; and the third (which is much drawn upon by Jean de Meun's *Vieille* and her followers, including the Wife of Bath) advises women on how to win the love of men. The whole work is concerned with social procedure in love, described in a lightly cynical spirit.

At the opening of Book I the poet offers his credentials as a 'magister amoris', a teacher of love. He then tells his novice lover to frequent places where women of nubile inclination are to be found: law-courts, horse-races, the theatre, banquets. Turning to the process of winning the selected lady, he stresses the importance of getting to know her handmaid.

VI

But first let it be your concern to get to know the handmaid[15] of the lady who is to be won; she will facilitate your approaches. Make sure that she is the one nearest to the deliberations of the lady and an entirely trustworthy confidante in your secret games. Break her loyalty with promises and by entreating. You will easily gain what you wish if she is willing. Let her choose a time (just as doctors too keep to times) at which her mistress' mood is relaxed and ready for the taking. Her mood will be ready for winning when as the most joyful of creatures she feels voluptuous, like the corn in rich earth. When hearts are joyful and not pinched by sorrow they lie open; then Venus creeps in with her insinuating art. When Troy was gloomy it was defended by its warriors; while celebrating it let in the horse weighed down with soldiers. Also, she should be attempted when she grieves, injured by a rival mistress. Then you will do your work, and she will not be unavenged. Let the maid as she combs her hair in the morning urge her on, and add to the sail the force of an oarsman. And let her say, sighing to herself with a little murmur, 'But I do not suppose that you could pay him back yourself'.[16] Then let her talk about you, adding persuasive words, and swear that you are dying out of insane love. But hurry, lest the sails fall and the breezes sink away. Anger dies by delay like thin ice. You ask whether it is a good thing to violate the helper herself? There is great risk in such deeds. One woman is made alert by sex, another is made slower. One prepares you as a gift for her lady, another for herself. The proof of the gamble lies in the outcome; even if a particular case favours the attempt, my advice is nevertheless to leave it untouched. I am not going to travel dangerously and on jagged peaks, and none of the youths under my leadership will be captured. Yet if, while she gives and receives your letters, she pleases you not only by her assiduousness but by her body too, make sure you have the lady first, and let the other follow as a companion. Your intercourse should not be begun by the servant. I urge this alone, if you just trust my skill and the greedy wind does not sweep my words out to sea: either do not attempt the enterprise or complete it successfully. The accusatory finger disappears as soon as she herself becomes a party to the crime. It is no use having the bird's wings limed if it flies away; it is a bad thing if the boar escapes from nets which are loose-meshed.[17] (Book I, lines 351/92)

Book II turns to the problem of keeping the lady once she has been won. Amongst the things to avoid are quarrels, which are more appropriate for husbands and wives.

VII

Stay far off, disputes and bitter-tongued battles; tender love must be nurtured with sweet words. Let wives pursue husbands and husbands wives with a quarrel and let each of them believe that there must always be contention between them. This befits wives; the wifely dowry is a quarrel. Let your love always hear wished-for sounds. You have not come to the one bed by command of law; in your case love discharges the function of law. (II, 151–8)

The calculating nature of all these recommendations is justified by a comparison of love with war (an association very familiar in the Provençal poets and their followers).

VIII

Love is a species of war; lazy people, keep out! These standards are not to be manned by nervous men. Night and winter and long roads and terrible sorrows and every hardship are native to this gentle camp. Often you will bear the rain dispensed from the cloud of heaven, and often you will lie cold on the bare earth. The Cynthian is said to have pastured the cows of Admetus of Pherae[18] and to have sheltered in a small cottage. That which was good enough for Phoebus, who is it not good enough for? Strip off your arrogance, whoever you are who have a care for love which is to last. If it is denied you to go by a safe and smooth progress, and the door facing you is secured by a bolt, you can still slip down straight through the roof-opening. A high windows too will afford you a secret route.[19] She will be glad, and she will know that she is a cause of risk to you. To your lady this will be a tender of certain love. Often, Leander, you might have been absent from your mistress; but you swam across so that she would see your resolve.[20] (II, 233–50)

Book III offers advice to women, mostly involving their preparations for presenting themselves to men: dress, toilet, accomplishments such as singing and dancing. Much of the advice is the corresponding obverse of the advice to men: make the suitor attentive through uncertainty, for instance, by considered repulses (580). In a passage closely corresponding to that quoted from Book II immediately above, the *magister* advises women to make the tryst seem dangerous even when it is not. (Much of this section is copied by Jean de Meun; the vieille's advice concerning teeth and bad breath – *Roman*, 13365–6 – comes from III, 277–80, and she also borrows the advice in the following extract to let the lover in by the window even when the door is open.)

IX

The pleasure which comes in safety is less prized. Invent a fear, even if you are safer than Thais.[21] Let him in by the window even though it is easier through the doors, and in your face have the signs of one in fear. Let your artful maid burst in and say 'We are done for!'. You hide the terrified youth wherever you like. However, safe sexual fulfilment must be mixed with the terror, so that he will not think that nights with you are not worth it.

By what measures a clever husband or an attentive guardian can be deceived I was going to pass over.[22] Let the wife fear her husband: let the guarding of a wife be calculated. This is proper, being what the laws and justice and decency demand. But who could tolerate that you too should be guarded, a girl who has just been bought into freedom by decree? Come to my mysteries, so that you may deceive! So long as your will is determined, let as many keep guard as the number of Argus's eyes, you will still deceive successfully. How can your guardian prevent you from being able to write when you are accorded the time to have a wash? — when your confederate can carry a written message which she hides in a wide band across her warm breast? — when she can hide a folded document on her calf, and carry your seductive writing under her sandalled foot? If the guardian gets to know of this, let the confidante offer her back as notepaper and bear your words upon her body. (III, 603–26)

From *Amores*

X

Although much of *Amores*, particularly of Book III, shares the calculating and cynical spirit of the advice to lovers in *Ars Amatoria* and *Remedia Amoris*, the work also contains some purer elegiac love-poetry which has affinities with the medieval poets of love rather than with the *magister amoris* Andreas. The eloquent *janitor* (doorkeeper) poem and the *alba* from Book I are evocative of the troubadours and *Minnesänger*, although the characteristic charm of this poetry comes from Ovid's saturation in the love writings of his Greek and Latin predecessors.

You, doorkeeper bound with a hard chain (a degrading task!), open the intractable door on its turning hinge. What I ask is a small thing: leave the door be half open to take me sideways through a small opening. Protracted love has thinned off my body for such exigencies, and has made my limbs fit for them by reducing my weight. Love shows me how to go softly past the watches of the guards; he guides my feet without a stumble. Yet at one time I used to fear the night and its ghostly images. I used to be astonished at whoever would go out in the dark. Cupid, along with his gentle mother, laughed for me to hear, and lightly he said 'You too will become brave'. And love came without delay: I do not fear the shadows gliding in the night nor hands raised for my destruction. I fear you who are too indifferent, and to you alone do I plead. You have the thunderbolt with which you can shatter me.

Look (and open the merciless bolt so you can see) how the door has been made damp with my tears. For a fact, when you stood before the whip with your clothes stripped off, I put in a word with your mistress for you as you trembled. So the favour which at one time helped you in your turn, now (alas, the villainy of it!) does it help me so little? Make return for my favours! Whatever you want will come to you if you are obliging. The hours of night are passing; take the bolt from the door![23]

Take it down! In this way, I tell you, you will be free of your long chain, and a slave's water-allowance will not always be your drink. You listen like steel, doorkeeper, as I beg in vain, and the bolted door holds stiff with its solid oaken bolts. Locked gates furnish a defence for besieged cities; why do you fear arms amid peace? What will you do to an enemy if you lock out a lover like this? The hours of night are passing; take the bolt from the door!

I do not come attended by soldiers and arms; I would be alone if terrible Love were not with me. If I wished it, I cannot turn him away anywhere. First, rather, I will be divided from my own person. So Love and a certain amount of wine around my temples and a garland slipping off my dye-soaked hair are with me. Who would fear this army? Who would not march out against them? The hours of night are passing; take the bolt from the door!

You are incorrigible. Or is it that sleep (and may it be the death of you!) casts to the winds the lover's words driven off by your ears? Yet, I remember that at first, when I wanted to escape you, you were alert until the stars of midnight. Maybe your sweetheart rests now with you too. Ah, how much better your luck is than mine! Come to me, hard chains, if only I could be in such a state. The hours of night are passing; take the bolt from the door!

Am I wrong, or did the doors resound at the turning of a hinge, and did the shaken doors make that raucous noise? I am wrong; the door was struck by a gust of wind. Ah, how far from me has that breeze swept my hope away! If, Boreas, you remember well enough your stolen Orithyia,[24] come here and buffet down these deaf doors with your breath. Things are silent throughout the city, and, soaked with the crystal dew, the hours of night are passing; take the bolt from the door!

Otherwise I myself, better prepared with steel and the fire I carry in my torch, will seek out your proud house. Night and Love and wine urge nothing moderate; the first is empty of shame, Bacchus and Love empty of fear. I have used up all resources; we have moved you neither with entreaties or threats, you who are harder yourself than your doors. It was not fitting for you to guard the threshold of my lovely girl; you were fit for a turbulent dungeon.

And already the frosty Morning-star is setting his axles in motion,[25] and the cock is urging unhappy people to their work. But you, garland wrenched from my unhappy hair, lie the whole night on the hard doorstep! You will be a witness before my mistress, when she sees you thrown there tomorrow, to the time spent so miserably. And you, doorkeeper, whatever you are like, farewell! Have the honour of my leavetaking: farewell, relentless one, not shamed by an admitted lover! And you also, cruel doorposts with your unyielding threshold, hard beams and doors, slavish accessories, fare you well! (I, vi)

XI

Already the golden-haired lady who brings the day with her frosty axle comes over the ocean from her ancient husband.[26] Where are you hastening to, Aurora? Wait! – so can the bird of Memnon make ritual sacrifice by the annual solemn slaughter to his shades.[27] Now it delights me to have lain in the gentle arms of my mistress; now, of all times, it is bliss to have her joined to my side. Now too sleep is rich and the air is cool, and the bird sings serenely from his slight throat. Where are you hastening to, unwelcome to men and girls alike? Hold back with your shining hand the dew-covered reins. Before your rising, the sailor observes his stars better and does not wander blindly amid the sea. When you come the traveller gets up, however tired he is, and the soldier fits his brutal hands to arms. You first see the labourers tilling the fields with the fork; you first call the ponderous oxen under the bent yoke. You cheat boys of their sleep and give them over to their masters so that their soft hands should submit to the brutal lash. And you send the guileless likewise to swear before the courts, so that they may suffer huge losses through a single word. You cheer up neither lawyer nor barrister; both of them have to get up to new cases. When womanly labours might be suspended, it is you who call back to its benches the hand that works the wool.

I would tolerate all these things; but who, except somebody who has no girl-friend, could bear that girls should get up in the morning? How often have I wished that night should refuse to give place to you and that the stars should not feel impelled to flee before your face! How often have I wished that either the wind would break your axle, or that your horse should fall, hindered by a thick cloud. Jealous one, where are you hastening to? For your son was black, and that was the colour of his mother's heart.[28] I would like Tithonus to be free to talk about you; there would be no more disgraceful tale in heaven. While you are fleeing from him because he is older by a great deal, you get up early from the old man to go to the hated chariot-wheels. But if you held Cephalus in your embrace, as you would like, you would call: 'Run slowly, horses of night!' Why should I be penalised as a lover, because your husband is wasted by years? Did you marry an old man with my compliance? Look how much sleep Luna gave to the boy she loved![29] And her beauty is not inferior to yours. The father of the gods himself put two nights together for his purposes, so as not to see you so often.

I had finished my complaints. You would know she had heard: she blushed! And yet the day broke no later than usual. (I, xiii)

But *Amores* contains a good deal in the same cynical and humorous vein as the two works of advice to lovers. The last chapter of Book II echoes the *Ars Amatoria*, particularly Book III which influenced Jean de Meun.

XII

If you, fool, do not need to have your girl watched for yourself, at least have her watched over for me, so that I should desire her the more.[30] Whatever is allowed gives no pleasure; what is not allowed stings more sharply. If anyone loves what another permits him, he is made of iron. Let us hope and fear equally, we lovers, and let the odd rejection make room for a prayer. What is that good fortune to me that never takes the trouble to deceive? I love nothing that never wounds.

Crafty Corinna had seen this weakness in me and cleverly

saw the resource by which I could be captured. Ah, how often
did she invent aches for a clear head and ordered me to go as I
delayed with hesitant foot! Ah, how often did she make up
some fault and (as much as was possible towards an innocent
man) assume the appearance of one attacking me! (II, xix,
1–14)

So will I, unhappy as I am, never be prohibited from going to
her? Will the night always be without an avenger for me? Will I
have nothing to fear? Will I enjoy sleep with no signs? Will you
do nothing whereby I might wish you dead with reason? What
am I to do with an easygoing husband who is a pander? With
his weakness he wrecks our delights. Why do you not seek
someone else who likes such patience? If you want me to be a
rival for you, forbid it! (II, xix, 53–60)

ANDREAS CAPELLANUS
From *De Arte Honeste Amandi*
(or *De Amore*) – c. 1185

This very influential book of advice to lovers in which the author
appears as an Ovidian *magister amoris* is usually thought to have
been written by a chaplain Andreas at the court of Marie de
Champagne who is cited as the arbiter in cases of difficulty in Book
II of the work. It displays a wide knowledge of early medieval
encyclopoedic writers, and it exerts considerable influence on Jean
de Meun; but its spirit is almost entirely that of Ovid, and the
principal significance of the book is in transmitting awareness of
Ovid's writings on love, particularly the more humorous *Ars
Amatoria* and *Remedia Amoris*, to the tradition of medieval love
poetry. The book is an inferred code of practice for lovers, based to
some extent on the twelfth-century school, but drawn mostly from
Ovid even in detail. Ovid's classical illustrations are omitted, to be
replaced by stories of Andreas's time or of King Arthur. Christian
teaching on illicit love is asserted at the very beginning and in the
course of Book III which is an even more dramatic retraction than
those at the end of *The Canterbury Tales*, *Troilus and Criseyde* and

Decameron; but Andreas is simply attempting, and not without success, to be a medieval Ovid. It is very curious that his tone has been called enigmatic; Books I and II are in the lightly cynical vein of Ovid, and Book III, quite different from them, is a typical retraction. Denomy (*The Heresy of Courtly Love*, p. 34ff) says that Books I and II are *De Amore*, concerned with mundane man, and Book III is *De Reprobatione Amoris*, concerned with spiritual man.[31]

The excerpts here are taken from the translation by J. J. Parry (published as *The Art of Courtly Love*, Columbia University Press, New York 1941), whose introduction seems a much better outline of Andreas than Lewis's in *The Allegory of Love*. The Preface begins with the author's offer of the book to his (unidentified) friend Walter, making it clear in the first sentence that the scope of the book will correspond precisely to the *Ars Amatoria* and the *Remedia Amoris*.

XIII   **Author's Preface**

I am greatly impelled by the continual urging of my love for you, my revered friend Walter, to make known by word of mouth and to teach you by my writings the way in which a state of love between two lovers may be kept unharmed and likewise how those who do not love may get rid of the darts of Venus that are fixed in their hearts. You tell me that you are a new recruit of Love, and, having recently been wounded by an arrow of his, you do not know how to manage your horse's reins properly and you cannot find any cure for yourself. How serious this is and how it troubles my soul no words of mine can make clear to you. For I know, having learned from experience, that it does not do the man who owes obedience to Venus's services any good to give careful thought to anything except how he may always be doing something that will entangle him more firmly in his chains; he thinks he has nothing good except what may wholly please his love. Therefore, although it does not seem expedient to devote oneself to things of this kind or fitting for any prudent man to engage in this kind of hunting, nevertheless, because of the affection I have for you I can by no means refuse your request; because I know clearer than day that after you have learned the art of love your progress in it will be more cautious, in so far as I can I shall comply with your desire. (Parry, p. 27)

Book I, which takes up about two thirds of the whole work, is concerned with the definition of love and rulings about procedure in love in such matters as the people who are fit for love and love of the clergy. There are twelve chapters but chapter VI, 'In what manner love may be acquired, and in how many ways', takes up five-sixths of Book I. This chapter consists of eight dialogues between a man and a woman of various classes, increasing in length as they rise in the social scale.

XIV Book One: Introduction to the Treatise on Love

We must first consider what love is, whence it gets its name, what the effect of love is between what persons love may exist, how it may be acquired, retained, increased, decreased, and ended, what are the signs that one's love is returned, and what one of the lovers ought to do if the other is unfaithful.

Chapter 1. What Love Is

Love is a certain inborn suffering derived from the sight of and excessive meditation upon the beauty of the opposite sex, which causes each one to wish above all things the embraces of the other and by common desire to carry out all of love's precepts in the other's embrace.

That love is suffering is easy to see, for before the love becomes equally balanced on both sides there is no torment greater, since the lover is always in fear that his love may not gain its desire and that he is wasting his efforts. He fears, too, that rumors of it may get abroad, and he fears everything that might harm it in any way, for before things are perfected a slight disturbance often spoils them. If he is a poor man, he also fears that the woman may scorn his poverty; if he is ugly, he fears that she may despise his lack of beauty or may give her love to a more handsome man; if he is rich, he fears that his parsimony in the past may stand in his way. To tell the truth, no one can number the fears of one single lover. This kind of love, then, is a suffering which is felt by only one of the persons and may be called 'single love'. But even after both are in love the fears that arise are just as great, for each of the lovers fears that what he has acquired with so much effort may be lost through the effort of someone else, which is certainly much worse for a man than if, having no hope, he sees that his efforts are accomplishing nothing, for it is worse to lose the things you are seeking than to be deprived of a gain you merely hope for. The lover fears, too, that he may offend his loved one in some way; indeed he fears so many things that it would be difficult to tell them.

That this suffering is inborn I shall show you clearly, because if you will look at the truth and distinguish carefully you will see that it does not arise out of any action, only from the reflection of the mind upon what it sees does this suffering come.[32] For when a man sees some woman fit for love and shaped according to his taste, he begins at once to lust after her in his heart; then the more he thinks about her the more he burns with love, until he comes to a fuller meditation. Presently he begins to think about the fashioning of the woman and to differentiate her limbs, to think about what she does, and to pry into the secrets of her body, and he desires to put each part of it to the fullest use. Then after he has come to this complete meditation, love cannot hold the reins, but he proceeds at once to action; straightway he strives to get a helper and to find an intermediary. He begins to plan how he may find favor with her, and he begins to seek a place and a time opportune for talking; he looks upon a brief hour as a very long year, because he cannot do anything fast enough to suit his eager mind. It is well known that many things happen to him in this manner. This inborn suffering comes, therefore, from seeing and meditating. Not every kind of meditation can be the cause of love, an excessive one is required; for a restrained thought does not, as a rule return to the mind, and so love cannot arise from it . . . (Parry, pp. 28–9)

XV   Chapter IV: What the Effect of Love Is

Now it is the effect of love that a true lover cannot be degraded with any avarice. Love causes a rough and uncouth man to be distinguished for his handsomeness; it can endow a man even of the humblest birth with nobility of character; it blesses the proud with humility; and the man in love becomes accustomed to performing many services gracefully for everyone. O what a wonderful thing is love, which makes a man shine with so many virtues and teaches everyone, no matter who he is, so many good traits of character! There is another thing about love that we should not praise in few words: it adorns a man, so to speak, with the virtue of chastity, because he who shines with the light of one love can hardly think of embracing another woman, even a beautiful one. For when he thinks deeply of his beloved the sight of any other woman seems to his mind rough and rude. (Parry, pp. 31–2)

XVI   Chapter V: What Persons are Fit for Love

We must now see what persons are fit to bear the arms of love. You should know that everyone of sound mind who is capable of doing the work of Venus may be wounded by one of Love's arrows unless prevented by age, or blindness, or excess of passion. Age is a bar, because after the sixtieth year in a man and the fiftieth in a woman, although one may have intercourse his passion cannot develop into love; because at that age the natural heat begins to lose its force, and the natural moisture is greatly increased, which leads a man into various difficulties and troubles him with various ailments, and there are no consolations in the world for him except food and drink. Similarly, a girl under the age of twelve and a boy before the fourteenth year do not serve in love's army. However, I say and insist that before his eighteenth year a man cannot be a true lover, because up to that age he is overcome with embarrassment over any little thing, which not only interferes with the perfecting of love, but even destroys it if it is well perfected. But we find another even more powerful reason, which is that before this age a man has no constancy, but is changeable in every way, for such a tender age cannot think about the mysteries of love's realm. Why love should kindle in a woman at an earlier age than in a man I shall perhaps show you elsewhere.

Blindness is a bar to love, because a blind man cannot see anything upon which his mind can reflect immoderately, and so love cannot arise in him, as I have already fully shown. But I admit that this is true only of the acquiring of love, for I do not deny that a love which a man acquires before his blindness may last after he becomes blind.

An excess of passion is a bar to love, because there are men who are slaves to such passionate desire that they cannot be held in the bonds of love – men who, after they have thought long about some woman or even enjoyed her, when they see another woman straightway desire her embraces, and they forget about the services they have received from their first love and they feel no gratitude for them. Men of this kind lust after every woman they see; their love is like that of a shameless dog. They should rather, I believe, be compared to asses, for they are moved only by that low nature which shows that men are on the level of the other animals rather than by that true nature which sets us apart from all the other animals by the difference of reason. Of such lovers I shall speak elsewhere.[33] (Parry, pp. 32–3)

In the course of the Fifth Dialogue in Book I, between a nobleman and a noblewoman, the nobleman tries to win the lady away from her slowness to love by telling her a story of the type of Breton lai illustrated by Gower's Rosiphilee (*Confessio Amantis* IV,

1245–446). The man relates that one day while out riding he came upon troops of ladies, led by a man with a diadem. These, he learns, are women from the world of the dead, led by the god of Love, who live in circumstances pleasant or unpleasant according to how well they obeyed love's behests in life. He asks the god of Love for the rules of love:

XVII

"To my request he answered, 'You have been permitted to see our mighty works that through you our glory may be revealed to those who know it not, and that this sight which you now see may be a means of salvation for many ladies. We therefore command and firmly enjoin upon you that wherever you find a lady of any worth departing from our pathway by refusing to submit herself to love's engagements, you shall take care to relate to her what you have seen here and shall cause her to leave her erroneous ideas so that she may escape such very heavy torments and find a place here in glory. Know, then, that the chief rules in love are these twelve that follow:[34]

I. Thou shalt avoid avarice like the deadly pestilence and shalt embrace its opposite.

II. Thou shalt keep thyself chaste for the sake of her whom thou lovest.

III. Thou shalt not knowingly strive to break up a correct love affair that someone else is engaged in.

IV. Thou shalt not choose for thy love anyone whom a natural sense of shame forbids thee to marry.

V. Be mindful completely to avoid falsehood.

VI. Thou shalt not have many who know of thy love affair.

VII. Being obedient in all things to the commands of ladies, thou shalt ever strive to ally thyself to the service of Love.

VIII. In giving and receiving love's solaces let modesty be ever present.

IX. Thou shalt speak no evil.

X. Thou shalt not be a revealer of love affairs.

XI. Thou shalt be in all things polite and courteous.

XII. In practicing the solaces of love thou shalt not exceed the desires of thy lover.

There are also other lesser precepts of love which it would not profit you to hear, since you can find them in the book written to Walter. (Parry, pp. 81–2)

The self-referring last sentence is a device familiar in *The Canterbury Tales*.

Book II turns to Ovid's concern in the *Remedia Amoris*. Chapter 3 deals with the qualities in a lover which leads to diminution of love for him, and it strikingly adds to personal deficiencies a religious disqualification from a Christian standpoint, in the same paragraph as a series of more traditional courtly disqualifications: revealing of love or taking another lover.

XVIII

It also decreases love if one discovers any infamy in the lover or hears of any avarice, bad character, or any kind of unworthiness; so it does for him to have an affair with another woman, even if he is not in love with her. Love decreases, too, if the woman finds that her lover is foolish and indiscreet, or if he seems to go beyond reasonable bounds in his demands for love, or if she sees that he has no regard for her modesty and will not forgive her bashfulness. For a faithful lover ought to prefer love's greatest pains to making demands which deprive his beloved of her modesty or taking pleasure in making fun of her blushes; he is not called a lover, but a betrayer, who would consider only his own passions and who would be unmindful of the good of his beloved. Love decreases, too, if the woman considers that her lover is cowardly in battle, or sees that he is unrestrained in his speech or spoiled by the vice or arrogance. For nothing appears more seemly in the character of any lover at all than that he should be clad in the garment of humility and wholly lack the nakedness of pride. The utterance of silly and foolish words frequently decreases love. Many men, when with a woman, think that they will please her if they utter the first silly words that come into their heads, which is really a great mistake. The man who thinks he can please a wise woman by doing something foolish shows a great lack of sense.

Other things which weaken love are blasphemy against God or His saints, mockery of the ceremonies of the Church, and a deliberate withholding of charity from the poor.[35] We find that love decreases very sharply if one is unfaithful to his friend, or if he brazenly says one thing while he deceitfully conceals a different idea in his heart. Love decreases, too, if the lover piles up more wealth than is proper, or if he is too ready to go to law over trifles. We could tell you many more things about the weakening of love, but we leave you to find these out for yourself, for we see that you are so devoted to the practice of love as to neglect all other business and so determined to love that nothing in the art of love can escape you, since there is not a thing in it that you leave undiscussed. But we do not want you to overlook the fact that when love has definitely begun to decline, it quickly comes to an end unless something comes to save it. (Parry, pp. 155–6)

XIX Chapter IV: How Love may Come to an End

Now having treated briefly of the lessening of love we shall try next to add for you an explanation of how it may come to an end. First of all we see that love comes to an end if one of the lovers breaks faith or tries to break faith with the other, or if he is found to go astray from the Catholic religion. It comes to an end also after it has been openly revealed and made known to men. So, too if one of the lovers has plenty of money and does not come to the aid of the other who is in great need and lacks a great many things, then love usually becomes very cheap and comes to an ignominious end. An old love also ends when a new one begins, because no one can love two people at the same time. (Parry, p. 156)

The longest and most interesting part of Book II is chapter 7, a series of legal cases in love, put for judgement to Marie of Champagne. The first one below is an interesting parallel to the impossible but undeniable tasks imposed upon knights by their ladies, such as by Guinevere on Lancelot in Chrétien's *Lancelot*; number 4 considers the problem presented in *The Parlement of Fowles*; number 9 makes an immensely important distinction between married love and courtly love, declaring them to belong to different realms, neither of which is said to be superior (a judgement not noted by many modern authorities on courtly love, led by Lewis, perhaps disingenuously); and number 14 pronounces touchingly on the psychology of *amor de lonh*, evoking by contrast the story of Jaufre Rudel and the Countess of Tripoli (XLII here).

XX   Chapter VII: Various Decisions in Love Cases

Now then, let us come to various decisions in cases of love:

I. A man who was greatly enamoured of a certain woman devoted his whole heart to the love of her. But when she saw that he was in love with her, she absolutely forbade him to love. When she discovered that he was just as much in love with her as ever, she said to him one day, 'I know it is true that you have striven a very long time for my love, but you can never get it unless you are willing to make me a firm promise that you will always obey all my commands and that if you oppose them in any way you will be willing to lose my love completely.' The man answered her, 'My lady, God forbid that I should ever be so much in error as to oppose your commands in anything; so, since what you ask if very pleasing, I gladly assent to it.' After he had promised this she immediately ordered him to make no more effort to gain her love and not to dare to speak a good word of her to others. This was a heavy blow to the lover, yet he bore it patiently. But one day when this lover and some other knights were with some ladies he heard his companions speaking very shamefully about his lady and saying things about her reputation that were neither right nor proper. He endured it for a while with an ill grace, but when he saw that they kept on disparaging the lady he burst out violently against them and began to accuse them of slander and to defend his lady's reputation. When all this came to her ears she said that he ought to lose her love completely because by praising her he had violated her commands.

This point the Countess of Champagne explained as follows in her decision. She said that the lady was too severe in her command, because she was not ashamed to silence him by an unfair sentence after he had wholly submitted himself to her will and after she had given him the hope of her love by binding him to her with a promise which no honourable woman can break without a reason. Nor did the aforesaid lover sin at all when he tried to deliver a well-deserved rebuke to those who were slandering his lady. For although he did make such a promise in order the more easily to obtain her love, it seems unfair of the woman to lay upon him the command that he should trouble himself no more with love for her. (Parry, pp. 167–8)

IV. Another question like this came up: two men who were in all things absolutely equal began to pay court at the same time and in the same manner and demanded urgently that they be loved. Therefore it was asked which man's love could be chosen in such a case. We are taught by the admonition of the same countess that in such a case the man who asks first should be given the preference; but if their proposals seem to be simultaneous, it is not unfair to leave it to the woman to choose the one of the two toward whom she finds her heart inclining. (Parry, pp. 169–70)

IX. A certain man asked the same lady to make clear where there was the greater affection – between lovers or between married people. The lady gave him a logical answer. She said: 'We consider that marital affection and the true love of lovers are wholly different and arise from entirely different sources, and so the ambiguous nature of the word prevents the comparison of the things and we have to place them in different classes.[36] Comparisons of more or less are not valid when things are grouped together under an ambiguous heading and the comparison is made in regard to that ambiguous term. It is no true comparison to say that a name is simpler than a body or that the outline of a speech is better arranged than the delivery. (Parry, p. 171)

XIV. A certain lady, while her lover was on an expedition overseas and she had no hope of his early return and nearly everybody had given up all hope that he would ever come, sought for herself another lover. But a confidant of the first lover, who was very much grieved by the lady's change of faith, forbade her this new love. The woman did not accept his advice and defended herself by saying, 'If a woman who is left a widow by the death of her lover may seek a new love after two years have elapsed, this should be much more permissible for a woman who is left a widow while her lover is still alive and who for this length of time hasn't had the satisfaction of any messenger or letter from him, especially when there has been no lack of messengers.' After the question had been disputed pro and con for a long time it was referred to the Countess of Champagne, who settled it with this decision. 'It is not right for the lady to give up her love because her lover has been away for a long time (unless she knows that he was the first to fail in his love or that he has clearly been unfaithful) in cases in which it is obvious that his absence is due to necessity or to some especially praiseworthy cause. Nothing should bring more joy to the soul of a woman who is in love than to hear from distant regions the praise of her lover or to know that he is respected by honourable assemblages of great men. That he is said to have refrained from communicating with her by letters or messengers may be considered great prudence on his part, since he may not reveal this secret to any third party. If he had sent letters, even though their contents were kept secret from the bearer, it might easily happen, through the wickedness of the bearer or because he died on the journey, that the secret of their love would be made public.' (Parry, p. 173)

The last chapter of Book II contains the story of the Briton who wins the love of his lady by capturing a hawk in perilous circumstances and is given the rules of loving declared by the god of Love (the rules referred to in Book I, Dialogue 5 by the god of Love).

XXI

    I. Marriage is no real excuse for not loving.

    II. He who is not jealous cannot love.

    III. No one can be bound by a double love.

    IV. It is well known that love is always increasing or decreasing.

    V. That which a lover takes against the will of his beloved has no relish.

    VI. Boys do not love until they arrive at the age of maturity.

    VII. When one lover dies, a widowhood of two years is required of the survivor.

    VIII. No one should be deprived of love without the very best of reasons.

    IX. No one can love unless he is impelled by the persuasion of love.

    X. Love is always a stranger in the home of avarice.

    XI. It is not proper to love any woman whom one would be ashamed to seek to marry.

    XII. A true lover does not desire to embrace in love anyone except his beloved.

    XIII. When made public love rarely endures.

    XIV. The easy attainment of love makes it of little value; difficulty of attainment makes it prized.

    XV. Every lover regularly turns pale in the presence of his beloved.

XVI. When a lover suddenly catches sight of his beloved his heart palpitates.

XVII. A new love puts to flight an old one.

XVIII. Good character alone makes any man worthy of love.

XIX. If love diminishes, it quickly fails and rarely revives.

XX. A man in love is always apprehensive.

XXI. Real jealousy always increases the feeling of love.

XXII. Jealousy, and therefore love, are increased when one suspects his beloved.

XXIII. He whom the thought of love vexes eats and sleeps very little.

XXIV. Every act of a lover ends in the thought of his beloved.

XXV. A true lover considers nothing good except what he thinks will please his beloved.

XXVI. Love can deny nothing to love.

XXVII. A lover can never have enough of the solaces of his beloved.

XXVIII. A slight presumption causes a lover to suspect his beloved.

XXIX. A man who is vexed by too much passion usually does not love.

XXX. A true lover is constantly and without intermission possessed by the thought of his beloved.

XXXI. Nothing forbids one woman being loved by two men or one man by two women.

(Parry, pp. 184–6)

The short third Book is the Christian retraction, a warning to pay no heed to everything that has gone before since extra-marital love is sinful.

XXII   **Book Three: The Rejection of Love**

Now, friend Walter, if you will lend attentive ears to those things which after careful consideration we wrote down for you because you urged us so strongly, you can lack nothing in the art of love, since in this little book we gave you the theory of the subject, fully and completely, being willing to accede to your requests because of the great love we have for you. You should know that we did not do this because we consider it advisable for you or any other man to fall in love, but for fear lest you might think us stupid; we believe, though, that any man who devotes his efforts to love loses all his usefulness. Read this little book, then, not as one seeking to take up the life of a lover, but that, invigorated by the theory and trained to excite the minds of women to love, you may, by refraining from so doing, win an eternal recompense and thereby deserve a greater reward from God. For God is more pleased with a man who is able to sin and does not, than with a man who has no opportunity to sin.

Now for many reasons any wise man is bound to avoid all the deeds of love and to oppose all its mandates. The first of these reasons is one which it is not right for anyone to oppose, for no man, so long as he devotes himself to the service of love, can please God by any other works, even if they are good ones. For God hates, and in both testaments commands the punishment of, those whom he sees engaged in the works of Venus outside the bonds of wedlock or caught in the toils of any sort of passion. What good therefore can be found in a thing in which nothing is done except what is contrary to the will of God? (Parry, p. 187)

LATIN LYRICS

XXIII	*Alba*	
Phoebi claro	nondum orto iubare,	
fert Aurora	lumen terris tenue:	
spiculator	pigris clamat 'surgite.'	
L'alba part umet mar atra sol		
Poy pasa bigil	*mira clar tenebras.*	5
En incautos	hostium insidie	
torpentesque	gliscunt intercipere	
quos suadet	preco clamans surgere.	
L'alba part umet mar atra sol		
Poy pasa bigil	*mira clar tenebras.*	10
Ab Arcturo	disgregatur aquilo	
poli suos	condunt astra radios.	
orienti	tenditur septentrio.	
L'alba part umet mar atra sol		
Poy pasa bigil	*mira clar tenebras.*	15

(10th century. MS Vatican Reg. 1462)

XXIII

Before the clear star of Phoebus is shining yet, Dawn brings a faint light over the land. The watcher shouts 'get up' to the idle ones.

Refrain: The dewy dawn bears the sun over the dark sea; as it breaks through the darkness, the watchman then ends his guard.[37]

See, the enemy's ambush swells up to intercept them, unguarded and sluggish, and the watchman clamouring urges them to rise:

(Refrain)

The north wind parts from Arcturus and the stars set aside their rays of heaven; the Plough moves towards the East:

(Refrain)

XXIV

Levis exsurgit Zephyrus,
et sol procedit tepidus;
iam terra sinus aperit,
dulcore suo diffluit.

Ver purpuratum exiit,   5
ornatus suos induit:
aspergit terram floribus,
ligna silvarum frondibus.

Struunt lustra quadrupedes,
et dulces nidos volucres;   10
inter ligna florentia
sua decantant gaudia.

Quod oculis dum video
et auribus dum audio,
heu, pro tantis gaudiis   15
tantis inflor suspiriis.

Cum mihi sola sedeo
et hec revolvens palleo,
si forte caput sublevo,
nec audio nec video.   20

Tu saltim, Veris gratia,
exaudi et considera
frondes, flores et gramina;
nam mea languet anima.

(Ms. of St Augustine)

XXIV

The western breeze[38] rises light, and the sun turns warm; now the earth lays bare her breast and flows with her own sweetness.

The purpled spring goes forth and puts on its embellishments. It sprinkles the earth with flowers and the bare wood with the groves' leaves.

Animals build their lairs and birds their sweet nests. Within the flower-filled woods they sing their joys.

While with my eyes I see this and hear it with my ears, alas, I am inflated with so many sighs in place of so many joys.

When I sit with myself alone and grow pale recording these things, if I lift my head by chance, I neither hear nor see.

You at least, pleasure of spring, listen to and note the leaves, flowers and plants. For my spirit is listless.

From the *Carmina Burana*
(Benedictbeuern Ms.)

XXV

Terra iam pandit gremium
vernali lenitate,
quod gelu triste clauserat
brumali feritate;
dulci venit strepitu   5
favonius cum vere,
sevum spirans boreas
iam cessat commovere.
tam grata rerum novitas
quem patitur silere?   10

Nunc ergo canunt iuvenes,
nunc cantum promunt volucres;
modo ferro durior
est, quem non mollit Venus,
et saxo frigidior,   15
qui non est igne plenus.
pellantur nubes animi,
dum aer est serenus.

Ecce, iam vernant omnia
fructu redivivo,   20
pulso per temperiem
iam frigore nocivo,
tellus feta sui partus
grande decus flores
gignit odoriferos   25
nec non multos colores.
Catonis visis talibus
inmuterentur mores.

Fronde nemus induitur,
iam canit philomena;   30
cum variis coloribus

XXV

The earth now lays open her breast to spring mildness which she had closed up before the hard cold in winter's fierceness. With spring comes the west wind in its sweet rustling; the north wind breathing cruelty now ceases to blow. Whom can this pleasant freshness of things allow to be silent?

So now young people sing, now the birds bring forth their song. He is simply harder than iron, that man that love does not soften, and colder than the rock he who is not full of fire. The mind's clouds are driven off while the air is calm.

Look, all things now declare spring with new burgeoning, now that the harmful cold has been repulsed by mild weather. The pregnant earth brings forth great beauty as its offspring, the sweet-smelling flowers of many colours. Seeing such things, the nature of Cato would change.[40]

The grove is dressed in foliage, already the nightingale sings, while the meadows are charming with various colours. It is

iam prata sunt amena.
spatiari dulce est
per loca nemorosa,
dulcius est carpere   35
lilia cum rosa,
dulcissimum est ludere
cum virgine formosa.

Verum cum mentes talia
recensent oblectamina,   40
sentio quod anxia
fiunt mea precordia.
si friget in qua ardeo
nec mihi vult calere,
quid tunc cantus volucrum   45
mihi queunt valere,
cum tunc circum precordia
iam hyems est vere.

XXVI

Volo virum vivere viriliter,
diligam, si diligar equaliter.
sic amandum censeo, non aliter.
hac in parte fortior quam Jupiter
nescio precari   5
commercio vulgari;
amaturus forsitan
volo prius amari.

Mulieris animi superbiam
gravi supercilio despiciam,   10
nec maiorem terminum subiciam,
neque bubus aratrum preficiam;
displicet hic usus
in miseros diffusus;
malo plaudens ludere   15
quam plangere delusus.

sweet to walk through wooded places, sweeter to pluck lilies and roses, sweetest to dally with a lovely girl.

Nevertheless, when minds review again such delights, I feel how troubled my heart becomes. If she on whose account I burn is cold and does not want to glow to me, what then can the songs of the birds avail me, while then around my heart it is already winter in spring?

XXVI

I wish a man to live in a manly way; I shall love if I am loved equally. Thus I think one must love; not otherwise. In this respect stronger than Jupiter, I do not know how to implore in common commercial terms. If I am perhaps to love, first I wish to be loved.

I shall despise with heavy disdain the pride of woman's spirit. I shall not put the greater last and put the plough in charge of the ox.[41] This practice, widespread amongst miserable wretches, displeases me. I prefer to play with acclaim than to weep as a dupe.

Que cupit ut placeat, huic placeam,
prius ipsa faveat, ut faveam:
non ludemus aliter hanc aleam,
ne se granum reputet, me paleam;   20
pari lege fori
deserviam amori,
ne prosternar impudens
femineo pudori.

Liber ego liberum me iactito   25
casto fore similem Hippolyto;
non me vincit mulier tam subito
que seducat oculis ac digito.
dicat me placere,
et diligat sincere;   30
hoc mihi protervitas
placet in muliere.

Ecce, mihi displicet quod cecini,
et meo contrarius sum carmini,
tue reus, domina, dulcedini,   35
cuius elegantie non memini.
quia sic erravi,
sum dignus pena gravi;
penitentem corripe,
si placet, in conclavi.   40

　　　XXVII
Clausus Chronos et serato
carcere ver exit,
risu Jovis reserato
faciem detexit,
purpurato   5
floret prato.
ver tene primatum
ex algenti

She who wishes to please me, I shall please her. First let her show favour, in order that I should. We will not play dice on other terms, and she will not think herself grain and me chaff. I shall serve love devotedly with equal law of judgment, and I shall not be shamelessly prostrated to her woman's honour.

Being free, I repeatedly boast myself free, as being like chaste Hippolytus. The woman who seduces with eyes and finger does not overcome me that suddenly. Let her say that I am pleasing and love me sincerely. Boldness in a woman of this kind pleases me.

Look, what I have sung displeases me, and I am my own enemy in my song. I am the prisoner of your charm, my lady, and I did not remember your elegance. Because I have strayed in this way I am worthy of heavy punishment. Seize upon me, a penitent, if it pleases you in your own chambers.[42]

XXVII

Time[43] is locked up and spring breaks out of its bolted prison. The sun, with its smile set free, has revealed its face and blooms in the purple meadow. Spring, maintain your primacy, reborn

renitenti
specie renatum.   10

Vernant veris ad amena
—thyma, rosa, lilia,
his alludit filomena,
melos et lascivia.

Satyrus hoc excitatur,   15
et Dryadum chorea,
redivivis incitatur
hoc ignibus Napea.

O Cupido, concitus
hoc amor innovatur,   20
hoc ego sollicitus,
hoc mihi mens turbatur.

Ignem alo tacitum,
amo, nec ad placitum,
utquid contra libitum   25
cupio prohibitum,
votis Venus meritum
rite facit irritum,
trudit in interitum
quem rebar emeritum.   30

Si quis amans per amare
amari posset mereri,
posset amor mihi velle mederi,
quod facile sit, tandem beare,
perdo querelas absque levare.   35

Hoc amor predicat,
hec macilenta
hoc sibi vendicat
absque perempta . . .

to beauty, over the struggling cold.

Thyme and rose and lilies show the spring in pleasant, vernal places. The nightingale plays on to them, tuneful and suggestive.

The Satyr wakens at this and the chorus of Dryads. The dell-nymph is roused by this to renewed fires.

O Cupid, love roused together is thus renewed and so I am violently moved; my mind because of this is in turmoil.

I nourish a hidden fire; I love, but not to satisfaction; rather in such a way that unwillingly I desire that which is forbidden. Venus justly renders useless my service by vows, and pushes to his ruin one worn out in her service.

If any lover could deserve to be loved by loving, love could choose to cure me, because it would be easy to make me happy in the end. I waste my complaints which are unrelieved.

Love boasts of this; he claims these leannesses as his own without ending them . . .

Parce dato pia   40
Cypris agone,
et quia vincimur,
arma repone,
et quibus es Venus,
esto Dione.   45

    XXVIII
Nobilis, mei
miserere precor,
tua facies
ensis est quo necor,
nam medullitus   5
amat meum te cor,
subveni!
Amor improbus
omnia superat,
subveni!   10

Come sperulas
tue eliciunt
cordi sedulas,
flammas adjiciunt,
hebet animus,   15
vires deficiunt:
subveni!
Amor improbus
omnia superat,
subveni!   20

Odor roseus
spirat a labiis;
speciosior
pre cunctis filiis,
melle dulcior,   25
pulchrior liliis,

O good Venus, spare the struggle you have given. And because I am overcome, lay down your arms, and be Dione to those to whom you are Venus.[44]

XXVIII

Noble one,[45] I pray have mercy on me. Your face is a sword on which I am killed, for from the very marrow my heart loves you. Help me!

Cruel love overcomes everything. Help me!

Your hair lures out the ambitious seeds of hope from my heart; it adds to the flames. My spirit grows faint; my strength grows less. Help me!

Cruel love overcomes everything. Help me!

The smell of roses breathes from your lips. You are more beautiful than all girls, sweeter than honey, fairer than lilies.

subveli!
Amor improbus
omnia superat,
subveni!   30

Decor prevalet
candori etheris;
ad pretorium
presentor Veneris;
ecce pereo,   35
si non subveneris;
subveni!
Amor improbus
Omnia superat,
subveni!   40

XXIX

O comes amoris dolor,
cuius mala male solor,
nec habent remedium,
dolor urget me, nec mirum,
quem a predilecta dirum   5
en vocat exilium,
cuius laus est singularis,
pro qua non curasset Paris
Helene consortium.

Gaude vallis insignita,   10
vallis rosis redimita,
vallis flos convallium,
inter valles vallis una,
quam collaudat sol et luna,
dulcis cantus avium,   15
quam collaudat philomena.
nam quam dulcis et amena
mestis dan solatium!

Help me!

Cruel love overcomes everything. Help me!

Your beauty surpasses the shining of the sky. At the headquarters of Venus I present myself. Look, I am dying if you do not help. Help me!

Cruel love overcomes everything. Help me!

XXIX

O sorrow, love's comrade, whose ills I comfort poorly (and indeed they have no cure), sorrow drives me (and it is no wonder), a wretch that exile,[46] alas, calls away from his love. Her worth is unique; in competition with her, Paris would not have cared for the company of Helen.

Rejoice, distinguished valley, valley crowned with roses, valley the flower among surrounding ones, valley one amongst valleys whom the sun and moon praise greatly. Sweet is the song of birds for you whom the nightingale praises highly. For how sweet and pleasant you are, giving solace to sad people.

NOTES

1 *Propertius: Select Elegies*, ed. J. P. Postgate (London 1885), p. lxxix.
2 *Medieval Latin and the Rise of European Love Lyric* (Oxford University Press 1968); vol. 1, pp. 221ff.
3 *Mediaeval Latin Lyrics*, p. 341.
4 1948. English Translation by W. R. Trask, London 1953.
5 Poem 5 in Book 2 of the Elegies is Tibullus's longest poem, written not long before his early death in 19–18 B.C. in celebration of the elevation of Messalinas (the eldest son of Messalla, the patron of the poets) to the *Quindecimviri, XV viri*, the administrative college responsible for holding the Saecular Games and for keeping the Sybilline Books. Love as an illness and a pleasing pain, familiar as a piece of Petrarchism paralleled in the twelfth-century poets, is a *motif* common to poetry of all ages, according to Kirby Flower Smith in his 1913 American Book Company edition of Tibullus who quotes Horace and Seneca (p. 476). The conflicting claims of love and war are an age-old theme too, very prominent in troubadours such as Bertran de Born. The Latin texts of the excerpts from Tibullus and Propertius are taken from G. G. Ramsay, *Selections from Tibullus and Propertius* (Oxford 1887).
6 Macer is not definitely known, though he seems to be a love-poet from lines 1 and 5. It has been suggested (by Postgate and K. Flower Smith) that he may be the Aemilius Macer of Verona (died 16 B.C.) whose only known poems, however, are on botany and zoology. There is another Macer, a friend of Ovid, who wrote on the Trojan war (accordingly called 'Iliacus' in *Pont*. V, 16.6); cf. *Amores* II, 18.
7 The metaphor is of a runaway slave, the punishment for whom was branding.
8 *Hic* (more usually 'hic homo') means 'this man here', i.e. 'I myself'.
9 This recalcitrant leavetaking, more typical of Propertius's dealings with Cynthia, is a recurrent phenomenon in Latin elegy.
10 The poet has retreated to the woods, driven away by Cynthia's accusation of disloyalty. Hence, his protests are heard only by 'silent doorways' in this desert. His quiet acceptance of the lady's ill-founded perversity is strikingly reminiscent of the courtly lover. 'Divini', here translated 'inhuman', does not seem to make much sense; 'inhuman' in a pejorative sense is not a normal sense of 'divinus'.
11 'The boy' is Cupid who fires the arrow which inspires love. The idea is that his love is too profound to be lightly forgotten.
12 Attalus III, king of Pergamus, who gave up his cares of government to concentrate on precious metals. He died without an heir, leaving in his will the words 'P.R. meorum haeres esto' which the Romans interpreted as 'Let the Roman Republic be my heir' as an excuse to

take over his kingdom in 133 B.C. From this great bequest, the adjective 'Attalicus' comes to mean 'magnificent', as here.

13 *Tres;* used, as often, to mean 'two or three', and not to be taken to refer to the exact number of the works of Propertius. The gift to Persephone corresponds to the golden bough which the priestess tells Aeneas to give as his gift to Proserpina (*Aeneid* VI, 142).

14 The reference is to Syrian perfumes. The onyx casket is the jar made of precious stone used to carry anointing oil.

15 Cf. *Amores* I, xi, the appeal to Nape, and the repeated use of servant-messengers in *The Knight in the Tiger's Skin*. It is a very familiar feature of medieval romance, most famously perhaps in Yvain's dealings with the maid Lunete in Chrétien's *Yvain*; she presses his suit for him more than once (Lines 1589ff, 6659ff.).

16 A. S. Hollis notes in his edition of Book I of *Ars Amatoria* (Oxford University Press 1977) that Ovid uses the imperfect to suggest a tentative hint.

17 Hollis's interpretation which I have followed in the translation (see previous note) greatly improves on the sense of these lines offered by the translation of J. H. Mozley (Loeb Classical Library 1929, p. 39 and p. 41). The sense of the metaphor is that it is no good trapping something if you fail to hold it.

18 Apollo is said to have tended the flocks of Admetus of Pherae in Thessaly for nine years after he was banished from Heaven. He then promised Admetus that he would live for ever if someone could be found to lay down their life for him, a sacrifice which Admetus's wife Alcestis performs. See *Alcestis* by Euripides.

19 This deliberate choosing of the arduous way is paralleled in Book III, 604ff (IX here) and by Jean de Meun in the *Roman de la Rose* where La Vielle's practical advice to women is largely drawn from *Ars Amatoria*: see the third excerpt in LXVI here.

20 The story of Leander's swimming across the Hellespont to reach Hero each night and of his drowning is the subject of the letters in *Heroides* 18 and 19.

21 Thais, the courtesan, held great sway because Alexander was at her bidding. At her whim he burned down Persepolis.

22 We might note that in Ovid, as amongst the medieval poets, the husband was by no means always the *jalous* or *gilos*. For one example of many, cf the 'oncle' in Arnaut's 'Lo ferm voler', LIII here; and see A. R. Press's entirely persuasive article, 'The Adulterous Nature of Fin' Amors' in *Forum for Modern Language Studies* 6, 1970, pp. 327–41 for a great deal more evidence.

23 The refrain of the *alba* can be compared with 'Phoebi claro' (XXIII here), Guiraut de Borneil's 'Reis glorios' (L here), and Heinrich von Morungen's 'Owe, sol' (LXXIII here).

24   Orithyia, the daughter of King Erechtheus of Athens, was carried off by Boreas, the North wind, to Thrace (*Metamorphoses* VI, v, 706).

25   The sentimental but eloquent lines from 65 to the end are thought by some commentators to be an interpolation.

26   The goddess Aurora granted Tithonus, her lover, the gift of everlasting life, but he forgot to ask for everlasting youth to accompany it. Hence her anxiety to leave her ever-ageing bed-companion in the morning.

27   Memmon, the son of Aurora and Tithonus, was killed in combat at the siege of Troy by Achilles. Aurora asked Jupiter to mark his death in a special way, and Jupiter caused a flock of birds to issue from Memnon's burning pyre and fight a fierce battle in the air above it.

28   Phaethon (in *Metamorphoses* I, xvii, 2) was sometimes said to be the son of Aurora and Cephalus (though more generally he was said to be the son of Phoebus and Clymene). When he drove his chariot too near the sun, the blood of the Ethiopians dried up and turned black.

29   Diana, the moon, fell in love with Endymion when she saw him sleeping naked on the hillside. Night, the period of her influence, is entirely devoted to sleep, Ovid suggests, so that she can be in bed with him.

30   This, the most cynical passage in all the *Amores*, urges the complacent husband to be more jealously on his guard to make the lover's suit more exciting.

31   Although the full title of *De Amore* is '*De Amore: Libri Tres*' (see edition of E. Trojel, Copenhagen 1892).

32   That the suffering of love results from the reflection of the mind on the findings of the eyes is a view of love, in its half-philosophical basis, corresponding to the kinds of definition of love given by the stilnovisti. See, for example, XCIV here.

33   Like the troubadours, Andreas insists that the love he is talking about is guided by Reason, and is not to be identified with animal passion (the *amars* of Marcabru and his followers).

34   The list of rules for loving given here are strikingly more idealistic than the list given by Andreas at the end of Book II, or those told to the lover by La Vielle in Jean de Meun (13001ff.). It is notable that in each case the more cynical, amended list is a correction to rules offered by the god of love.

35   Again, it is emphasised that love must be consistent with Christian virtue in general, even if it is adulterous. The Christian chivalry which must characterise the courtly lover here corresponds to the virtues of the Arthurian knights in the romances.

36   This refusal to declare courtly love to be superior to, or even comparable with, married love has been under-emphasised by the critics since Gaston Paris who have always implied that adulterous love surpasses married relations in courtly writings.

37 The texts of the following seven lyrics are taken with generous permission from *Mediaeval Latin Lyrics* by Helen Waddell. The first poem is celebrated as the first medieval *alba*; cf. those by Guiraut de Borneil (L), Wolfram (LXXXII), and Heinrich von Morungen (LXXIII) here. The translation of the refrain is somewhat speculative; it is not certain to which of the medieval Latin languages it should be assigned. Both North Italian and Provençal have claimed it.

38 The theme of the contrast between the renewing joys of spring and the poet's misery is found here in an eleventh-century poem in the MS. of St Augustine. Helen Waddell says it has 'the wistfulness of German minnesong' (*Mediaeval Latin Lyrics*, p. 333). It is not made explicit here that love is the cause of the poet's gloom; it is probably to be assumed, as in some medieval English lyrics, or in *The Bok of the Duchesse*, lines 30–42.

39 The remaining five poems are taken from the *Carmina Burana*. The manuscript was written, probably in Bavaria, at the end of the thirteenth century, but its contents, where they are certainly identifiable, are concerned with the last quarter of the twelfth century. The poems are in German as well as Latin, and some of the poems are by known writers such as the Archpoet, Walther von der Vogelweide and Gautier de Chatillon. So it does not need argument that they are connected with some of the vernacular lyric poetry in this anthology.

40 Presumably Marcus Cato Uticensis (?95–46 B.C.), great-grandson of Cato the Censor. He was a Stoic, famous for his austerity and his scorn for the cybaritic way of life. Dante, out of regard for his virtue and in spite of his suicide, makes him guardian of the Christian Purgatory (*Purgatorio* I, 31ff.).

41 This anti-courtly love poem with its twist at the end, modelled on rebellion against the moral law, follows a common pattern. The plough pulling the ox is a 'world upside down' image, an *adynata*; cf. Curtius, *European Literature and the Latin Middle Ages*, pp. 94–8, with its references to Chrétien's *Cligés* 3849ff and Arnaut Daniel, particularly 'En Cest Sonet', (LII here), lines 43–5. The topos is, of course, particularly associated with the madness of the lover.

42 *Conclavis* was originally a private room but it meant a Papal conclave by the thirteenth century, so the pun on a place of religious trial as well as bedroom is probably intended. The last stanza uses the terminology (*domina*) and the religious parallel of courtly love in a classic way.

43 Many features of courtly love can be seen here: the spring opening contrasted with the lover's tribulations; the power of Cupid, Venus and love; the burning of the lover and his lack of fulfilment; desire, merit and the nightingale.

44 The last line is an emendation which remains obscure, since Dione, the nymph who was Venus's mother, does not have associations of

fulfilment in love particularly. The appeal perhaps means: 'do not display the tyranny of Venus'. The line is an emendation of the manuscript reading, 'Est et Dione' which makes less sense.

45   The goliardic metre, rhyme-scheme and refrain are notable in this love appeal.

46   The *amor de lonh* of the exile is the theme of this poem; cf XLIII here. The ecstatic praise of the valley (where the beloved lives presumably) as a *locus amoenus* is unusual in that it praises the place apt for love, even when the lover must be absent from it, for the consolatory things (nightingale, roses and moon) which are traditionally said to be useless in the absence of love.

Poetry outside the main European Tradition: Georgian and Arabic

This section could have been made very large, to include a wide selection of works that have an affinity with the forms and themes of courtly love. The Arabic parallels, along with the Platonic literature associated with them, would be a large section on their own, as the examples of Dronke, de Rougement's arguments and the references in A. R. Nykl's editions show. Dronke's evidence of close parallels in the Mozarabic *kharjas*, the Germanic *winileodas*, the Icelandic Skaldic poems and a long tradition extending back to Egyptian is undeniable proof of his thesis that the elements of courtly love cannot be said to have originated *ex nihilo* in eleventh-century Provence. But the material would have been far beyond the scope of this book if everything were represented. More important, it would have distracted attention from what is clearly a condensed period of courtly love literature in the twelfth and thirteenth centuries. Much criticism of courtly writings has dispersed concentration in this way.

Only two works are represented here, both apparently removed from the centres of European literature, but closely linked in different ways with the other writings in this book. *The Knight in the Tiger's Skin* by Shot'ha Rust'haveli[1] is dated 1184–1207 by the Moscow editors (p. xxvii) and even more narrowly by Dronke between 1196 and 1207.[2] It therefore (perhaps coincidentally) comes from the precise period of the high point of French and German courtly poetry. As the poem's introduction (XXX here) shows, the demands the poet makes of the lover are strikingly reminiscent of the cult of perfection associated with courtly love romances and lyrics: common features, for instance, are devotion to a single beloved, assertion of her glory, sighs for her from afar, and secrecy in love. In the story itself many episodes suggest comparison with courtly love; a striking case is the occasion (in the second extract here) when Avt'handil sleeps with the lady P'hatman who is helping him to attain his beloved, with no sense of offence to P'hatman. This is reminiscent of Ovid's sanctioning sexual relations with the handmaid who is helping the lover's suit[3] and of the occasion in *Tristan* when Brangane's virginity is sacrificed to Mark without thought for any consideration other than the protection of the love of Tristan and Isolde. The common element in all these cases is the ruthless single-mindedness of the courtly lover: 'all's fair in love'. Whatever their implications for the universality of courtly love or its emanation from Provence, the resemblances are very remarkable.

Mozarabic poetry is particularly under-represented here, if one considers the prevalence of theories of Arabic influence on courtly love since the sixteenth century,[4] the strong possibility of Moorish influence, and the similarity of Arabic pronouncements on the theory and practice of love. An ultimate influence of Arabic on Provençal, both in poetic forms and in ideas about love, has generally been credited from the sixteenth century to the present day, and this influence was argued and evidenced fully by the Spanish Jesuit Andres (1740–1817). It is an aspect of courtly love that writers since about 1970 have been inclined to play down; but nobody would deny that there was some influence through Mozarabic Spain. This is hardly surprising in view of the general Arabic influence on European thought in the eleventh and twelfth centuries, most importantly in the transmission of Aristotelian philosophy. It has been argued that, if there *are* Neoplatonic elements in courtly love, they have come down from Arabic literature, since there is a strong Neoplatonic colouring in that from the *Liber de Causis* and Plotinus. But discussions of such influences, interesting though they are, take the reader of poetry far from the romances and lyrics of 1200.

The Arabic work from which a section is included here, *The*

Dove's Neck-Ring of Ibn Hazm, is dated by its editor A. R. Nykl at about 1022.[5] It is full of resemblances to medieval writings on love, from its first declaration of intent to write on 'love, its aspects, its causes and its accidents' (p. 2), an aspiration typical in its inclusiveness of writers from the first troubadours to Guillaume de Lorris, and reminiscent of the stilnovisti in its use of the terminology of Aristotelian philosophy. Its definitions are of a Neoplatonic nature, suggesting a philosophical origin for the idea that love from afar and fixity in love are definitive qualities of the true lover. Love ennobles; the lover is wakeful at night and can think of nothing but his beloved; he is desolate when apart from her. Love histories are told in exemplification of each of the poet's themes and subjects. In structure the book is like Andreas's *De Arte Honeste Amandi* with a more philosophical *and* a more personal-sounding basis: an evocation of what it feels like and what it means to be in love, rather than a set of rules for procedure in love, seen from the outside. It could be said to be a primary source for love poetry while Andreas is secondary. Expression in perfect poetic form is of great importance (as for the troubadours), as is secrecy and the role of the messenger. When obedience in love is discussed, the excesses of the demands made by Guinevere on Lancelot in Chrétien are brought to mind: a man must avoid his beloved if she bids him to; if she accuses him of a fictitious crime, he must plead guilty if she wishes it and incur whatever punishment that entails, as in the episode of the cart in *Lancelot*. The roles of slanderer and watchman are debated at length. Nykl notes that similarities in terminology have 'been pointed out by previous writers, such as: *gardador* and *raqib*, *lausengier* and *wasi*', to which he adds *hasid* for *gilos*.[6] He also proposes Arabic poetry as the origin of the curious and often-noted use of the masculine *midons* in Provençal for the female beloved (no doubt rightly explained by all commentators as the logical consequence of presenting the lady as the metaphorical equivalent of the male fuedal lord). Nykl's lengthy analysis of the earlier troubadours in the context of Hispano–Arabic poetry (the same in substance in his introduction to *The Dove's Neck-Ring* and in his *Hispano–Arabic poetry and its Relations with the Old Provençal Troubadours*[7]) gives an admirable condensed view of the nature and history of the troubadour lyric, presenting powerful evidence for his conclusion:

'Even if we disregard a large number of coincidences as belonging to the common stock of human experience in matters of love, the 'greifbare Übergänge' and 'konkrete Spuren' are strong enough to point decisively to Arabic, and especially Andalusian–Arabic influence' (*The Dove's Neck-Ring*. p. ciii).

In view of this it may appear that not enough space has been given to the Arabic literary background here. However, it seems that the nature and extent of that influence is well suggested by the *Neck-Ring* on its own. The principal concern of this volume is to present the literature of Europe of around 1200 which was such an important foundation of the European literary tradition, whatever its own origins, and the inspiration of that literature, whether in Ovid or the *kharjas*, is secondary. But it would be a very incomplete corpus of that literature that did not include and emphasise its Arabic parallels.

RUST 'HAVELI
The Knight in the Tiger's Skin
(Georgian, *c.* 1196–1207)

Although this long love-poem was written in Georgian, it claims to be based on a Persian story and it is set in Arabia[8] and India. The poem is an epic of love which has many features in common with courtly love. In the introduction to the story itself (from which the first excerpt here comes), the poet speaks of his own love in terms reminiscent of Boccaccio's addresses to Maria d'Aquino and of the Queen T'hamar (called king) as Chrétien speaks of Marie de Champagne, before turning to the roles of the poet and the lover.

XXX

I, Rust'haveli, have composed this work by the folly of my art. For her whom a multitude of hosts obey, I lose my wits, I die! I am sick of love, and for me there is no cure from anywhere, unless she give me healing or the earth a grave.[9]

This Persian tale, now done into Georgian, has hitherto been like a pearl of great price cast in play from hand to hand; now I have found it and mounted it in a setting of verse; I have done a praiseworthy deed. The ravisher of my reason, proud and beautiful, willed me to do it.

Eyes that have lost their light through her, long to look on her anew; lo! my heart is mad with love, and it is my lot to run about the fields. Who will pray for me? The burning of the body sufficeth, let the soul have comfort! The verse in praise of the three like heroes cannot but affect the hearer.

With what Fate gives to a man, therewithal should he be content, and so speak of it. The labourer should ever work, the warrior be brave. So, also, should the lover love Love, and recognise it. Neither must he disdain the love of another, or that other disdain his.

Minstrelsy is, first of all, a branch of wisdom; the divine must be hearkened to divinely, and wholesome is to them that hearken; it is pleasant, too, if the listener be a worthy man; in few words he utters a long discourse: herein lies the excellence of poetry.

Like a horse is tested in a great race on a long course, like a ball-player in the lists striking the ball fairly and aiming adroitly at the mark, even so is it with the poet who composes and indites long poems, and reins in his horse when utterance is hard for him and verse begins to fail.

Then, indeed, behold the poet, and his poesy will be manifest. When he is at a loss for words, and verse begins to fail, he will not weaken the verse, nor will he let the verse grow poor. Let him strike cunningly with the polo-mallet; he will show great virtue.

He who utters, somewhere, one or two verses cannot be called a poet; let him not think himself equal to great singers. Even if they compose a few discrepant verses from time to time, yet if they say, 'Mine are of the best!' they are stiff-necked mules.

Secondly, lyrics which are but a small part of poetry and cannot command heart-piercing words – I may liken them to the bad bows of young hunters who cannot kill big game; they are able only to slay the small.

Thirdly, lyrics are fit for the festive, the joyous, the amorous, the merry, for pleasantries of comrades; they please us when they are clearly sung. Those are not called poets who cannot compose a lengthy work.

The poet must not spend his toil in vain. One should seem to him worthy of love; he must be devoted to one, he must employ all his art for her, he must praise her, he must set forth the glory of his beloved; he must wish for nought else, for her alone must his tongue be tuneful.[10]

Now let all know that I praise her whom I erstwhile praised; in this I have great glory, I feel no shame. She is my life; merciless as a leopard is she. Her name I pronounce hereafter praising her allegorically.

I speak of the highest love — divine in its kind. It is difficult to discourse thereon, ill to tell forth with tongues. It is heavenly, upraising the soul on pinions. Whoever strives thereafter must indeed have endurance of many griefs.

Sages cannot comprehend that one Love; the tongue will tire, the ears of the listeners will become wearied; I must tell of lower frenzies, which befall human beings; they imitate it when they wanton not, but faint from afar.

In the Arabic tongue they call the lover 'madman', because by non-fruition he loses his wits. Some have nearness to God, but they weary in the flight; then again, to others it is natural to pursue lovely women.

To a lover, beauty, like unto the sun, wisdom, wealth, generosity, youth and leisure are fitting; he must be eloquent, intelligent, patient, a conqueror of mighty adversaries; who is not all these lacks the qualities of a lover.

Love is tender, a thing hard to be known. True love is something apart from lust, and cannot be likened thereto; it is one thing; lust is quite another thing, and between them lies a broad boundary; in no way do thou mingle them — hear my saying![11]

The lover must be constant, not lewd, impure and faithless; when he is far from his beloved he must heave sigh upon sigh; his heart must be fixed on one from whom he endures wrath or sorrow if need be. I hate heartless love — embracing, kissing, loud smacking of the lips.

Lovers, call not this thing love: when any longs for one today and another to-morrow, bearing parting's pain. Such base sport is like mere boyish trifling; the good lover is he who suffers a world's woe.

There is a noblest love; it does not show, but hides its woes; the lover thinks of it when he is alone, and always seeks solitude; his fainting, dying, burning, flaming, all are from afar; he must face the wrath of his beloved, and he must be fearful of her.

He must betray his secret to none, he must not basely groan and put his beloved to shame; in nought should he manifest his love, nowhere must he reveal it; for her sake he looks upon sorrow as joy, for her sake he would willingly be burned.

How can the sane trust him who noises his love abroad, and what shall it profit to do this? He makes her suffer, and he himself suffers. How should he glorify her if he shame her with words? What need is there for man to cause pain to the heart of his beloved!

I wonder why men show that they love the beloved. Why shame they her whom they love, her who slays herself for them, who is covered with wounds? If they love her not, why do they not manifest to her feelings of hatred? Why do they disgrace what they hate? But an evil man loves an evil word more than his soul or heart.

If the lover weep for his beloved, tears are his due. Wandering and solitude befit him, and must be esteemed as roaming. He will have time for nothing but to think of her. If he be among men, it is better that he manifest not his love. (Introduction, §§ 8–31)

The story begins with the ageing King Rostevan of Arabia who abdicates in favour of his beautiful daughter T'hinat'hin, loved by Avt'handil. One day Rostevan and Avt'handil see a knight in a tiger's skin (later revealed as Tariel). Tariel Kills Rostevan's slaves and disappears. T'hinat'hin declares her love to Avt'handil and tells him to search for Tariel for three years. Avt'handil sets off, leaving his slave Shermadin in his place and telling him of his love 'because of his worthiness' (§163). After three years he finds Tariel, weeping in the arms of a weeping lady called Asmat'h who tells Avt'handil about Tariel in his absence: Tariel is the son of one of the seven kings of India, in love with the princess Nestan. The rest of the story is occupied with the attempt to rescue the banished Nestan which the two heroes accomplish with the help of another king P'hridon. Avt'handil goes home briefly but then returns to the aid of the tiger knight, leaving a letter of explanation to Rostevan in which he quotes Plato. During his absence from T'hinat'hin, Avt'handil sleeps with his lady helper P'hatman (in excerpt XXXI below).

In the end all the suits are successful and the three kings often visit each other's kingdoms. What is most evocative of courtly love is the nobility of the lovers and their loves, their use of confidantes and swearing of secrecy in love, and their sense of the absoluteness and single-mindedness of love. Much of the poetic terminology and language is different; many things are compared with the rose, the lady is called the sun and the moon, the knight is the aloe-tree and the lion, and sorrow turns his heart into soot. But despite these differences, there is much that parallels what has often been thought to be peculiar to courtly love, including two of the three qualities which Denomy says are definitive:[12] the superiority of the lady and the ennobling power of love.

In the course of the search for Tariel's beloved Nestan, Avt'handil in disguise is helped by P'hatman who becomes enamoured of him. Because he is disguised and cannot declare his identity, Avt'handil has to sleep with her.[13]

XXXI

P'hatman thought of herself; therefore she was again burned up. The knight kept his secret, he lent himself to love; P'hatman embraced his neck, she kissed his sun-like face.

That night P'hatman enjoyed lying with Avt'handil; the knight unwillingly embraces her neck with his crystal neck;

remembrance of T'hinat'hin slays him, he quakes with secret fear, his maddened heart raced away to the wild beasts and ran with them.

Avt'handil secretly rains tears, they flow to mingle with the sea; in an inky eddy floats a jetty ship. He says: 'Behold me, O lovers, me who have a rose for mine own! Away from her, I, the nightingale, like a carioncrow, sit on the dungheap!'

The tears which flowed there from him would have melted a stone, the thicket of jet dammed them up, there is a pool on the rose-field. P'hatman rejoiced in him as if she were a nightingale; if a crow find a rose it thinks itself a nightingale.

Day dawned; the sun whose rays were soiled by the world went forth to bathe. The woman gave him many coats, cloaks, turbans, many kinds of perfumes, fair clean shirts. 'Whatsoever thou desirest,' said she, 'put on; be not shy of me!' Avt'handil said: 'This day will I declare my affair.' (§§ 1229–34)

The lack of sympathy or consideration towards P'hatman is explained by the first line here: her love is selfish, not the noble, aristocratic love extolled by the poet and by the courtly commentators on love. It is only in love that P'hatman is not admired; throughout the rest of the poem her behaviour is heroic, and the hero Tariel adopts her as his sister at the end.

IBN HAZM
The Dove's Neck-Ring
(Arabic, *c.* 1022)

If Arabic is regarded as an influence on courtly love writings, then the date of this text stands at about the right distance from the first troubadours, a half-century before the birth of Guilhem IX. The programme of the work as a whole is of great significance for the development of a theory in medieval love poetry; the work will contain three sections, on origins of love, accidents of love (philosophically defined), and calamities in love (Nykl, p. 4). At the outset the poet says what aspects of love he will treat. They are a very familiar list: the messenger, keeping love a secret, divulging the secret, submissiveness to the beloved, the faultfinder, the helping friend, the watcher, the slanderer, union, break-off, loyalty, betrayal, separation, contentment and so on. It will end with a chapter on illicit practices and the excellence of continence, which is reminiscent of the motif of retraction.

The poet opens with a dedication to God, saying that he is writing in response to the request of a friend that he write on 'love, its aspects, its causes, and its accidents', and turns to his definition of love, making it clear that the definition is Neoplatonic rather than Islamic.

XXXII

There is a good deal of dispute among people about the *nature of love*, and there is much lengthy discussion. What I believe myself is that it is a *reunion of parts of the souls, separated in this creation, within their original higher element*, not according to what Muhammad b. Dawud, may God have mercy on him, said, basing himself upon the views of some philosophers that: 'Spirits are divided spheres' but along the line of the resemblance of their motive forces in the *abode of their higher world* and their mutual approximation to the form of their make-up. We well know that the secret of commingling and estrangement in creation is nothing but attraction or repulsion; and so one kind zealously yearns for one of its kind, and like dwells with its like, and the resemblance of forms has a psychological action and an evident influence: the mutual repulsion of opposites and mutual accord of likes, and yearning between things mutually similar, all this is found among us.[14]

How much more is it true of the *soul* whose world is a pure, ethereal world and its essence is the essence of a straight, well-balanced lance; it is basically shaped to take on mutual agreement, and inclination, and sympathy, and aversion, and passionate desire and avoidance: all this is known in our day in the various circumstances as man fluctuates between them and dwells in them; and God, Most High and Exalted, says: 'He it is who created you *from one soul*, and made therefrom its mate to dwell therewith', and as the cause of this dwelling He made the fact that she is made of him. If the cause of love were the beauty of bodily form it would be necessary to find that something more defective in form would not find approval – but we find many people who prefer something worse, and though they know something better than that, yet they find for their heart no swerving from it – and were it on account of mutual agreement of character then man would not fall in love with someone who does not help him or does not agree with him. We know, then, that it is something within the soul *itself*: and maybe love is caused by certain causes and such a love passes away when its cause passes away; so that if someone loves you on account of something he will turn away from you when that something passes away. And on that subject I say:

My affection for you is permanent in accordance with its *being*: It attains its utmost limit, and then does not decrease in any way, nor increase;
There is no cause for it except *will*,
And there is no other cause but this that anyone could know;
Whenever we find a thing to be its own cause
Such an existence does not pass away in all eternity:
And if we do find in something to have its cause in something

different from it,
The coming to naught of that thing will be caused by our being bereft of that to which it owed its existence!

Anf what corroborates this saying is our knowing that there are *various kinds of love.* (Nykl, pp. 7–8)

This long and rigorous introductory definition shows that, in Arabic poetry at least, the philosophical view of secular love, linked to the creative activity of God (which the poet discusses next), has a very long heritage in love poetry and is by no means new in the troubadours of the *trobar clus* or the stilnovisti.

Later in this definition of love, the poet goes on to define the mutual attraction of lovers as naturally inevitable, using imagery like Guinicelli's in LXXXIX here.

XXXIII

And the soul of the one who loves is free, knows of the place where it was its companion in proximity, is asking for it, endeavoring to reach it, searching for it, ardently desirous of meeting it, gravitating toward it when it can – like magnet and iron. The force of the essence of the magnet which is bound up with the force of the essence of iron does not reach out, as a result of its make-up nor its purity towards iron, although it is of its kind and element, but rather the power of iron, on account of its strength, inclines towards its kind and is attracted to it: since motion always comes from the stronger: and the force of iron when left to itself is not prevented by an obstacle to desire what resembles it and to giving itself up to it, hurrying toward it according to nature and necessity, not because of choice and firm purpose. But while you take iron in your hand it will not be attracted, since there has not also come from it an overpowering force which would be more powerful than the strength of him who has picked it up. When the particles of iron are numerous they only act upon one another and check their kind from the desire to follow a small part of their forces far removed from it. But when the volume of the magnet is large and its force matches all the force of the volume of iron, the latter will come back to its usual nature. Similarly, fire in a flint;[15] the latter does not overcome the force by fire by simple joining and approximation of its particles wherever they might be, except after rubbing and approaching the two pieces of stone by mutual pressure and friction; otherwise, fire will remain hidden in its inside, and will not start or become visible. And an argument in favor of this is also the fact that you will not find two persons who love each other except if there is between them an accord and agreement of natural qualities. This is absolutely necessary, even if it be in a small measure. And whenever the resemblance is greater the similarity (of species) increases and love becomes firmer. And if you look around you will see this plainly yourself. (Nykl, p. 10).

The cause of love is described in the same natural, material psychology as the Stilnovisti use (see page 259 here).

XXXIV

As regards the cause because of which love ever occurs in most cases, it is an outwardly beautiful form; because the soul is beautiful and passionately desires anything beautiful, and inclines toward perfect images: and if it sees such an image it fixes itself upon it; and if it discerns, after that, something of its nature in it, draws close to it, and true love comes to pass: and if it does not discern behind it something of its kind, its affection does not go beyond the *form*. Thus it is with *passion*. Truly, images are a wonderful vehicle of bringing about a union between parts of the souls distant from each other. (p. 11)

Plato is cited in support of this view of the process.

The whole section on the signs of being in love is very familiar from the medieval and post-Petrarchan tradition. The following is evocative of a whole tradition, from *Lancelot* to Yeats's 'She is foremost of those I would hear praised':[16]

XXXV

Another sign of love is: you find that the lover provokes hearing the name of the person beloved, and takes delight in talking about him and makes of such talk a subject of constant repetition and nothing pleases him so much as this, and he is not checked in this by the fear of the one who hears comprehending, and he who is present understanding his secret. If you love a thing it makes you blind and deaf! And if the lover could so arrange it that in the place where he is there should be nothing mentioned but the person he loves he would not wish to go beyond it; and it happens to a man truly in love that he begins eating when he has a desire for it, yet the very moment when he becomes excited by the mention of the beloved the meal becomes a choking obstruction in his throat and a throttling morsel in his oesophagus: thus it is with both water and talk; when he begins to talk to you he may be exceedingly gay, but then some casual thought comes to him concerning his beloved, and there at once becomes evident a sudden change of his enunciation and cutting short of his talk: and a sign of this is his remaining silent with downcast eyes, and perplexed hanging down of the head, and self-concentration: and while before his face was beaming and his motions were light, it becomes as if rigidly covered up and inert, his soul confused, his motions rigid, he is annoyed and weary in his speech, ill at ease when questioned. (p. 19)

The poet boasts that, in celebration of such deep love, he has written poems in which were comparisons of two, three, four and even five things, all in the form and metre required by the tradition. 'It seemed as if I and she, and the goblet, and the wine, and the starless night were softened ground, and rain, and pearls, and gold sand, and jade.' He comments: 'neither versification nor the construction of words allows more than this' (p. 21). The importance of the connexion here between love and writing poetry about it is as prominent as it is in the troubadours and the *Vita Nuova*. Indeed the whole enterprise of the

Neck-Ring, setting poems within the framework of an anatomy of love, is like that in the *Vita Nuova*. There is a different emphasis, however; while Dante seems to construct the framework at least partly for the purpose of exposition of the poetry, this poet seems to use the poems, important as they are to him, as illustrations of his general argument. Here I am quoting the argument rather than the poems, partly for this reason, but mainly because the poems depend very largely on their form, which is lost in translation.

The poet has interesting things to say about the requirement of secrecy (he questions whether this is because being in love is the activity of a bad man, but rejects this explanation) and the necessity of obedience to every demand of the beloved, even if it is not accordant with reason. The watcher is a significant figure in love affairs, whether inadvertent or inquisitive or a chaperon; a heritage for Pandarus could be seen here.

XXXVI

Then comes the watcher who when he perceived something of what is going on between the two, and made himself an idea of their condition, wants to verify the truth of it: and he becomes used to visiting them, and sits with them for a long while, and observes their movements, and looks fixedly at their faces, and counts every breath of theirs: and this is worse than war! . . .

Then comes the guardian of the beloved: with him, there is no trickery to be employed, except in trying to please him: and when he is pleased with a gift, then it is the limit of delight! This is the watcher whom the poets mentioned in their poems. And I have seen cases where one has been so kind in trying to propitiate the watcher that the watcher, instead of spying on him, was spying for him, pretending not to see when he was expected to be negligent, and averting dangers from him and working in his behalf. . . .

The most despicable watcher is the one who has experienced love in days gone by, and was smitten by it, and was in love for a long time: then freed himself of it after becoming wise to its meanings, and wishes to protect the person whom he is watching. And blessed be Allah — what a watcher such a person is, and what a woe laid like a snare comes upon the people in love on account of him! (Nykl, pp. 73–5)

When the poet treats of separation, he calls it the greatest misfortune in the world and 'the brother of death'. He dwells at some length, with illustrative stories, on the pain of loving from afar.

XXXVII

There are various kinds of separation. The first is for a period of time of which one is sure to see the end, and one is certain of a return shortly. But verily even then it is a heavy weight upon the heart and a bitter swallow in the throat, from which one is not relieved except by return. And I know a man whose beloved was absent from his sight only one day, and he was taken by so much agitation and sadness and worry and continuous chagrin that it nearly caused his death.

Then comes the separation caused by the prevention of meeting and by the seclusion of the beloved from her lover's sight: and this, even though your sweetheart were together with you in one house, is separation: because she is removed from you, and this indeed causes no little sadness and grief: we have experienced it and it was bitter! And on that subject I say:

I see her dwelling at each time and hour,
But the one who is in the house is concealed from me:
Does it profit me if the house is near,
When there is a watcher over its inhabitants watching that I should not come near them? . . .

Then comes separation purposely intended by the lover, in order to be far away from the slanderers' talk, or for fear that his stay might be the cause of preventing the meeting with the beloved and be a means for idle talk being spread about, and thus a strict seclusion of the beloved coming to pass.

Then comes the staying away caused by the lover because of some unfortunate vicissitude of Time obliging him to it, and then his excuse is either to be accepted or rejected, according to the motive that makes him undertake the sudden journey. (Nykl, pp. 122–3)

The greatest and most desolating separation is death, movingly described. The poet speaks of his beloved Nu'm, who, Nykl is anxious to establish, was the poet's great and only love; the description here, Nykl insists, is '*por experiencia*' (p. xiv).

XXXVIII

Then comes the parting at death: this is the passing away, and this is a parting where there is no hope of return; it is an overwhelming misfortune, which breaks the spine, and the greatest blow of Fate, and a great woe, which enshrouds more than the darkness of the night, and breaks off all hope, and wipes out all desire, and makes one despair of meeting. Here tongues are baffled, and the possibility of a remedy is cut off, and there is no way out of it except bearing it patiently willy-nilly: and this is the most grievous thing by which lovers are afflicted. And for him who has been struck by it there is nothing except lamentation and tears, until one perishes or becomes tired of it; and it is a wound which never heals, and a pain which never passes, and a grief which is renewed in proportion to the misfortune of whom you have enfolded in the darkness of the earth; and on that subject I say:

In every parting that occurs – hope is not gone;
Do not hasten despair – he who has not died is not gone:
But he who died, the despair concerning him is certain!

And we have seen many to whom this happened. Concerning myself I shall tell you that I am one of those who was struck by this adversity, and upon whom this misfortune has suddenly come: namely, I was most passionately infatuated and violently in love with a slave-girl of mine, whose name, in the past, was Nu'm;[17] she was the very ideal of everything one may wish, exceedingly beautiful in body and character, and very congenial to me. And I was her first lover, and we were mutually corresponding to each other in affection; and God's decree brought upon me a great calamity when nights and the passing of the day took her away: and she became the third with dust and stones!

When she died I was less than twenty years old and she was younger than I: and after her death I remained seven months without taking off my clothes, and my tears did not cease to flow, despite the dryness of my eyes and their little help: however it may be, by God, I have not forgotten to this day! And if a ransom were accepted I would ransom her with everything I possess in properties both inherited and acquired, and by some limbs of my body which are dear to me, promptly and willingly! And life was not sweet to me afterwards, and I have not forgotten her memory. (pp. 130–1)

Towards the end of the book, the poet turns to consider the ugliness of illicit practices, describing immorality in a very Augustinian– Robertsonian way when he considers 'the custom of God with those who practise immorality, striving towards something else but Him' (p. 195). Passion is condemned, and the poet concludes with a firm religious retraction, solidly based in reason. Indeed, given the hardships suffered by the poet and his people in the sack of Cordoba,[18] it is remarkable that his treatise on the subject of love is as worthy even as it is.

XXXIX

Here, my dear friend, ends what I have recalled in response to you with a view to gladden your heart, and in fulfilment of your request. And I did not refrain from mentioning to you in this essay things which poets mention and speak frequently of, treating them completely from various points of view, separating them into chapters and accompanying them with commentary: such as the exaggeration in the description of growing thin and the comparison of tears to rainfalls, and that they can quench the thirst of travelers, and a complete absence of sleep, and a total ceasing to eat food; only (I must say that) these latter are things to which there is no truth and lying is not the right way of acting. Everything has a limit and God has given to everything its proportioned measure; hence emaciation when it is made too great (and if a person became as they describe it he would be the size of a small ant or smaller), and would exceed the limit of the reasonable;[19] staying awake may reach the limit of several nights; but if a person lacked food for two weeks he would perish. However, if we said that the power to go without sleep is smaller than that of going without food (because sleep is the food for the spirit and meals are the food of the body, though they both do co-participate in each other's share), we only have had reference to the preponderating cases. As regards water I myself saw Meisur, the architect, our neighbour in Córdoba, who could go without water for two weeks in the hottest part of the summer and contented himself with the moisture that was in his food. And qādi Abū Adb-ur-Rahmān b. Gihhaf told me that he knew a man who had not drunk water for a month.

However, I have confirmed myself in this treatise of mine to wellknown truths beside which nothing can exist at all; and with the many instances I have already cited about the aforementioned aspects, let it suffice, so as not to deviate from the custom of poets and their ways of doing things; and many of our friends will find in this essay stories about them with their names disguised, according to what we have stipulated in its beginning. And I ask God, Most High, for pardon from what the two angels write and what the two watchers compute, on account of this and what resembles it, with the heart of him who knows that his talk is a part of his actions: but, in case it be not of the vanities for which a man is not taken to task, I hope, if it please God, that it will be of the pardonable venial sins; and at least, that it surely is not of the evils and abominations upon which falls eternal punishment; and at any rate, it is not of the great sins concerning which Revelation came.

And I know that some of those who are fanatically against me will find fault with me on account of having written something like this, and will say: 'It is contrary to his religious views,' and: 'It far departs from his chosen way': but I do not permit any one to suspect of me something which I did not mean to convey. Said God, Most High and Exalted: 'Oh ye who believe! carefully avoid suspicion; verily, some suspicion is sin.'[25]

Here ends the treatise known as Tauq-ul-Hamama by Abu Muhammad Ali b. Ahmad b. Sa'id Ibn Hazm, may God be pleased with him, after abbreviating *most of its poems*, and *letting stand only the best of them,* so as *to improve it,* and *show better its beauties*, and *reduce its volume,* and *make it easier to find out the strange meanings of its expressions*, with the praise of God, Most High, and His help, and kind succor. The copying of it was ended at the beginning of Regeb, the Only, 738.[20]

NOTES

1   Translated M. S. Wardrop; revised by E. Orbelyani and S. Jordanshili, Co-operative Publishing Society of Foreign Workers in the U.S.S.R., Moscow 1938. This edition is a corrected version of Marjory Wardrop's original translation (London 1912). The poem has received a good deal of attention in English recently: the 1912 Wardrop version was reprinted in 1966 ('Literatura Da Kheloveneba' (U.S.S.R.) Tbilisi), and a new translation by Venera Urushadze was published in Tbilisi in 1968. A 'free translation in prose' by Katharine Vivian, with a good introduction and a more readable style than most of the others, was published by the Folio Society (London) in 1977. The excerpts here are taken with permission from the 1938 version, chosen because it is the corrected version of what had aimed to be a close literal translation.

2   *Op. cit.*, p. 16.

3   For instance in *Ars Amatoria* I, 383–98 (and elsewhere in *Ars Amatoria* and *Amores*).

4   See R. Boase, *The Origin and Meaning of Courtly Love* (Manchester University Press 1977), pp. 11ff, and the summary, p. 18.

5   *A Book Containing the Risala, known as The Love's Neck-Ring, about Love and Lovers.* Trans. A. R. Nykl, Paris 1931. The excerpts here are taken from this edition, except that I have removed some of Nykl's many parentheses.

6   P. ci ff.

7   Baltimore 1946; Chapter VII, 'Relations between the Hispano-Arabic poetry and that of the first Aquitanian troubadours' (pp. 371–411). Compare *The Dove's Neck-Ring* Chapter IV, 'Poetry on the two sides of the Pyrenees', pp. lxi–ciii.

8   Wardrop says (1912, p. 6) that Arabia stands for Georgia, comparing Aeschylus, *Promentheus Bound*, 436–40.

9   Here Rust'haveli offers his own experience of love as his credentials in claiming to be a *magister amoris*, just as Ibn Hazm and many of the troubadours do. There is variation in the order of the sections between Wardrop 1912 and all the rest.

10   This is a very full statement of the identification of the courtly poet with the lover, a constant theme from Ibn Hazm to Petrarch.

11   This *amors/amars* distinction comes in the middle of a series of pronouncements that show the poem to be concerned with the same kind of love as the courtly poets.

12   Denomy, *The Heresy of Courtly Love*, p. 20.

13   Wardrop (1912, p. vii) says that this is one of 'three unpleasant incidents in the story', supposing it to have been 'as repugnant to Rust'haveli as to ourselves', accounted for by the fact that the three

'were all for the sake of women and directly instigated by women' (p. viii). But the repeated occurrence in courtly texts of the central lover's sexual distraction from his main suit might suggest that some less censorious explanation is called for: perhaps that an absolute distinction must be made between noble love and passing, selfish love.

14 This philosophical and physiological explanation of love can be compared with the definitions of the Stilnovisti: cf in particular 'Donna me prega', lines 58ff. (XCIV here) for the attraction of like things for each other.

15 It would be interesting to trace the history of this metaphor, familiar from *Timon of Athens* I.i.22 and the title of Seamus Heaney's essay on Hopkins taken from the poet's speech in *Timon* ('The Fire I' The Flint'; British Academy Lecture 1974; Oxford University Press 1974). The definition of the poet's activity, which seems somewhat uncalled for in *Timon*, clearly belongs to the same tradition as this passage of love definitions.

16 'Her Praise'. *Collected Poems*, Macmillan (London), 2nd ed. 1950, etc., p. 168.

17 See Nykl translation, p. lv and *passim*.

18 The sacking of Cordoba in 1012 is referred to on page xlvi in the course of Nykl's excellent outline of the historical background to Ibn Hazm and his poem.

19 No doubt the incompatibility of the reasonable with what love enjoined was as absolute a theme in Arabic love-poetry as in *Lancelot* and Arnaut Daniel. Accordingly, this retraction contradicts what has gone before as flatly as Andreas, Boccaccio and the fourteenth-century English poets do.

20 i.e. A.D. 1337–8.

The troubadours

Whether or not one accepts C. S. Lewis's view of courtly love that 'every one knows that it appears quite suddenly at the end of the eleventh century in Languedoc' in the poetry of the troubadours,[1] there can be no doubt about the importance of the Provençal poets of the twelfth and thirteenth centuries in the development of European love poetry. Wherever the ultimate sources of the impulses and terms of courtly love are to be sought, the characteristics and forms usually ascribed to it (a feudal respect for the dominant loved lady; the figures of jealous husband, tale-bearer, votive and lady; the cult of joy from love; ideas such as *mesura, solace, pretz, valors*) are all found fully articulated in the first surviving *cansos*, those of Guilhem IX of Aquitaine. The first of the poets already follow the systematic practices of courtly love (use of the term *fin amor*, for instance, and all that it entails) before its system had been defined.

Yet much of the poetry itself remains obscure in many ways. The repeated terminology noted in the last paragraph is more familiar than clearly comprehended. Poet after poet says he is choosing the *trobar clus* (obscure style) or the *trobar leu* (simple style); yet it is by no means self-evident what these terms mean precisely, or whether the distinction is one of form or content. Many pages have been written, not fully conclusively, about the exact senses of the terms *jois* and *amor*. In spite of the great appeal of this poetry, the troubadour poems which can be read with immediate understanding by a modern reader are few.[2]

This uncertainty has been compounded by the pseudo-biographical information supplied by the thirteenth- and fourteenth-century writers of the *vidas* of the troubadours, who concocted lives of the troubadours to introduce compilations of their work. Most of these are deduced from situations apparently described in the poems, where they are almost certainly only metaphorical; famous examples are the story of Jaufre Rudel and the Countess of Tripoli (XLII here) inferred from such poems as 'Lanquan li jorn' (XLIII here) and 'Quan lo rius', and the story of how Peire Vidal dressed in a wolfskin to be hunted by hounds in celebration of the name of his lady Loba de Pennautier (see note 52 to this section). Even before the *vidas*, no doubt, the troubadours were cult figures, a status which it seems they courted, to judge from the repeated self-references in their poetry. The culmination of this cult-making process was the late sixteenth-century collection of troubadour biographies by John Nostrodamus,[3] brother of the soothsayer and no more reliable than him, whose accounts were regarded as historical until the nineteenth century. This literal interpretation was entirely misleading for understanding of the poetry, since the poetic, religious or metaphorical significance of a poem was lost by a reading that took it as a simple statement of fact.

Although modern commentators feel that they can outline with more certainty the developments in troubadour poetry between 1090 and 1323, a consideration of the views of twentieth-century authorities since Jeanroy shows how much interpretations still vary. For instance, Jeanroy says that after Guilhem IX the poetry divides into two schools: one of poetry of divine love, such as Marcabru's (Jeanroy calls these poets 'realistic', using in a loose way a distinction drawn from medieval theological philosophy perhaps), and the other of more secular poetry which Jeanroy calls 'idealist', such as that of Eblo of Ventadorn (of whose work nothing survives) and Jaufre Rudel.[4] We would not now think of Jaufre as distinctively secular. The distinction becomes more useful, perhaps, when we look at the followers of the 'idealist' tradition, such as Bernart de Ventadorn in his 'romantic' poetry (though he dissociates himself from Eblo's school in 'Lo tems vai', lines 22–3, and we should heed L. T.

Topsfield's warning against regarding Bernart as 'a Wordsworth of the twelfth century').[5] Entirely opposed to Jeanroy's distinction is A. J. Denomy's argument[6] that Marcabru and Bernart are united by the same kind of high-minded love, as opposed to the lustful love of the school of Eblo, and that the difference between them is one of style: the crude 'realism' of Marcabru against the subtler 'idealism' of Bernart (using these terms in more normal moral senses than in Jeanroy's distinction). And indeed if one takes a different kind of poetry from Bernard's *oeuvre* (such as 'Lo tems vai' or even 'Non es mervelha' (XLIV here), where the 'romantic' elements are not so prominent), it does seem to be a good deal less different from the writing of Marcabru.

This religious–secular contrast, or absence of it, is of central importance because one of the principal means of classification among historians of troubadour poetry has been the extent to which a particular poet is religious or secular in purpose. Moreover, the historical and geographical links of these poets with Catharism and the Albigensian heresy make possible religious interpretations crucial. Broadly speaking, there seems to be a development from the early, purely sensual poetry of Guilhem IX, through the increasingly moralising work of Marcabru and Peire d'Alvernhe, to the late, religious poetry of Guiraut Riquier. But this sequence has to be applied with great caution to particular poets within its historical scope, as is clear from views such as Jeanroy's in the last paragraph. The argument, familiar to readers of the Middle English lyric, about the mutual influence of secular and religious poetry and the difficulty of assigning particular poems in the twilight area between them to one category or the other, applies in a marked way to the troubadours. Just as it has been argued that a phrase such as 'best of bone and blood' in Middle English poetry cannot be used without provoking a religious association, so the question of the connotations of a word like '*amors*' (as contrasted, say, with Marcabru's '*amars*') is a vexed one. Troubadour poetry, both as an influence and as a parallel, can valuably be adduced as evidence in this argument about Middle English.[7]

The influence of the Provençal poets is soon evident in other European literature. In Dante's *De Vulgari Eloquentia*, written very early in the fourteenth century, there are references to, and quotations from Arnaut Daniel, Folquet de Marseilles and Guiraut de Borneil. Dante clearly sees a direct descent from these poets to the Italian poets of the *stil nuovo*: Cino da Pistoia, Cino's friend (Dante himself), Guinicelli, Cavalcanti and others. Indeed he links all these poets together as writers in the vernacular in his lists of illustrations, at one point showing the similarity of the senses of the word *amor* in various languages with illustration from Guiraut, the King of Navarre and Guinicelli.[8] But Dante's criticism, concerned primarily with formal considerations as it is, does not help greatly in the matter of interpretation. The one interpretative observation he makes is rather puzzling, when he nominates the poets pre-eminent in various fields: Bertran de Born in arms, Arnaut in love and Guiraut in rectitude. The most striking qualities of Arnaut seem now to be formal virtuosity and difficulty of expression, and of Guiraut the formal perfection of his solutions to the problems set by the requirements of the love poem. Few of the troubadours seem less explicitly concerned with righteousness than Guiraut.[9] But we must believe and attempt to understand Dante's testimony about these writers, since he followed them and, in some lines of development of the *trobar clus*, brought them to perfection.

Nothing so clearly illustrates the influence of the troubadours on other European poetry[95] as the effect that the meanings of technical words in Provençal had on the cognate words in Italian (as well as in the Northern French of the trouvères and, less obviously, in the German of the *Minnesänger*). This influence is shown very interestingly by Valency (*In Praise of Love*, p. 198). *Umile* comes to mean 'simple'; *canoscenza* 'wisdom'; *sofferenca* 'patience'; *cattivo* 'unhappy'; *caro* 'rare'; *invidia* 'longing' (side by side with 'envy'); and *ira* 'grief' (side by side with 'wrath'). One might add the critical use of the word 'ragione', suggested by the Provençal 'razo'.

Modern assessment of the merits of these poets can be guided in part by their early admirers. The thirteenth-century *vida* of Guiraut tells us that he was known as the *'maestre dels trobadors'*, and few later critics have diverged violently from that accolade. Guinicelli, in *Purgatorio* XXVI (XCVIII here) is made to say (perhaps reflecting his real views) that Arnaut surpasses everyone in verses of love, and that those who think Guiraut ('he of Limoges') is the foremost are fools. Petrarch too calls Arnaut 'il primo . . . Gran maestro d'amor'

(*Trionfo d'Amore* iv, 40–1). For the most part, only Bernart de Ventadorn of the other poets has since been elevated to a rank equal to these two. Judgements of the worth of troubadour poetry must rely heavily on formal criteria: music, versification and metre. Often the material for such a judgement is absent, as in the case of Guilhem IX when he praises himself for the melody of 'Pus vezem', (XL here) 'good and excellent'. It is important to remember that any assessment based only on the words on the page is a partial one; one feels uneasy about Topsfield's omission of Guiraut de Borneil from his survey of the development of troubadour ideas on the grounds that his 'significance in the development of the troubadour love lyric appears to lie more in the manner and style rather than the substance of his work' (*Troubadours and Love*, p. 1). Much of troubadour poetry (like the poetry of many ages) is *about* composition and its difficulties, with the love theme apparently used only as a structure to contain the discussion. Generally in poetry we expect fixed forms (the sonnet, say, or rhyme royal) to be used to contain new ideas; in troubadour poetry, fixed ideas are very often used as a vehicle for new and brilliant forms. The courtly love situation and the poems' circumstances in the *alba, pastorela* or *planh* are more conventional than the forms, such as Arnaut's invented *sestina*. The roles of tenor and vehicle are reversed, as Valency says (*In Praise of Love*, p. 123).

An anthology like this one inevitably under-emphasises the formal and musical side of troubadour composition. It is also unrepresentative in concentrating on love poetry, even though that is what the poets are most celebrated for. Their satirical, moralising poems (*sirventes*) are of great importance in content and number, though they are not the concern of an anthology of love poetry. But even the poems included here show that a collection of Provençal love-writings containing no observations on contemporary ideas, events or methods of composition would be an impossibility. It is clear from almost every troubadour poem that these poets were never concerned to write a simple poem in praise of a particular lady. Their scope extends a great deal more widely, into metrics, politics and theology than the amorous prescriptions of Andreas and the summary of C. S. Lewis have taught readers to expect.

Unless the contrary is specified, the texts here are taken from the invaluable edition of A. R. Press (Edinburgh University Press 1971), which has made wide familiarity with the troubadours possible for English readers.

GUILHEM IX OF AQUITAINE
(1071–1127)[10]

XL

Pus vezem de novelh florir
Pratz e vergiers reverdezir,
Rius e fontanas esclarzir,
Auras e vens,
Ben deu quascus lo joy jauzir   5
Don es jauzens.

D'amor non dey dire mas be.
Quar no n'ai ni petit ni re?
Quar ben leu plus no m'en cove;
Pero leumens   10
Dona gran joy qui be.n mante
Los aizimens.

A totz jorns m'es pres enaissi
Qu'anc d'aquo qu'aimiey non jauzi,
Ni o faray ni anc no fi;   15
Qu'az esciens
Fas mantas res que.l cor me di:
'Tot es nïens.'

XL

When we see the fields flowering again and the gardens
growing green, the streams and the fountains becoming bright,
breezes and winds, certainly everyone should rejoice in the joy
by which he is made happy.

Of love I ought to say nothing but good. Why do I have little
or nothing of it? Perhaps because more would not suit me. Yet
it freely gives great joy to the man who abides by its rules.

What has always happened to me is this: that I have never
found joy in the quarter where I loved. I never will, and I never
have yet. So quite consciously I perform many actions while
my heart says to me: 'all is useless'.

(XL)

Per tal n'ai meyns de bon saber:
Quar vuelh so que no puesc aver;   20
E si.l reproviers me ditz ver
Certanamens:
'A bon coratge bon poder'—
Qui's ben suffrens.

Ja no sera nuils hom ben fis   25
Contr'amor, si non l'es aclis,
Et als estranhs et als vezis
Non es consens,
Et a totz sels d'aicels aizis
Obedïens.   30

Obedïensa deu portar
A motas gens, qui vol amar,
E coven li que sapcha far
Faigz avinens,
E que.s gart en cort de parlar   35
Vilanamens.

Del vers vos dig que mais en vau,
Qui ben l'enten, e n'a plus lau,
Que.l mot son fag tug per egau
Cominalmens,   40
E.l sonetz, qu'ieu mezeis m'en lau,
Bos e valens.

Mon Esteve, mas ieu no.i vau,
Sïa.l prezens
Mos vers, e veulh que d'aquest lau   45
.M sïa guirens.

(XL)

Because of this I have less happiness,[11] because I want what I cannot have. And still the proverb surely tells me the truth: 'If there's a will, there's a way' – for the man who is very patient.

No man will ever be wholly faithful[12] towards Love if he does not pay homage to it, acting agreeably towards strangers and neighbours alike, and obediently to all the natives of the place.

The man who wishes to love must display obedience to many people; and it is fitting for him to know how to behave graciously and to guard against speaking churlishly in the court.

Concerning this poem, I tell you that it is more meaningful and more to be praised for the man who construes it well. For the words are all alike made to the same measure, and the tune (for which I praise myself) is good and noble.

May my poem present itself before my friend Stephen, though I am not going to him myself. And I wish that he should be the seconder of this praise for me.

MARCABRU
(c. 1110–c. 1150)

XLI

Cortesamen vuoill comenssar
Un vers, si es qui l'escout'ar,
E puois tant m'en sui entremes,
Veirai si.l poirai affinar,
Qu'eras vouill mon chan esmerar,   5
E dirai vos de maintas res.

Assatz pot hom villanejar
Qui Cortezïa vol blasmar,
Que.l plus savis e.l mieills apres
Non sap tantas dire ni far   10
C'om no li posca enseignar
Petit o pro, tals hora es.

De Cortezïa.is pot vanar
Qui ben sap Mesur'esguardar;
E qui tot vol auzir quant es,   15
Ni tot cant ve cuid'amassar,
Del tot l'es ops a mesurar,
O ja non sera trop cortes.

Mesura es de gen parlar,
E Cortezïa es d'amar;   20
E qui non vol esser mespres,
De tota vilanïa.is gar,
D'escarnir e de folleiar,
Puois sera savis, ab qu'el pes.

XLI

I want to begin a poem of a courtly[13] kind, if there is anyone who listens to such nowadays. And since I am so far embarked on it, I will see if I can refine it, because I want to perfect my song now; and I will tell you about many things.

The man who wants to find fault with Courtesy is certainly capable of acting churlishly. For the most wise and informed is not able to say or do so much that he cannot be taught something, slight or significant, at some time.

The person who can keep well to Moderation can boast of courtliness; and the man who wants to hear everything there is, or who is determined to gather together all that he sees, he must be moderate in everything, or he will never be very courtly.

Moderation is speaking graciously, and it is Courtliness to love; and the man who does not want to be in error must guard against all discourtesy, against sneering and speaking evil. Then he will be wise, by remembering this.

C'aissi pot savis hom reignar,   25
E bona dompna meillurar;
Mas cella qu'en pren dos ni tres
E per un non si vol fïar,
Ben deu sos pretz asordeiar,
E sa valors a chascun mes.   30

Aitals amors fai a prezar
Que si meteissa ten a car;
E s'ieu en dic nuill vilanes
Per mal que la.n vueilh encolpar,
Be.ill lauzi fassa.m pro muzar,   35
Qu'ieu n'aurai so que.m n'a promes.

Lo vers e.l son vuoill envïar
A.N Jaufre Rudel outra mar,
E vuoill que l'aujon li Frances
Per lor coratges alegrar;   40
Que Dieus lor o pot perdonar:
O sïa pechatz, o merces.

JAUFRE RUDEL
(died before 1167)

XLII   *Vida*

Jaufres Rudels de Blaia si fo molt gentils hom, princes de Blaia; et enamoret.se de la comtessa de Tripol ses vezer, per lo ben q'el n'auzi dir als pelegrins que vengron d'Antiochia; e fetz de lieis mains vers ab bons sons, ab paubres motz.

E, per voluntat de liei vezer, el se crozet e mes.se en mar; e pres.lo malautia en la nau, e fo condug a Tripol, en un alberc, per mort. E fo faich asaber a la comtessa, et ella venc ad el, al sieu lieich, e pres.lo entre sos bratz; et el saup q'ella era la comtessa, e recobret lo vezer e.l flazar, e lauzet Dieu e.l grazi qe.ill avia la vida sostenguda tro q'el l'ages vista; et enaissi el moric entre sos bratz. Et ella lo fetz a gran honor sepeillir en la maison del Temple; e pois en aqel dia ella se rendet monga, per la dolor qe ella ac de la soa mort.

So can the wise man act and the good lady become better.[14] But she who takes two or three and does not want to keep faith with one only, certainly her reputation and her worth must decline every month.

Such love as prizes itself highly is to be valued.[15] And if I say anything discourteous of it because of some misfortune that I want to blame love for, then I readily give my approval that it should waste my time in such a way that I do not have what it promised me.

This poem and tune I wish to send to M. Jaufre Rudel[16] across the sea; and I would like the French to hear it, to lighten their spirits. For God can grant them this: wherever there be sin, let there be mercy.

XLII   *Life*[17]

Jaufre Rudel of Blaia was a very noble man, a prince of Blaie; and he fell in love with the countess of Tripoli, without seeing her, through the good things which he heard said about her by the pilgrims who came from Antioch; and he composed many songs about her, with good tunes but poor words.

And, because of his wish to see her, he became a crusader and set to sea; and he became ill on the ship, and he was brought to Tripoli, into an inn, for dead. And this was made known to the countess, and she came to him, to his bed, and took him into her arms; and he knew it was the countess, and he recovered his sight and his sense of smell, and he praised God and thanked him for having sustained his life until he saw her; and thus he died within her arms. And she had him buried with great honour in the house of the Temple; and then the same day she entered a monastery, because of the sorrow which she had at his death.

XLIII

Lanquan li jorn son lonc, en may,
M'es belhs dous chans d'auzelhs de lonh;
E quan mi suy partitz de lay,
Remembra.m d'un'amor de lonh;
Vau de talan embroncx e clis,   5
Si que chans ni flors d'albespis
No.m valon plus qu'iverns gelatz.

Be tenc lo Senhor per veray
Per qu'ieu veirai l'amor de lonh;
Mas, per un ben que m'en eschay,   10
N'ai dos mals, quar tant suy de lonh.
Ai! car no suy lai pelegris,
Si que mos fustz e mos tapis
Fos pels sieus belhs huelhs remiratz.

Be.m parra joys quan li querray,   15
Per amor Dieu, l'ostal de lonh;
E, s'a lieys platz, alberguarai
Pres de lieys, si be.m suy de lonh.
Qu'aissi es lo parlamens fis,
Quan drutz lonhdas es tan vezis   20
Qu'ab cortes ginh jauzis solatz.

Iratz e dolens m'en partray,
S'ieu no vey sest'amor de lonh.
Non sai quora mais la veyrai,
Que tan son nostras terras lonh;   25
Assatz hi a pas e camis,
E per aisso no.n suy devis—
Mas tot sïa cum a lieis platz!

Ja mais d'amor no.m jauziray
Si no.m jau d'est'amor de lonh,   30
Que melhor ni gensor no.n sai
Ves nulha part, ni pres ni lonh;

XLIII

When the days are long in May,[18] I love the sweet songs of the birds from far away; and, when I am separated from that place, I remember a far-off love. I go around depressed and bowed with desire, so that neither birdsong nor hawthorn blossom is any more good to me than frozen winter.

Certainly I regard as trustworthy that Lord through whom I shall see that distant love. But for every benefit that comes to me from it I have two miseries, because I am so far away. Ah! why am I not a pilgrim there so that my staff and my coat would be seen by her beautiful eyes?

Certainly joy will come to me when I ask her for hospitality, for the love of God, in that distant place. And if it is pleasing to her, I will lodge near her, even though I am one from far away. For thus is the exchange admirable, when the lover from far is so near at hand that he rejoices in comfort in courtly manner.

In grief and sorrowing will I set out if I do not see this distant love. I do not know when I will ever see her, so far away are our countries from each other. There are enough roads and highways, and I am not separated from her because of that. But let all be as she pleases!

Never ever will I take joy in love if I do not rejoice in this distant love. For I know none that is better or more noble in any region, near or far. So high and elevated is her worth that

Tant es sos pretz ricx e sobris
Que lay, el reng dels Sarrazis,
Fos ieu per lieys chaitius clamatz.   35

Dieus que fetz tot quant ve ni vai
E formet sest'amor de lonh,
Mi don poder, que cor ben ai,
Qu'ieu veya sest'amor de lonh
Verayamen, en luec aiziz,   40
Si que la cambra e.l jardis
Mi resemblon novels palatz.

Ver ditz qui m'apella lechay
Ni deziros d'amor de lonh;
Que nulhs autres joys tan no.m play   45
Cum jauzimens d'amors de lonh.
Mas so qu'ieu vuelh m'es tant ahis
Qu'enaissi.m fadet mos pairis:
Qu'ieu ames e non fos amatz.

there, in the kingdom of the Saracens, I would for her sake be called a captive.[19]

May God who made everything that comes or goes, and shaped that distant love, give me the strength (for I certainly have the will) that I might see this distant love in reality, in a place nearby, so that the room and the garden may seem to me a new palace.

The man who calls me anxious for and desirous of distant love is right. For no other joy pleases me as much as rejoicing in a distant love. But that which I want is so ill-disposed to me because my godfather made it thus, that I should love and not be loved.[20]

BERNART DE VENTADORN
(*fl. c.* 1140–1175?)[21]

XLIV

Non es meravelha s'eu chan
melhs de nul autre chantador,
que plus me tra.l cors vas amor
e melhs sui faihz a so coman.
cor e cors e saber e sen   5
e fors' e poder i ai mes;
si.m tira vas amor lo fres
que vas autra part no.m aten.

Ben es mortz qui d'amor no sen
al cor cal que dousa sabor;   10
e que val viure ses valor
mas per enoi far a la gen?
ja Domnedeus no.m azir tan
qu'eu ja pois viva jorn ni mes,
pois que d'enoi serai mespres   15
ni d'amor non aurai talan.

Per bona fe e ses enjan
am la plus bel' e la melhor.
del cor sospir e dels olhs plor,
car tan l'am eu, per que i ai dan.   20
eu que.n posc mais, s'Amors me pren
e las charcers en que m'a mes,
no pot claus obrir mas merces,
e de merce no.i trop nien?

Aquest' amors me fer tan gen   25
al cor d'una dousa sabor:
cen vetz mor lo jorn de dolor
e reviu de joi autras cen.
ben es mos mals de bel semblan,
que mais val mos mals qu'autre bes;   30

XLIV

It is no wonder if I sing better than any other singer,[22] for my heart draws me more towards love and I am better made for its command. In it I have placed my heart and body, intelligence and mind and strength and ability. The reins draw me so much towards love that I cannot pay attention to anything else.

That person is certainly dead who does not feel in his heart some sweet taste of love; and what does it achieve to live without worth, except to cause boredom to people? May the Lord God never detest me so much that I should ever live a day or a month after I have been guilty of tediousness or of lacking a taste for love.

In good faith and without artifice do I love the most beautiful and best. From my heart I sigh and from my eyes I weep, because I love her so much that I am injured by it. What can I ever do if Love holds me prisoner and no key except mercy can open the dungeon in which it has put me, and I can find no mercy whatever?

This love strikes me so graciously in the heart with a sweet taste. A hundred times a day I die of sorrow, and I revive with joy another hundred. Certainly my malady has a beautiful

e pois mos mals aitan bos m'es,
bos er lo bes apres l'afan.

Ai Deus! car se fosson trian
d'entrels faus li fin amador,
e.lh lauzenger e.lh trichador   35
portesson corns el fron denan!
tot l'aur del mon e tot l'argen
i volgr'aver dat, s'ue l'agues,
sol que ma domna conogues
aissi com eu l'am finamen.   40

Cant eu la vei, be m'es parven
als olhs, al vis, a la color,
car aissi tremble de paor
com fa la folha contra.l ven.
non ai de sen per un efan,   45
aissi sui d'amor entrepres;
e d'ome qu'es aissi conques,
pot domn' aver almorna gran.

Bona domna, re no.us deman
mas que.m prendatz per servidor,   50
qu'e.us servirai com bo senhor,
cossi que del gazardo m'an.
ve.us m'al vostre comandamen,
francs cors umils, gais e cortes!
ors ni leos non etz vos ges,   55
que.m aucizatz, s'a vos me ren.

A Mo Cortes, lai on ilh es,
tramet lo vers, e ja no.lh pes
car n'ai estat tan lonjamen.

face, and my ill is worth more than another good. And since my ill pleases me so much, the good after the pain will be great.

Ah God! if only true lovers could be distinguished from the false, and the flatterers and tricksters wear horns on their brows. I would readily have given all the gold and all the silver in the world, if I had it, if only my lady could recognise how devotedly I love her.

When I see her, surely it appears in my eyes and face and complexion, because I tremble with fear just as the leaf does against the wind. I have not the judgment of a child, so captive am I by love. And for a man who is so defeated a lady may have great pity.

Good lady, nothing do I ask of you but that you take me as your servant, for I will serve you as I would a good lord, whatever I have in the way of reward. See me at your bidding, you who are a noble and modest person, joyful and courtly. You are not at all a bear or a lion that you should kill me if I give myself up to you.

To my courtly Lady, there where she is, I send the poem, and let it not in any way distress her that I have not been there for such a long time.

XLV

Can vei la lauzeta mover
De joi sas alas contra.l rai,
Que s'oblid'e.s laissa chazer
Per la doussor c'al cor li vai,
Ai, tan grans enveya m'en ve   5
De cui qu'eu veya jauzïon,
Meravilhas ai car desse
Lo cor de dezirer no.m fon.

Ai las, tan cuidava saber
D'amor, e tan petit en sai!   10
Car eu d'amar no.m posc tener
Celeis don ja pro non aurai.
Tout m'a mo cor e tout m'a me,
E se mezeis e tot lo mon,
E can se.m tolc, no.m laisset re   15
Mas dezirer e cor volon.

Anc non agui de me poder
Ni no fui meus de l'or'en sai
Que.m laisset en sos olhs vezer,
En un miralh que mout me plai.   20
Miralhs, pus me mirei en te,
M'an mort li sospir de prëon,
C'aissi.m perdei com perdet se
Lo bels Narcisus en la fon.

De las domnas me dezesper;   25
Ja mais en lor no.m fiarai,
C'aissi com las solh chaptener,
Enaissi las deschaptenrai.
Pos vei c'una pro no m'en te
Vas leis que.m destrui e.m. cofon,   30
Totas las dopt'e las mescre,
Car be sai c'atretals se son.

XLV

When I see the lark[23] moving its wings against the sun's rays for joy, until it forgets itself and lets itself drop because of the sweetness that comes into its heart, ah! such great envy of whatever I see rejoicing comes to me that I am surprised that my heart is not immediately taken from me through desire.

Alas, I presumed to know so much of love, and how little of it I do know! For I cannot keep myself from loving her from whom I shall never have benefit. She has taken from me my heart and myself, and herself and the whole world. And when she took herself from me, she left me nothing but desiring and a wishful heart.

Never have I had power over myself, nor have I to this day been mine, since the hour when she let me look into her eyes, into a mirror which pleases me greatly. Mirror,[24] since I gazed at myself in you, sighs from deep down have killed me; and so I lost myself, just as the beautiful Narcissus lost himself in the fountain.

I despair of the ladies. Never again shall I trust myself to them. And, just as I used to protect them, now I shall abandon them. Since I see that not one of them gives me help against her who destroys and ruins me, I suspect and mistrust them all, because I know well that they are all the same.

D'aisso.s fa be femna parer
Ma domna, per qu'e.lh o retrai,
Car no vol so c'om deu voler   35
E so c'om li deveda. fai
Chazutz sui en mala merce,
Et ai be faih co.l fols en pon;
E no sai per que m'esdeve
Mas car trop puyei contra mon.   40

Merces es perduda per ver,
Et eu non o saubi anc mai.
Car cilh qui plus en degr'aver
No.n a ges. et on la querrai?
A, can mal sembla, qui la ve,   45
Qued aquest chaitiu deziron
Que ja ses leis non aura be
Laisse morir, que no l'āon!

Pus ab midons no.m pot valer
Precs ni merces ni.l dreihz qu'eu ai,   50
Ni a leis no ven a plazer
Qu'eu l'am, ja mais no.lh o dirai.
Aissi.m part de leis e.m recre;
Mort m'a e per mort li respon,
E vau m'en, pus ilh no.m rete,   55
Chaitius, en issilh, no sai on.

Tristans, ges non auretz de me,
Qu'eu m'en vau, chaitius, no sai on.
De chantar me gic e.m recre,
E de joi e d'amor m'escon.   60

By this my lady declares herself a woman for certain, and because of it I accuse her thus: that she does not want what should be wanted, and that she does that which is forbidden her. I have fallen upon harsh mercy, and I have behaved just like the fool on the bridge.[25] And I do not know why this has befallen me, except that I aspired too high.

Mercy is indeed lost, and I never once experienced it. Because she who ought to have it most has none at all; so where shall I search for it? Ah! how little it seems to someone who sees her that she leaves to die this yearning prisoner, and does not help him who never will have good without her.

Since neither prayer nor mercy can help me with my lady nor the justice that is on my side, and it does not happen to please her that I love her, never more will I tell her so. So I depart from her and give up. She has killed me and with my death I answer her; and, since she will not hold me, I go away as a slave into exile, I do not know where.

Tristan,[26] you will learn not a thing from me, for I am going away as a slave, I do not know where. I leave my singing and give up, and depart from joy and love.

RAIMBAUT D'AURENGA
(*c.* 1144–1173)[27]

XLVI

Non chant per auzel ni per flor
Ni per neu ni per gelada,
Ni neis per freich ni per calor,
Ni per reverdir de prada;
Ni per nuill autr'esbaudimen   5
Non chan, ni non fui chantaire,
Mas per midonz en cui m'enten,
Car es del mon la bellaire.

Ar sui partitz de la pejor
C'anc fos vista ni trobada,   10
Et am del mon la bellazor
Dompna, e la plus prezada.
E farai ho al mieu viven,
Que d'alres non sui amaire;
Car ieu crei qu'ill a bon talen   15
Ves mi, segon mon vejaire.

Ben aurai, dompna, grand honor
Si ja de vos m'es jutgada
Honranssa que sotz cobertor
Vos tenga nud'embrassada;   20
Car vos valetz las meillors cen,
Qu'ieu non sui sobregabaire.
Sol del pretz ai mon cor gauzen
Plus que s'era emperaire!

De midonz fatz dompn'e seignor,   25
Cals que sïa.il destinada,
Car ieu begui de la amor,
Que ja.us dei amar, celada.
Tristan, qan la.il det Yseus gen,

XLVI

I do not sing because of bird or flower or snow or frost, nor even because of cold or heat or because of the field growing green again. I do not sing for any other happiness, nor have I ever been a singer except on account of my lady for whom I yearn, for she is the most beautiful in the world.

Now am I parted from the worst that ever was seen or discovered, and I love the most beautiful lady in the world and the most prized. And I shall do that all my life because I am in love with nothing else. And I believe that she has a good inclination towards me, according to my judgement.

Certainly, lady, I shall be greatly honoured if ever the privilege is granted to me in a judgement of yours that under the bedclothes I should hold you naked in my embrace. For you are worth a hundred times the best, and I am not exaggerating. In that prize alone my heart has delight, more than if I were emperor!

Of my beloved I make lady and lord, whatever may be my destiny. For I have drunk that secret love, so that always I must love you. Tristan, when noble Iseult the Fair granted it to

La bela, no.n saup als faire,   30
Et ieu am per aital coven
Midonz, don no.m posc estraire.

Sobre totz aurai gran valor
S'aitals camisa m'es dada
Cum Yseus det a l'amador,   35
Que mais non era portada.
Tristan, mout presetz gent presen:
D'aital sui eu enquistaire.
Si.l me dona cill cui m'enten,
No.us port enveja, bels fraire!   40

Vejatz, dompna, cum Dieus acor
Dompna que d'amar s'agrada:
Q'Iseutz estet en gran paor,
Puois fon breumens conseillada
Qu'il fetz a son marit crezen   45
C'anc hom que nasques de maire
Non toques en lieis: mantenen
Atrestal podetz vos faire!

Carestïa, esgauzimen
M'aporta d'aicel repaire   50
On es midonz qu.m ten gauzen
Plus q'ieu eis non sai retraire.

XLVII

Ar resplan la flors enversa
Pels trencans rancx e pels tertres.
Cals flors? Neus, gels e conglapis
Que cotz e destrenh e trenca;
Don vey morz quils, critz, brays, siscles   5
En fuelhs, en rams e en giscles.
Mas mi ten vert e jauzen joys
Er quan vey secx los dolens croys.

him, could not do anything else, and I love my lady by a similar necessity from which I cannot extricate myself.[29]

Above all men I shall have great success if such a shirt is given to me as Iseult gave to her lover, for it was never worn again.[30] Tristan, you greatly esteemed the noble gift; I am on the quest of such a one. If she for whom I yearn gives me one, I bear no envy towards you, beautiful brother.

See, Lady, how God helps the lady who rejoices in loving. For Iseult was in great dread and then immediately was counselled so that she made her husband believe that no man who was born of a mother had ever touched her.[31] Now you can do just the same.

O Abstinence,[32] bring me happiness from the place where my lady is who keeps me joyful more than I can describe it.

XLVII

Now the reverse flower[33] shines along the sharp rocks and the hills. What flower? Snow, ice and frost which burns and pains and cuts. Because of it I see that the cries, shrills, songs and whistlings in the leaves are dead. But Joy keeps me green and exultant, now when I see desiccated the gloomy, miserable ones.

Quar enaissi m'o enverse
Que bel plan mi semblon tertre,   10
E tenc per flor lo conglapi,
E.l cautz m'es vis que.l freit trenque,
E.l tro mi son chant e siscle.
E paro.m fulhat li giscle.
Aissi.m suy ferm lassatz en joy   15
Que re non vey que.m sïa croy—

Mas una gen fad'enversa
Cum s'eron noirit en tertres,
Que.m fan pro pieigz que conglapis,
Q'us quecx ab sa lengua trenca   20
E.n parla bas et ab siscles.
E no.y val bastos ni giscles
Ni menassas; ans lur es joys
Quan fan so don hom los clam croys.

Qu'ar en baizan no.us enverse   25
No m'o tolon pla ni tertre,
Dona, ni gel ni conglapi,
Mas non-poder trop en trenque.
Dona, per cuy chant e siscle,
Vostre belh huelh mi son giscle   30
Que'm castïon si.l cor ab joy
Qu'ieu no.us aus aver talan croy.

Anat ai cum cauz'enversa,
Sercan rancx e vals e tertres,
Marritz cum selh que conglapis   35
Cocha e mazelh'e trenca;
Que no.m conquis chans ni siscles
Plus que folhs clercx conquer giscles.
Mas ar, Dieu lau, m'alberga joys
Malgrat dels fals lauzengiers croys.   40

Because I invert things for myself, so that hills seem to me beautiful plains and I regard the frost as a flower, and the heat seems to me to cut through the cold, and the thunder is songs and whistlings for me, and the dry sticks are leaved to me. I am so wholly taken up in Joy that I can see nothing which is miserable in my eyes —

but a stupid, inverted crowd of people (as if they had been nourished on the hills) whose effect on me is worse than frost! For each of them cuts with his tongue and speaks low and with whistles. And neither stick nor rod nor threats are any good. Indeed it is a joy for them when they do that for which they are called contemptible.

Now though, neither plains nor hills, my lady, stop me from laying you down to kiss you; neither does ice or frost, but stupefaction utterly cuts me off from it. Lady, because of whom I sing and whistle, your lovely eyes are rods to me which strike me in the heart with joy so that I dare not have low desire for you.

I have gone like a creature upside down, searching rocks and valleys and hills, demented like someone that the frost oppresses and destroys and cuts. For neither song nor whistle overcame me any more than the rod subdues undisciplined students. But now, praise to God! joy harbours me in spite of evil, contemptible slanderers.

Mos vers an, qu'aissi l'enverse
Que no.l tenhon bosc ni tertre,
Lai on hom non sen conglapi,
Ni a freitz poder que.y trenque.
A midons lo chant e.l siscle   45
Clar, qu'el cor l'en intro.l giscle,
Selh que sap gen chantar ab joy,
Que no tanh a chantador croy.

Doussa dona, amors e joys
Nos ajosten malgrat dels croys.   50

Jocglar, granren ai meynhs de joy,
Quar no.us vey, e.n fas semblan croy.

GUIRAUT DE BORNEIL
(c. 1165–c. 1212?)[35]

XLVIII

Amars, onrars, e char-teners,
Umiliars et obezirs,
Loncs merceiars e loncs grazirs,
Long'atendens'e loncs espers
Me degron far viur'ad onor,   5
S'eu fos astrucs de bo senhor,
Mas car no.m vir ni no.m bïais,
No vol Amors qu'eu sïa gais.

Pero mos sens e mos sabers,
E mos parlars e mos be-dirs,   10
Mos esperars e mos sofrirs,
E mos celars e mos temers
M'agron totztems onrat d'amor,
S'eu perchasses mo ben alhor.
Mas cilh que.m ten en greu pantais   15
No vol qu'eu l'am, ni que m'en lais.

E si.lh plagues mos enquerers,
Ni mos preiars ni mos servirs,

May my poem go (because I turn it round in such a way that neither woods nor hills should restrain it) to where no frost is felt and the cold has no power to cut. May someone who can sing nobly out of joy sing and whistle it clearly to my lady so that slips from it may enter her heart, for it is not appropriate to any mean singer.

Sweet lady, my love and joy unite us in spite of those mean-spirited people.

Ministrel,[34] it is a great lessening of my joy that I do not see you, and in that you appear mean.

XLVIII

Loving, honouring and holding dear,[36] acting humbly and obeying, long asking for grace and long making gracious approaches, long paying of attentions and long hoping should cause me to live in honour, if I were blessed with a good master. But because I do not turn back or bend, Love does not wish that I should be in joy.

Yet my reason and my understanding, my speech and my eloquence, my hope and my endurance, my concealment and my fear would have granted me honour in love on all occasions, if I had looked for my fulfilment somewhere else. But she who keeps me in heavy misery wants me neither to love her nor to leave her.

And if my attention pleased her, and my praying and

Ja.l trop velhars ni.l paucs dormirs,
Ni.lh mal qu'eu trac matis e sers   20
No.m pogron ja partir de lor.
Ans m'agra Jois per servidor
E ja no.m fora greus lo fais
Ni.l mals c'al cor me brolh'e.m nais.

Per qu'eu conosc e sai qu'es vers   25
Que viure.m val menhs que morirs?
Pos que.lh sofranh jois e jauzirs,
E.m falh Amors e sos poders.
Per qu'eu sospir e planh e plor?
Car Jois no.m val ni no.m socor;   30
Qu'eu sui aquel c'am melhs e mais
E no manei, ni tenh, ni bais.

Era.m combat sobre-volers,
E sobr'amars e loncs dezirs;
E fa.m chassar sobr'enardirs   35
E foleiars e no-devers
So que no tanh a ma valor.
E s'eu volh trop per ma folor,
Mos sens en par alques savais,
Mas eu remanh fis e verais.   40

Car ma semblans'e mos parers,
E mos cudars e mos albirs
M'an dich totztems c'altr'enriquirs,
Ni altr'onors ni altr'avers,
No.m podon dar tan de ricor   45
Com cilh que.m fai viur'ab langor;
C'on plus languisc e dezengrais,
Cut et aten c'a me s'abais.

Domna valens, vostra valor
E vostre pretz e vostr'onor   50
Poiatz totztems e valetz mais,
Per qu'eu vos sui fis e verais.

service, then never could the long vigil and the lack of sleep, nor the ills I endure morning and night make me ever give them up. On the contrary, joy would have me as its servant and never would the burden be heavy, nor the pain which quickens and is born in my heart.

How do I recognise and know that it is true that to live avails me less than to die? Because it lacks joy and exultation, and Love and its power abandon me. Why do I sigh and complain and weep? Because joy does not help or aid me. For I am the man who loves best and most fully; yet I do not embrace or hold or kiss.

Now excessive desire attacks me, and excessive love and long yearning; and over-daring and recklessness and impropriety make me pay court to that which does not match my deserving. And if in my madness I wish for too much, my reason seems rather slight, but I remain faithful and true.

Since what appears and what is evident to me, my belief and my judgement, have at all times told me that other riches, other honour and other possessions cannot give me as much wealth as she who makes me live in sorrow, then as I languish more and grow thinner, I trust and expect that she will incline towards me.

Worthy lady, you elevate and increase in value your deserving and your worth and your honour at all times. Therefore I am faithful and true to you.

XLIX

Ailas, com mor! – Quez as, amis?—
Eu sui traïs!—
Per cal razo?—
Car anc jorn mis m'ententïo
En leis que.m fetz lo bel parven.—   5
Et as per so to cor dolen?—
Si ai.—
As enaissi to cor en lai?—
Oc eu, plus fort.—
Est donc aissi pres de la mort?—   10
Oc eu, plus fort que no.us sai dir.—
Per que.t laissas aissi morir?—

Car sui trop vergonhos e fis.—
No l'as re quis?—
Eu, per Deu, no!—   15
E per que menas tal tenso
Tro aias saubut so talen?—
Senher, fai me tal espaven.—
Que.l fai?—
S'amors que.m ten en greu esmai.—   20
Be n'as gran tort;
Cudas te qu'ela t'o aport?—
Eu no, mas no.m n'aus enardir.—
Trop poiras tu to dan sofrir.

Senher, e cals conselhs n'er pres?—   25
Bos e cortes.—
Et lo.m diatz!—
Tu venras denan leis vïatz
Et enquerras la de s'amor.—
E si s'o ten a dezonor?—   30
No.t chal!—
E s'ela.m respon lach ni mal?—
Sïas sofrens,

XLIX

Alas, how I die![37] *What is the matter, friend?* I am betrayed!
For what reason? Because one day I set my affections on her
who gave me an encouraging glance. *And is your heart
sorrowing because of that?* Indeed it is. *Is your heart thus set
on her?* I have set it so, very strongly. *Are you therefore so
close to death?* I am indeed: more completely than I can tell
you. *Why do you leave yourself die thus?*

Because I am too retiring and too faithful. *Have you asked
nothing of her?* I certainly have not, by God. *And why do you
prolong this agony before you know her inclinations?* Sir, it fills
me with such fear. *What does?* Her love which keeps me in
great distress. *Certainly you are quite wrong. Do you think she
will bring it to you?* I do not, but I dare not presume to it. *You
could suffer much hurt from this.*

And what course, sir, should be taken? *A good and courtly
one.* Tell it to me at once. *You will come before her quickly and
ask her for her love.* And if she takes it as an affront? *Do not
disturb yourself!* And if she answers me dismissively or
angrily? *Be patient, because patience is always triumphant.*

Que totztems bos sofrire vens.—
E si.s n'apercep lo gilos?—   35
Adonc no'obraretz plus ginhos.—

Nos?—Oc be.—Sol qu'ilh o volgues!—
Er.—Que?—Si.m cres.—
Crezutz sïatz!—
Be te sera tos jois doblatz,   40
Sol lo dichs no.t fassa päor.—
Senher, tan senti la dolor
Mortal,
Per qu'es ops c'o partam egal.—
Er donc tos sens   45
Que te valh'e tos ardimens.—
Oc, e ma bona sospeissos.—
Garda te que gen t'i razos!—

Razonar no.m sabrai ja be.—
Dïas, per que?—   50
Per leis gardar.—
No.n sabras donc ab leis parlar?
Est aissi del tot esperdutz?—
Oc, can li sui denan vengutz . . .—
T'espertz?—   55
Oc eu, que no sui de re certz.—
Aital fan tuch
Cilh que son per amor perduch.—
Oc, mas eu forsarai mo cor!—
Era non o torns en demor!—   60

Be m'a aduch
Amors a so, que sabon tuch
Que mal viu qui deziran mor,
Per qu'eu no sai planher mo cor.—

Vas to desduch   65
Vai, amics, ans c'o sapchon tuch,
Per que no perdas to resor;
Que levet pert om so demor.

And if the jealous one finds out about it? *Then you will both act more stealthily.*

Both of us? *Of course, yes.* If only she wished that! *So it will be.* How? *If you trust me.* Trusted you are! *Certainly your joy will be doubled, but only if your words are not fearful.* Sir, I feel the mortal pain so much that we must divide it equally. *Then may your reason and your devotion avail you!* Yes, and my good hope. *Make sure that your arguments are correct.*

I shall never be able to argue well. *Tell me why not?* In order to protect her. *So you will not then know how to talk to her? Are you so utterly in despair?* Yes, when I have come into her presence. *You despair?* I do indeed, so that I am certain of nothing. *All those who are in despair because of love feel thus.* Yes, but I will make my heart do it. *Now do not make any delay.*

Certainly love has brought me to this, because everyone knows that the man who dies yearning lives badly, so I cannot mourn for my heart.

Go, friend, towards your delight before everyone knows about it, so that you do not lose your determination. Because one loses easily what one hesitates over.

L
Reis glorïos, verais lums e clartatz,
Deus poderos, Senher, si a vos platz,
Al meu companh sïatz fizels aiuda;
Qu'eu no lo vi pos la nochs fo venguda,
Et ades sera l'alba.   5

Bel companho, si dormetz o velhatz,
No dormatz plus, süau vos ressidatz;
Qu'en orïen vei l'estela creguda
C'amena.l jorn, qu'eu l'ai be conoguda,
Et ades sera l'alba.   10

Bel companho, en chantan vos apel;
No dormatz plus, qu'eu auch chantar l'auzel
Que vai queren lo jorn per lo boschatge,
Et ai päor que.l gilos vos assatge,
Et ades sera l'alba.   15

Bel companho, issetz al fenestrel,
E regardatz las estelas del cel!
Conoisseretz si.us sui fizels messatge.
Si non o faitz, vostres n'er lo damnatge,
Et ades sera l'alba.   20

Bel companho, pos me parti de vos,
Eu no.m dormi ni.m moc de genolhos,
Ans preiei Deu, lo filh Santa Marïa,
Que.us me rendes per leial companhïa,
Et ades sera l'alba.   25

Bel companho, la foras als peiros
Me preiavatz qu'eu no fos dormilhos,
Enans velhes tota noch tro al dïa.
Era no.us platz mos chans ni ma parïa,
Et ades sera l'laba.   30

L

Glorious king,[38] true light and brightness, mighty God, Lord, be a loyal helper to my comrade, if it pleases you. For I have not seen him since the night came, and soon it will be dawn.

Fair friend, whether you are sleeping or lying awake, sleep no more, but get up quietly. For in the east I see growing the star which leads in the day, and I have noted it for certain. And soon it will be dawn.

Fair friend, I call you in song. Sleep no more, for I hear the bird singing as it goes looking for the day among the leaves, and I am afraid that the jealous one might attack you. And soon it will be dawn.

Fair friend, go to the window and look at the stars in the sky. You will know whether I am a trustworthy news-bearer to you. If you do not do it, the loss will be yours. And soon it will be dawn.

Fair friend, since I left you I have not slept nor moved off my knees; rather I prayed to God, the son of Holy Mary, that he should give you back to me in faithful friendship. And soon it will be dawn.

Fair friend, out there on the steps you asked me not to be asleep, but to keep watch all night until the day. Now neither my song nor my friendship pleases you. And soon it will be dawn.

—Bel dous companh, tan sui en ric sojorn
Qu'eu no volgra mais fos alba ni jorn,
Car la gensor que anc nasques de maire
Tenc et abras, per qu'eu non prezi gaire
Lo fol gilos ni l'alba.   35

LI

A penas sai comensar
Un vers que volh far leuger,
E si n'ai pensat des er
Que.l fezes de tal razo
Que l'entenda tota gens   5
E qu'el fass'a leu chantar;
Qu'eu.l fatz per pla deportar.

Be.l saupra plus cobert far,
Mas non a chans pretz enter
Can tuch no.n son parsoner.   10
Qui que.s n'azir, me sap bo
Can auch dire pet contens
Mo sonet, rauquet e clar,
E l'auch a la fon portar.

Ja, pos volrai clus trobar,   15
No cut aver man parer—
Ab so que ben ai mester
A far una leu chanso;
Qu'eu cut c'atretan grans sens
Es, qui sap razo gardar,   20
Co mes motz entrebeschar.

Fair, gentle friend,[39] *I am in such a fine place that I would not wish it to be dawn or day ever again. For I hold and embrace the noblest that ever was born of mother. So I hardly care for the foolish jealous one nor the dawn.*

LI

I hardly know how to start a poem which I want to make more simple,[40] and I have thought about it since yesterday, how I could make it of such matter that everyone will understand it and that it could be sung in the easy style. For I am making it up for amusement only.[41]

Certainly I could make it more obscure, but a song does not have total worth when not everyone is involved with it. No matter who is agitated by this, I feel happy when I hear my little song sung in competition, raucous or sweet, and hear it carried to the fountain.

If I did want to compose obscure poetry, I believe I would never have many performers, as long as I really need to compose an easy song. For I believe that that is just as reasonable, if one knows how to keep to its subject, as to interlace my words.[42]

D'als m'aven a consirar,
Qu'eu am tal que non enquer,
Per so car del consirer
Sai be que fatz mesprezo.   25
Que farai? C'us ardimens
Me ve qu'eu l'an razonar,
E päors fai m'o laissar.

Be lo.i volrïa mandar,
Si trobava messatger;   30
Mas si.n fatz altrui parler
Eu tem qu'ilh me n'ochaizo,
Car non es ensenhamens
C'om ja fass'altrui parlar
D'aisso que sols vol celar.   35

Tan be.m sap lo cor comtar
La beltat e.l pretz sobrer,
Que gran batalha.n sofer
Car no.i vauc ad espero.
Pois m'en ven us espavens   40
Que m'en fai dezacordar
E mon ardimen baissar.

Ges no la posc oblidar,
Tan me fai gran dezirer;
E volh peitz c'a mo guerrer   45
Celui que d'als me somo;
Car lai es mos pensamens,
E melhs no.m pot solassar,
Sol que.m lais de leis pensar.

Consirers m'en es guirens   50
C'anc re tan no.m poc amar,
Pos la vi, ni tener char.

I ought to work at something else, because I love such a one that I do not plead for love since I know well that I am committing a crime in the very thought. What shall I do? For a burning wish comes to me that I should declare myself to her, and fear makes me refrain.

I would certainly like to send her this, if I found a messenger. But if I make someone else speak in this matter, I am afraid that she will attack me for it, because it is not proper that a man should ever make someone else speak of a thing which he, left to himself, wants to hide.

So well my heart can describe to me her beauty and her supreme worth that I suffer a great blow that I do not go spurring on my way. Then there comes to me after that a fear that makes me undecided and my audacity lessen.

I cannot at all forget her, so much does she make me greatly yearn. And I wish worse than my enemy the man who invites me to anything else. For in that place is my concern, and he cannot comfort me better than in merely letting me think about her.

In that matter thinking is my salvation, for I can never love anything else as much nor hold it so dear since I saw her.

ARNAUT DANIEL
(*fl. c.* 1180–1200)[43]

LII

En cest sonet coind'e leri
Fauc motz, e capuig e doli,
Que serant verai e cert
Qan n'aurai passat la lima;
Q'Amors marves plan'e daura   5
Mon chantar, que de liei mou
Qui pretz manten e governa.

Tot jorn meillur et esmeri,
Car la gensor serv e coli
El mon – so.us dic en apert.   10
Sieus sui del pe tro q'en cima,
E, si tot venta.ill freid'aura,
L'amors q'inz el cor mi plou
Mi ten chaut on plus iverna.

Mil messas n'aug e.n proferi,   15
E.n art lum de cer'e d'oli
Que Dieus m'en don bon issert
De lieis, on no.m val escrima.
E, qan remir sa crin saura
E.l cors q'es grailet e nou,   20
Mais l'am que qi.m des Luserna.

Tant l'am de cor e la queri
C'ab trop voler cug la.m toli—
S'om ren per ben amar pert!
Q'el sieus cors sobre-tracima   25
Lo mieu tot, e non s'eisaura;
Tant a de ver fait renou
C'obrador n'a e taverna.

LII

In this little song, pretty and gay, I compose words, I plane and polish them, so that they will be true and certain when I have passed the file over them. For Love immediately smooths and gilds my singing, which originates from her who possesses and controls deserving.

Every day I become better and purified, because I serve and honour the most noble in the world. I tell you this openly. I am hers from the foot up to the head, and, even if the cold wind blows, the love that rains within my heart keeps me warm in the deepest winter.

I hear a thousand masses and offer them up for it, and for it I burn wax and oil, so that God should give me a good outcome from her where no worth is a defence for me. And, when I admire her golden hair and her build which is slim and youthful, I love her more than if someone gave me Luserna.[44]

So much I love her from my heart and long for her that from great desire I believe I will take her away from myself — if a person does lose something through loving well. For her heart submerges mine utterly and it does not dry up. So well, truly, has she practised usury that she owns both the worker and the shop.

No vuoill de Roma l'emperi,
Ni c'om m'en fass'apostoli,   30
Q'en lieis non aia revert
Per cui m'art lo cors e.m rima;
E si.l maltraich no.m restaura
Ab un baisar, anz d'annou,
Mi auci e si enferna.   35

Ges pel maltraich q'ieu soferi
De ben amar no.m destoli,
Si tot me ten en desert,
C'aissi.n fatz los motz en rima:
Pieitz trac aman c'om que laura,   40
C'anc plus non amet un ou
Cel de Moncli N'Audierna.

Ieu sui Arnautz, q'amas l'aura,
E chatz la lebre ab lo bou,
E nadi contra suberna.   45

LIII

Lo ferm voler qu'el cor m'intra
No.m pot ges becs escoisendre ni ongla
De lauzengier, si tot per mal dir s'arma;
E quar no l'aus batr'ab ram ni ab vergua,
Sivals a frau, lai on non aurai oncle,   5
Jauzirai joi, en vergier o dinz cambra.

Quan mi soven de la cambra
On, al mieu dan, sai que nuils hom non intra,
Ans mi son tug plus que fraire ni oncle,
Non ai membre no.m fremisca, ni ongla,   10
Plus que non fai l'enfas denant la vergua;
Tal päor ai que.ill sïa trop de m'arma.

I would not want the imperium of Rome, nor to be made pope there, if it meant that I could not come back to her for whom my heart burns and scorches me. And if she does not relieve my pain with a kiss before the new year, she will kill me and damn herself.

I do not at all cease to love nobly because of the pain I suffer, although it keeps me in the wilderness. And so out of it I make these words in verse: as a lover I suffer worse than the man who labours, and never did the man of Monclin love more Lady Audierna.[45]

I am Arnaut who gathers the wind and hunts the hare from the ox's back and swims against the rising tide.[46]

LIII

Neither beak[47] nor slanderer's nail can at all tear from me the strong desire that comes into my heart, even if he arms himself to speak evilly. And since I dare not strike him with branch or rod, then in secret at least, there where I have no uncle[48] I will experience joy, in garden or bedroom.

When I recall the bedroom where, to my ruin, I know that no man enters, but where, on the contrary, they are all more on guard against me than brother or uncle, I have no organ or nail which does not tremble more than the child does before the rod. I am so afraid that I am too much hers in my soul.

Del cors li fos, non de l'arma!
E cossentis m'a celat dinz sa cambra!
Que plus me nafra.l cor que colps de vergua,   15
Quar lo sieus sers, lai on ill es, non intra;
De lieis serai aisi com carns ez ongla,
E non creirai castic d'amic ni d'oncle.

Anc la seror de mon oncle
Non amei tan ni plus, per aquest'arma!   20
Que tan vezis com es lo detz de l'ongla,
S'a lieis plagues, volgr'esser de sa cambra;
De mi pot far l'amors qu'ins el cor m'intra
Mieils a son vol c'om fortz de frevol vergua.

Pois floris la seca vergua,   25
Ni d'En Adam foron nebot ni oncle,
Tan fin'amors com cela qu'el cor m'intra
Non cuig qu'anc fos en cors, ni eis en arma;
On qu'ill estei, fors en plan o dinz cambra,
Mos cors de lieis no.s part, tan com ten l'ongla.   30

C'aisi s'enpren e s'enongla
Mos cors en lieis com l'escors'en la vergua;
Qu'ill m'es de joi tors e palais e cambra,
Ez am la mais no fas cozin ni oncle.
Qu'en paradis n'aura doble joi m'arma,   35
Si ja nuils hom per ben amar lai intra.

Arnautz tramet son chantar d'ongl'e d'oncle
Ab grat de lieis que de sa vergua l'arma,
Son Dezirat, c'ab pretz en cambra intra.

Oh that I were hers in body, not soul! And that she might consent that I should be secretly in her room! For it wounds my heart more than a blow of a rod that her servant does not enter there where she is. I will always be by her, as flesh is by nail, and I will not regard the reproof of friend or uncle.

Never did I love as much or more my uncle's sister, by this soul of mine! For as close as is the finger to the nail, if it should please her, I would like to be to her bedroom. The love which enters within my heart can turn me better to its will than a strong man can a flimsy rod.

Since the dry rod flowered[49] and from Adam there were nephew and uncle, I do not believe there ever was in body nor even in soul such faithful love as this which enters my heart. Wherever she is, out in the open or within her room, my heart does not part from her by as much distance as the nail stretches.

So thus my body attaches itself and clings by the nail to her as its bark does to the rod. For she is to me tower and palace and chamber of joy, and I love her more than I do cousin or uncle. So in Paradise my soul will have doubl joy from this, if ever any man enters there through faithful loving.

Arnaut sends his singing of nail and uncle for the pleasure of her who arms him with her rod, his Beloved who worthily enters within the bedroom.

PEIRE VIDAL
(*fl.* 1180–1200)
Vida

LIV

Peire Vidals si fo de Toloza, filz d'un pelissier. E cantava mielhs
d'home del mon, e fo bos trobaire; e fo del plus fols homes que
mai fossen, qu'el crezia que tot fos vers so que a lui plazia ni q'el
volia. E plus leu li avenia trobars que a hulh home del mon: e fo
aquel que plus rics sons fetz e majors folias d'armas e d'amors.
E dis grans mals d'autrui; e fo vers que us cavaliers de San Gili
li fetz talhar la lengua, per so qu'el dava ad entendre qu'el era
drutz de sa molher; e N'Uc del Bauz si.l fetz garir e metgar. E
cant el fo garitz, el s'en anet outra mar, e de lai menet una
Grega que.il fon donada per moiller en Cipri. E.il fon donat a
entendre qu'els era netsa de l'emperador de Constantinople, e
qu'el per lieis devia aver l'emperi per razon. Don el mes tot can
poc guazanhar a far navili, qu'el crezia anar conquistar
l'emperi; e portava armas emperials, e.s fazia apelar emperaire
e sa molher emperairitz.

Et entendia en totas las bonas donas que vezia e totas las
pregava d'amor; e totas li dizian de far e dir so qu'el volgues:
don el se crezia drutz de totas e que cascuna moris per el; e
totas l'enganavan. E totas vets menava rics destriers e portava
ricas armas e cadieira e campolieit emperial: e crezia esser lo
melher cavaliers del mon per armas e.l plus amatz per donas.

LIV   *Life*[50]

Peire Vidal came from Toulouse, the son of a furrier. And he was the best singer in the world, and he was a good poet; and he was one of the maddest men that ever were, so that he believed that everything that pleased him or that he liked would be poetry. And composition came more easily to him than to any man in the world: and he was a man who made the richest tunes and deeds of great recklessness in war and love. And he spoke great evil of others. And he made a poem as a result of which one of the knights of San Gili had his tongue cut out, because he put it about that he was his wife's lover.[51] And M. Uc del Banz had him cured and treated. And when he was cured he set off across the sea, and from there he brought a Greek woman whom he was given as a wife in Cipri. And he was given to understand that she was the niece of the emperor of Constantinople, and that through her he should hold the empire by right. So he put all that he could earn to take a ship, because he intended to go and conquer the empire. And he wore the imperial arms, and he had himself called emperor and his wife called empress.

And he fell in love with all the fair women he saw, and he asked them all for their love.[52] And they all said to go and say whatever he liked, from which he believed himself the beloved of all of them and that each was dying for him. And they were all deceiving him. And he always rode splendid horses and bore rich arms and had an imperial throne and tent. And he believed himself to be the best knight at arms in the world and the most loved by women.

SORDELLO
(*c.* 1200–1269)[53]

LV

Bel m'es ab motz leugiers a far
Chanson plazen et ab guay so,
Que.l melher que hom pot trïar,
A cuy m'autrey e.m ren e.m do,
No vol ni.l plai chantar de mäestrïa;　　　5
E mas no.lh plai, farai hueymais mon chan
Leu a chantar e d'auzir agradan,
Clar d'entendre e prim, qui prim lo trïa.

Gen mi saup mon fin cor emblar
Al prim qu'ieu mirey sa faisso,　　　10
Ab un dous amoros esguar
Que.m lansero siey huelh lairo.
Ab selh esgar m'intret en aisselh dïa
Amors pels huelhs al cor d'aital semblan,
Que.l cor en trays e mes l'a son coman,　　　15
Si qu'ab lieys es, on qu'ieu an ni estïa.

Ai, cum mi saup gent esgardar—
Si l'esgartz messongiers no fo—
Dels huelhs que sap gent envïar
Totz temps per dreg lai on l'es bo!　　　20
Mas a sos digz mi par qu'aiso.s cambïa,
Pero l'esgar creirai, qu'ab cor forsan
Parl'om pro vetz, mas nulh poder non an
Huelh d'esgardar gen, si.l cor no.ls envïa.

E quar am de bon pretz ses par,　　　25
Am mais servir lieys en perdo
Qu'autra qu'ab si.m degnes colgar.
Mas no la sier ses guazardo,
Quar fis amicx no sier ges d'aital guïa,
Quan sier de cor en honrat loc prezan;　　　30

LV

I like to make a pleasant song with easy words and a gay tune because the best lady that a man can choose, to whom I vow and give and yield myself, neither wants nor is pleased by the elevated kind of singing. And because that does not please her, henceforth I will make my song easy to sing and pleasant to hear, clear to understand and light for someone who chooses it light.

By noble nature she knew how to rob me of my faithful heart the first time that I saw her, with a sweet amorous look that her thieving eyes threw me. With such a look and on such a day love penetrated through my eyes to my heart in such a form that it pulled my heart away and placed it at her command, so that it is with her wherever I go or stay.[54]

Ah, how she knew the way to look at me nobly (if the look was not a liar) with eyes which she can nobly send at all times straight wherever she chooses! But from her words it seems to me that this is changing. Yet I will trust the look, because a man sometimes speaks from a forced heart, but eyes have no power to look nobly if the heart does not send them.

And because I love with great and unparallelled worth, I prefer to serve her to no purpose than another who would think me worthy to let me sleep with her. But I do not serve her without reward, because a faithful lover does not at all serve in such a way when he serves from the heart in an honourable,

Per que l'onors m'es guazardos d'aitan
Que.l sobreplus non quier, mas be.u penrïa.

Vailla.m ab vos merces, dolz'enemïa;
No m'auzïez s'eu vos am ses enjan.
Qe me suffratz qe.us serv'ab ferm talan: 35
Tal don deman, ni estre non deurïa.

LVI

Qan plus creis, dompna, .l desiriers
Don languisc, quar no.m faitz amor,
De lauzar vostre pretz ausor
Creis plus mos cors, car jois entiers
No.m pot ges vinir, amija,   5
De vos, si.l pretz s'en destrija;
Q'aitan car teing vostre fin pretz valen
Com am ni voill vostre cors car e gen.

Aital m'autrei, fis, vertadiers,
A vos q'etz ses par de valor,   10
Q'eu am mais morir ab dolor
Qe de vos mi veng'aligriers
Q'al fin pretz q'en vos s'abrija
Puesca dan tener; e si ja
Mais me trobatz vas vos d'autre talen,   15
Ja non aiaz merce ni chausimen.

Q'amar non pot nuls cavaliers
Sa dompna ses cor trichador,
S'engal lei non ama sa honor.
Per qu.us prec, bels cors plazentiers,   20
Qe pauc ni gaire ni mija
Non fassatz de re qe.us dija,
Q'esser puesca contra.l vostr'onramen.
Gardaz s'ie.us am de fin cor, leialmen!

worthy place. So the honour is such reward for me that I do not ask for more, though of course I would accept it.

Sweet enemy, may mercy advance me with you. Do not kill me if I love you without calculating. May you allow me to serve you with fixed desire; such a privilege I ask, nor should there be a refusal.

LVI

My lady, the more the desire in which I languish grows because love is not granted to me, the more my heart swells to praise your elevated worth; because full joy[55] cannot at all come to me, beloved, from you if that worth is so denied you. Because I hold your noble and virtuous worth dear to the extent that I love and yearn for your dear and noble person.

Thus do I give myself, faithful and true, to you who are without equal in worth, so that I would prefer to die of sorrow than that there might come to me any happiness from you which in the end could bring damage to the noble worth which dwells in you. And if you ever find me of another disposition towards you, may you never show mercy or pity.

For no knight can love his lady without a treacherous heart if he does not love her honour as much as herself. So I beg you, beautiful and gracious one, not in the least, by a jot or iota, to do anything I tell you which could be contrary to your honour. Look how I love you faithfully from a pure heart.

Per merce.us prec, bell'amija, 25
Qez ab una qualqe brija
Del joi d'amor mi secoraz breumen,
Si far se pot salvan vostr'onramen.

Q'estiers non posc aver nul jauzimen,
Si pïetatz e merces no.us inpren. 30

ANONYMOUS,
PERHAPS ITALIAN, TROUBADOUR[56]

LVII

Aissi m'ave cum a l'enfan petit
que dins l'espelh esgarda son vizatge
e.i tast' ades e tan l'a assalhit
tro que l'espelhs se franh per son folatge,
adonca.s pren a plorar son damnatge: 5
tot enaissi m'avia enriquit
us bels semblans, qu'er an de mi partit
li lauzengier per lor fals vilanatge.

E per so ai conques gran consirier
e per so tem perdre sa drudaria 10
et aisso.m fai chantar per dezirier;
car la bela tan m'a vencut e.m lia
que per mos olhs tem que perda la via
com Narcisi, que dedins lo potz cler
vi sa ombra e l'amet tot entier 15
e per fol'amor mori d'aital guia.

Be fora de son perdo cobeitos,
car l'an de mi fals lauzengiers partida:
Deus lor do mal, car ses los enojos
agra gran gaug de leis e gran jauzida! 20
Membre.us, bela, la douss' ora grazida
que.m fetz baizar vostras belas faissos:
aisso.m ten en esperansa joios
que nostr'amors sia per be fenida.

A la bela t'en iras, ma chansos,
e digas li que sai sui de joi blos, 25
si no.m reve qualsque bona jauzida.

I beg you for mercy, fair beloved, that with some single fragment of the joy of love you help me immediately, if that can be done while preserving your honour.

For otherwise I cannot have any joy, if pity and mercy do not seize you.

LVII

I am like the little child who looks at his face in the mirror and goes on touching it, and hits it so much that the mirror breaks through his silliness, and then sets to bewailing his loss: in just the same way, a beautiful appearance has enriched me, which now the slanderers have taken from me through their lying villainy.

And so I have contracted a great obsession and yet I fear to lose her love; and this makes me sing out of longing. Because the fair one has overcome me and attached me to such an extent that I am afraid of losing my life through my eyes, like Narcissus who saw his reflection in the clear well and loved it quite totally and died in this way through a mad love.

Certainly I would hunger for her favours, but lying slanderers have parted me from them. May God punish them! For without those wretches I would have great joy and great rejoicing from her. Remember, fair one, the sweet and blessed hour that permits me to kiss your beautiful face. That keeps me joyful in the hope that our love should be concluded in success.

Go, my song, to the fair one, and tell her that I am here empty of joy, if some good happiness does not come to me.

NOTES

1   *The Allegory of Love*, p. 2.

2   Gaston Paris says that Bernart de Ventadorn is "perhaps almost the only one of all these singers of love who still touches our heart" (*Medieval French Literature*; Temple Primer 1903, p. 91). Modern critical opinion broadly agrees with this, although it might add Raimbaut d'Aurenga and some of Guiraut de Borneil.

3   Jean de Nostredame (1507–1577), *Les Vies des plus célèbres et anciens poètes provençaux* (1575). Ed. C. Chabaneau, introd. J. Anglade (Paris 1913).

4   A. Jeanroy, *La Poésie Lyrique des Troubadours*, (Toulouse and Paris 1934), Tome II, pp. 13ff.

5   *Troubadours and Love* (Cambridge University Press 1975), p. 113.

6   "Fin Amors: the pure love of the Troubadours, its Amorality and Possible Source", *Mediaeval Studies* 7 (1945), pp. 139–207.

7   See for example G. L. Brook, *The Harley Lyrics*, p. 16, and the argument with D. W. Robertson in E. T. Donaldson's *Speaking of Chaucer* (London 1970), pp. 151–2.

8   *De Vulgari Eloquentia*, I, ix and II, vi. For a convenient English version, see the translation of A. G. Ferrers Howell, London (Rebel Press) 1973, p. 29 and p. 62.

9   J. Anglade, *Les Troubadours* (Paris 1908) remarks how little this severity is in evidence in poems such as 'Ailas, com mor' (XLIX here) (p. 133). But Dante is referring to the strictly moral *sirventes* of Guiraut, not represented in this love anthology.

10   Although courtly poetry seems to have an established diction before him, Guilhem IX of Aquitaine is the first troubadour whose works survive. He was one of the most powerful European leaders of his time, and he led a Crusade in 1101. He was the grandfather of Eleanor of Aquitaine, the mother by different marriages of Marie de Champagne and Richard Coeur de Lion. For his historical importance, see Friedrich Heer, *The Medieval World* (trans. Janet Sondheimer, London 1962), chapter 7, "Courtly Love and Courtly Literature", especially pp. 154–5. Eleven of his poems survive (ed. A. Jeanroy, *Les Chansons de Guillaume IX, duc d'Aquitaine*, 2nd ed. Paris 1927), mostly profane love poetry, but one of which, "Pas de chantar" is a solemn personal statement and one of the greatest troubadour poems.

11   It is difficult to translate such terms as "bon saber" which are used by the troubadours in a tehnical way and are full of resonance. cf "Gai saber", the fourteenth-century Consistory of Toulouse which laid down rules and held competitions in love poetry as the exponents of the *Meistergesang* did in Germany.

12   "Fis", as in *fin amor*, derived from Latin *fidus*, "faithful". Originally

fin amor was admirable and refined *because* it was faithful, by definition.

13   Marcabru is said by Topsfield (*op. cit.*, p. 107) to be "one of the most original and important of all medieval poets". Forty-two poems are attributed to him by his twentieth-century editor J. M. L. Dejeanne (*Poésies Complètes du troubadour Marcabru*, Toulouse 1909), mostly difficult to interpret and moral in outlook. He developed the distinctions and terminology of troubadour love poetry more than almost any other poet, as this poem suggests ("Cortezia", "vilania", "mesura", "affinar" and so on), and important distinctions such as *Amars* (false earthly love) versus *Amors* (fin amor: noble earthly love), *amor frait* (fragmented) versus *amor entiers* (whole, integrated) and *Mesura* (moderation) versus *foudatz* (madness) in love, are at least first formulated, if not invented, by him. The writers of the *vidas* (who were attracted by the madness of Guilhem IX and Peire Vidal) found him poor material, being misogynistic and censorious. But the terminological oppositions he set up were the basis of courtly poetry from Guiraut de Borneil to Dante.

14   "meillurar" can be transitive or intransitive, so it is uncertain whether it is the lady herself or her lover that she improves.

15   Courtly poets always insist that, for all his humility towards the lady, the lover must have high self-regard.

16   Since in Jaufre *amor de lonh* is usually interpreted as a metaphor for the excellence of detached, unsexual love rather than a geographical fact, "outra mar" here is perhaps a recognition of the worth of that view of love. But in that case the dedication to the French (who could be soldiers, in the travails of war) is hard to explain. Jaufre *was*, almost certainly, abroad in the Crusade of 1148.

17   This famous story (translated with kind permission from the text in R. T. Hill and T. G. Bergin, *Anthology of the Provençal Troubadours*, Yale University Press 1973, vol. I, p. 31) is assumed not to be historical but to be a rationalisation of the yearning "amor de lonh" theme in his poems, in conjunction with his crusading activities. His poetry is always reconcilable with Christian morality, and some of his poems (such as "Quan lo rossinhols") contain crusading rallying calls which are as explicitly religious as those of Conon de Béthune (cf. LXIII here). Jaufre's poems were edited by Jeanroy (Paris 1924).

18   This is Jaufre's most famous poem and his phrase *amor de lonh* (line 4, etc.) has been used to describe one of the most constant themes of medieval love poetry, before as well as after him. As well as more traditional love-interpretations, the distant love has been identified as the Blessed Virgin and the Holy Land, in the Crusades. Rita Lejeune (in *Studi in onore di A. Monteverdi*, Modena 1959, pp. 403–42) argues for a different stanza order from that taken from Press's anthology

here, which is the order of Jeanroy's edition. (Lejeune's order can be found in Topsfield, pp. 62–3). Her arguments are well founded on the manuscripts, but her contention that her order gives a better sequential sense to the poem does not seem as certain as she claims. See Grace Frank, "The Distant Love of Jaufre Rudel", *Modern Language Notes*, 57 (1942), pp. 528–34.

19 Lines 33–5 are the major evidence for Appel's suggestion in his edition that the distant love is the Blessed Virgin. But the idea that the chivalric lover performed deeds of valour for the glory of his beloved is, of course, widely attested in romances from Chrétien to *Don Quixote*. The word *chaitius* is a common one for a captive of love: cf. Bernart de Ventadorn, "Can vei la lauzeta" (XLV here), line 56, for instance.

20 Lejeune (*op. cit.*, p. 436) identifies the godfather as Guilhem IX, not altogether convincingly. The godfather, as a kind of chaperon grudging towards love, might correspond to the uncle in Arnaut's "Lo ferm voler" (LIII here).

21 Bernart is the most popular troubadour in the modern judgement: with G. Paris, for example, (see note 2 above) and Jeanroy who lamented that he was under-rated by his contemporaries and by posterity (*La Poésie Lyrique des Troubadours*, Tome 2, p. 138). The explanation, it seems most likely, is that we have lost the key to the more obscure poetry valued by the twelfth and thirteenth centuries (and by Dante who never mentions Bernart), so we prefer the poetry, such as Bernart's love songs, which does not need decoding. Whatever the explanation, Bernart seems to be relatively over-rated now. He is an interesting and important figure in the literary history of courtly love, because we know that he lived for some time at the northern court of Eleanor of Aquitaine away from his native court of Ventadour where he was trained by the Viscount Eblo. But nobody can mistake the charm of his natural love-poetry, here exemplified by his most famous poem, "Can vei la lauzeta".

22 The text of this poem is taken, with kind permission, from Hill and Bergin's *Anthology*, vol. I, pp. 38–40.

23 As well as the poem, the haunting tune of this song is notable. It is performed by Nigel Rogers on the record "Chansons der Troubadours" (Telefunken 6.41126 AS, 1970). One of the most curious rationalising *razos* is published by S. G. Nichols and J. A. Galm in their edition of Bernart (Chapel Hill, N.C. 1962, p. 37): "And Bernart called her "Alauzeta" on account of the love of a knight who loved her, and she called him "Rai". Then one day the knight came to the Duchess and entered her chamber. She raised the border of his cloak, tucking it under his collar, and let herself fall on the bed. Bernart was able to see the whole thing because a maiden of the lady showed it to him secretly". The soaring and falling lark of the first stanza is often

said to have suggested Dante's simile in *Paradiso* XX, 73–5.

24   Narcissus is the inevitable figure of the courtly lover, since what he found in the woman's eyes was the possibility of his own perfectibility. Attention is focused primarily on the heart and soul of the lover, and the unrealised lady who is hardly ever differentiated in any personal way, is incidental. See Valency, *In Praise of Love*, chapter 1. For a very full discussion of the Narcissus theme, see F. Goldin, *The Mirror of Narcissus in the Courtly Love Lyric* (New York 1967) which discusses this poem (pp. 92–106) and the poem by Heinrich von Morungen (LXXVI here), pp. 151–50.

25   Lazar in his edition (quoted by Hill and Bergin, II, p. 19) and Appel in his (quoted Nichols p. 187) both refer to a proverb according to which the fool, unlike the wise man, does not dismount from his horse when crossing a bridge and falls into the river. This might make some sense in connexion with the aspiration "contra mon" of line 40 (against the slope). But see T. D. Hill (*Medium Aevum* 48, no. 2, 1979) who refers to a better proverbial parallel in Jacques de Vitry, according to which the fool stands on the bank, waiting for the river to pass by before he crosses. This fits very well the endless persistence in his madness of the courtly lover, even if the lady never relents.

26   Tristan is a *senhal* for a lady in the view of Lazar and Anglade (*Les Troubadours* p. 79), and for Raimbaut d'Aurenga according to others including the editor of Raimbaut, W. T. Pattison (p. 25, etc.).

27   In spite of his early death, thirty-nine of Raimbaut's poems survive. Most commentators have thought of him as a brilliantly talented but immature poet, and he is not mentioned by Dante. Recently he has been very highly admired, and he is the troubadour that Dronke examines at length to consider the relations between the religious and the secular in his poetry, in "Ara'm so del tot conquis". His poems, such as the two included here, have more vitality and availability than most troubadour poetry. His most recent editor in English is W. T. Pattison, *The Life and Works of the Troubadour, Raimbaut D'Orange* (University of Minnesota 1952).

28   It is noteworthy that the anti-spring opening with snow and frost is itself treated in an anti-conventional way here, reminding the reader perhaps of anti-Petrarchism.

29   For Tristan, cf. note 26 above. For the importance of the Tristan story as a love history, cf. D. de Rougemont, *L'Amour et L'Occident*, Book I (*Passion and Society*, pp. 19 ff).

30   Brangane, Iseult's servant, recounts the allegory of the two white shirts with which they set out from Ireland. Iseult was to wear hers on her wedding-night but she gave it to Tristan, so Brangane had to lend her unworn shirt when they came to King Mark. Cf. Gottfried von Strassburg *Tristan*, Penguin trans., pp. 209–10.

31 Pattison (p. 163) believes that the reference here is to Iseult's ordeal with the red-hot iron (see Penguin Gottfried, pp. 246–8), and that the version of the story known to Raimbaut was that of Thomas.

32 "Carestia" can be left as a proper name with significant overtones, as by Press and Pattison.

33 This poem is technically as brillaint as Arnaut's sestina (LIII here). Like "Non chant per auzel" (XLVI) it inverts the conventional opening.

34 "Joglar" is a repeated *senhal* in Raimbaut. Here, as in many of his poems, the *senhal* is puzzling and rather disconcerting. Cf "Carestia" (n. 32 above) and "lignaura" in the famous *tenso* with Guiraut de Borneil.

35 According to his *vida*, Guiraut was the "maestre dels trobadors" and only Bernart de Ventadorn and Arnaut Daniel have ever been said to rival or exceed him. Dante quotes him in *De Vulgari Eloquentia* I, ix and II, vi, although Guinicelli in *Purgatorio* XXVI is made to say that people who think that Guiraut exceeds Arnaut are fools (XCVIII here). Anglade (p. 130) praises him, surprisingly perhaps, for "a naive sincerity like Bernart de Ventadour's". About ninety compositions of his survive. Nowadays he is admired, not for the "rectitude" of his *sirventes* praised by Dante, but for the completeness and mastery with which he used the terminology and ideas of troubadour poetry in poems like "Amans, onrans" (XLVIII). He is the "maestre" because no other poet displays the courtly love lyric in all its aspects to the same extent. Topsfield omits him from his analysis in *Troubadours and Love* because what was developed in him was not the "substance of his work" as much as the style (p. 1). But precisely because of that, he is the culmination of the love tradition in Provence, and the poets after 1200 were a falling-off from him as writers of the love lyric. The edition is A. Kolsen, *Sämtliche Lieder des Trobadors Giraut de Bornelh* (Hallé 1910 and 1935, 2 vols.).

36 In taking the text of this poem from A. R. Press's *Anthology*, I have added a comma at the end of line 1 in accordance with Professor Press's kind suggestion. I have benefited in a number of ways from his expertise, generously offered, in preparing various parts of this volume.

37 I have chosen to include this *tenso* rather than the more celebrated Lignaura one because of the typical nature of the exchanges here which make it a classic of the species. Poetry of this kind must be borne in mind when reading the exchanges between Troilus and Pandarus in *Troilus and Criseyde*. The requirement to act stealthily to protect the lady's honour evokes the attitude towards Criseyde.

38 Guiraut was a famous exponent of the *alba*. This celebrated poem can be compared with the other *albas* in this book: from *Amores* (XI), in

medieval Latin (XXIII), and by Wolfram (LXXXII) and Heinrich von Morungen (LXXIII).

39 The first thirty lines of the poem are spoken by the lady and the last five by the departed lover. A religious interpretation of the last lines seems the only way to make sense of them without a slight to the lady speaker. But religious suggestions are already present in lines 1 and 23; the reference to Mary in the latter perhaps anticipates the conclusion. The balance, again, is very reminiscent of English courtly love poetry and Marian lyrics.

40 This poem is important evidence for the meaning of the *trobar leu* and the *trobar clus*: "leuger" (line 2) and "cobert" (line 8). Particularly striking is the observation in lines 3–4 that a day's reflexion is required to think of a *razo* (meaning) easy enough for everyone to understand.

41 The suggestion here, confirmed in lines 11–14, seems to be that the "trobar leu" is a song that anyone can sing for amusement rather than to provoke thought.

42 This line seems to define the *trobar clus* in terms of form, in the word *entrebeschar*, "interlace". For discussion of the terms, see A. Jeanroy *La Poésie Lyrique des Troubadours*, II, pp. 34ff. It is clear from this poem that the lady who is praised is secondary and merely the material on which the real substance of the poem can exist.

43 Commentators observe that Arnaut's poetry was slightly anachronistic because he was an exponent of the "*trobar clus*" rather than the "*trobar leu*" which was more popular amongst his contemporaries, the generation of 1200 (Topsfield, pp. 193ff). The later Middle Ages regarded him as the greatest poet of love; Guinicelli in *Purgatorio* XXVI (XCVIII here) points him out as the "miglior fabbro del parlar materno" (117), saying that he surpassed everyone in verses of love and tales of romance, and Petrarch confirms this judgement: "Fra tutti il primo Arnaldo Daniello, / Gran maestro d'amor, ch'a la sua terra / Ancor fa onor col dir polito e bello" (*Trionfo d'Amore*, iv, 40–2). Eighteen of his poems survive, of which all but one are love poems. The most recent edition of his poems is G. Toja, *Arnaut Daniel, Canzoni* (Florence 1960).

44 For Luserna, see the long note in Toja's edition, pp. 278ff. The reference is to a legendary Spanish city which is mentioned in *Anseis de Cartage* and various other *chansons de geste*.

45 The commentators have not succeeded in identifying this pair of lovers, though it is likely that the reference again is to the romances. But see Ezra Pound's intriguing speculative reference to Vergil, Eclogue IX, 10–11 and 44 (*Translations*, Faber 1970, p. 424).

46 These famous lines on the madness of love are quoted in Arnaut's *vida* (Toja, pp. 166ff). See note 41 on *Volo virum* in the Latin section here, and the *vida* of Peire Vidal here.

47 The sestina seems to have been invented by Arnaut, although previous poems did have a complex series of catchwords at the line endings. See Raimbaut's "Ar resplan" (XLVII here) the demands of which are even more searching than those of sestina.

48 The uncle as guardian inevitably evokes Pandarus for English readers. The reader of *Troilus and Criseyde* might bear in mind Topsfield's remarks about this poem: "*Oncle* in medieval poetry is synonymous with kinsman, as in Bernier's defence of his family to Raoul de Cambrai. . . . From Celtic days it was customary for the uncle to rear his nephew" (p. 217). Whether or not Pandarus was Criseyde's uncle by blood, the point that Chaucer is emphasising is that he is her guardian who should protect her from the depradations of the unserious lover.

49 The dry rod that flowers is a symbol of the Virgin Mary in St Bernard and generally in medieval Latin literature. See Toja, pp. 380ff. Obviously, it is also associated with the rod of Jesse (Isaiah II, 1–10) and the medieval exegesis of it.

50 The text of this *Vida* is taken with permission from the Hill–Bergin *Anthology*, vol. I, p. 119.

51 For this story, cf. Lo Monge de Montaudon's (*fl.* 1180–1215) song, "Pois Peire d'Alverne a chantat", lines 85–90. The monk's poem is a long *sirventes* on the model of that of Peire d'Alverne, about the lives of many troubadours, gathering together the notorious stories in circulation about them.

52 The *razo* of Peire Vidal mentions by name the many women he loved, including the often told story of the lady Loba ("wolf"). "And he loved the lady Loba de Puegnautier, and the lady Estefania de Son who came from Sardinia. And then he became enamoured anew of Lady Raymbauda de Biolh. . . . La Loba came from Carcassonne. And Peire Vidal had himself called "wolf" for her, and he bore the arms of a wolf. And on the mountains of Cabaret he had himself chased by shepherds." Loba is thought to have been the lady loved by Raimon de Miraval.

53 Sordello is the most famous of the Italian poets who were so impressed by the poetry of the troubadours that they wrote in Provençal. For this reason, as well as for his intermediate chronological position, he is an important link between the troubadours and the stilnovisti. Dante says in *De Vulgari Eloquentia* I, xv that he "who was so distinguished by his eloquence, forsook his native dialect, not only in poetry, but in every other form of utterance" (p. 40). His most distinguished poetry is on the subject of contemporary politics, and for this reason he is the guide of Dante and Vergil through the area of Ante-Purgatory assigned to kings and princes in *Purgatorio* VI–IX. His love poetry is not characterised by great originality or distinction in its own right;

but it purveys Provençal ideas and forms with accuracy into an Italian tradition. See H. J. Chaytor, *Troubadours of Dante* (Oxford University Press 1902), pp. 173–6.

54 The image of the look that penetrates to the heart is common in Provençal. But the inevitability of the physical process here is more typical of the Aristotelian physiology of the Stilnovisti. Cf. p. 259 below.

55 This paradoxical definition of "jois entiers" is very different from the spiritual characterisation of it in Marcabru. Again, Sordello is holding to the terms of Provençal poetry but using them in a way that is more familiar in the Stilnovisti.

56 This poem is taken, with generous permission, from *Trouvères et Minnesänger* by Istvan Frank (Saarbrucken 1952), pp. 113–15. The very close affinities between the troubadours, *trouvères* and *Minnesänger* are very fully demonstrated in this invaluable book. The present poem, thought to be from Italy, corresponds word-for-word in the first stanza to the poem by Heinrich von Morungen beginning "Mir ist geschehen" (LXXVI here) which Frank prints parallel with it, and its second stanza corresponds closely to Von Morungen's third.

The northern French tradition

The examination of courtly love writings in medieval Provençal, Latin, German or Italian is a reasonably well defined subject concerned with a number of works whose nature we can be certain about. The love poetry of northern France is a much larger and more wide-ranging phenomenon. Even that part of it which *is* confined to works which, altogether or in part, conform to the narrow definitions of Gaston Paris, Jeanroy and Lewis, is very large. It must be emphasised too that, if the Provençal poetry is important (as well as for its quality) for its place as the fount of a very major tradition of European literature, the French literature which appears to descend from it is of even greater moment. Writers such as Chrétien de Troyes, Marie de France, the compilers of the Vulgate romances and the authors of the *Roman de la Rose* are the most important general literary tradition of the Middle Ages. They are not as great as Dante nor to be credited with such originality as the troubadours; but they are the centrepiece of medieval literature.

An affinity with Provençal poetry is obvious from the *trouvère* poems included here. The fact that Bernart de Ventadorn visited the northern court, and the considerably earlier date of the first Provençal poetry, make it clear that the *trouvère* poems were not just cognate with but, at least to some extent, derivative from the troubadours. Moreover, the earlier *trouvère* poems are much closer to the Provençal originals than the later ones, so the argument of French critics such as Gaston Paris and Jeanroy[1] that the northern poets brought elements of their own to the tradition, is true only of the later, inferior writers. (The same progressive decadence noted in the *Minnesänger* and the troubadours, from early poetic talent to later lack of inspiration, is evident (if to a lesser degree, because even the early poets already seem rather flat and derivative) in the line from Chrétien and Blondel to writers of the generation of Thibaut de Champagne.) Provençal influence is also noticeable in the romances; the situation in Chrétien's *Lancelot* is clearly a classic instance (and the one on which Gaston Paris's definitions are founded)[2] of the occurrence of courtly elements first found in the troubadours. Besides, the fact that Chrétien wrote Provençal-derived lyric poems as well as romances, shows that there was troubadour influence on romance-writers, even without the internal evidence which also exists.

In this anthology there is not much representation of the lyric poetry of the *trouvères* because they added little that was new and inspired to the troubadour tradition. Not that we should entirely dismiss them because they are derivative any more than we dismiss the post-1180 Provençal, German or Italian poets for that reason; all the poetry after the first troubadours is, after all, derivative to some extent. French critics have been anxious to claim that the *trouvères* brought another, distinctively northern-French tradition into coalition with the Provençal poetry (just as the *Minnesänger* brought elements from the native German *trûtlied* into their poems of courtly love). Here is the lucid summary of the similarities and differences given by Gaston Paris: 'Those which are copied from the Provençal models are but faint reflections of these: such are the songs of Blondel de Nesle and the majority of those of Gui of Couci and Gace Brulé. We find here the conventions of the art of the trobadors; for matter, the lady's perfections, her rigours, the poet's hopeless love, the fear of slanderers; for form, the same laws of rhythmic construction and rhyme, the same material of expressions; however, the French did not adopt the use of the *senhal*, nor did they attempt the *trobar clus*, nor, in general, did they . . . follow the Provençals in their refined habit of rhyming'[3] (*Medieval French Literature,* Temple Primer 1903, p. 94). Paris goes on to stress the social and aristocratic nature of the *courtois* poetry of northern France. Along with other French critics of his day (notably Jeanroy), he emphasises as the peculiar virtue of French literature its 'social' quality, referring to the way in which that literature is rooted in the manners and practices of society. This emphasis has interesting implications for the history of courtly love writings. Courtly love is, in particular, love regarded in its social aspects, in relation to the royal or chivalric courts, to the framework of Christianity, or (in the thirteenth century) to the less refined context of the developing 'bourgeois' society. Indeed many of the features of courtly love defined by Paris are seen from a social point of view: secrecy, tale-bearing, concern for the lady's reputation, a sense of her social elevation, and so on. But it is unlikely that this aspect was introduced by the northern poets through their weaving songs and *chansons à personnages*, as Paris rather implies. It does not now seem that the lyric poems of the *trouvères* (as distinct, of course, from the related romances) contributed a great deal to the courtly tradition.

As well as the troubadours, there are two other major influences on the northern poets which make their work develop in a very different direction. The first is Andreas's Ovidian *De Arte Honeste Amandi*, probably written for the court of Marie de Champagne (who was also, of course, the patron of Chrétien's *Lancelot*) and dating from the mid-1180s. Its casuistry and legalism in discussing matters of love owe something, no doubt, to the love-reasoning of the troubadours, but it must also be addressing itself to a tradition of such debates within that court. There are common elements, perhaps, with the letter of troubadour writing in this work, but it is very foreign to that school in spirit. Its facile wit and worldliness could hardly be more different from the complicated and ingenious obscurities of the troubadours. Its alternative attitude to love (what all the critics from Gaston Paris to Charles Muscatine call the 'bourgeois' tradition)[4] affected the most significant French writing, and most importantly the *Roman de la Rose*, in the courtly tradition after 1200.

There is another, equally important tradition that bore upon northern French courtly writings from the first and whose subsequent history in inextricably linked with *courtoisie*: the Arthurian. Wace's Anglo-Norman rhymed version of Geoffrey of

Monmouth's *Historia Regum Britanniae* was presented at the court of Eleanor of Aquitaine in 1155, and a flourishing French Arthurian tradition immediately developed. A link between Arthurian and courtly love writing is immediately forged (that is, if it did not already exist): Bernart de Ventadorn, who came north under the aegis of Eleanor, declares his affection for an unidentified Tristan at the end of his poem beginning 'Lo Rossinhols s'Esbaudeya'.[5] Raimbaut d'Aurenga who died in 1173 compares the inexorability of his love-tie to that of Tristan ('Non Chant per auzel ni per flor', line 29; XLVI here) and Raimbaut's editor, W. T. Pattison, accordingly identifies Bernart's Tristan as Raimbaut.[6] Indeed these references are interesting, if unrepresentative, suggestions of a mutual French–Provençal influence, since there is no evidence for the existence of earlier Arthurian writing in Provençal.

So, when we turn to the major courtly work in French, the *Roman de la Rose*, there are influences from Andreas/Ovid towards a 'bourgeois', uncourtly view of love and a well-established Arthurian courtly tradition to be taken into account, as well as the Provençal origins. By 1200 it was already a much more ramified, if less intense, literary development that courtly writing had followed in Northern France than anywhere else. The social emphasis, mentioned by Paris, has become all-important, under the influence perhaps of the real court of Marie de Champagne as well as the literary court of Arthur. The social setting of love in the *Roman de la Rose* has become so central that the quality of feeling within the lover has disappeared almost entirely. There is no ecstasy in the lover in Jean de Meun; and Lewis's excellent phrase, 'his delighted apprenticeship in courtly usage'[7] suggests exactly the extent to which Guillaume de Lorris's section of the poem is an outline of social *mores* rather than an anatomy of the workings of a lover's mind. As with the Provençal poets, the concern is more with procedure in love than with its object, but there is an important difference. The troubadours, followed by a long tradition culminating in the Stilnovisti, especially Dante's *Vita Nuova*, examined the procedure of a lover from the point of view of the refining effect of courtly love upon him which necessarily involved, among other things, the state of his soul; the French writers, from Chrétien onwards and especially in the *Roman de la Rose*, are concerned more particularly with the correctness of the manners of a courtly lover – how admirable his social behaviour is and what kind of example he sets to other lovers. (In English a broad contrast along these lines could be made between the Italian-influenced *Troilus and Criseyde* and the French-influenced *Sir Gawain and the Green Knight*.)

Ultimately the limitation of psychological or spiritual interest in the French tradition enfeebled it, to result in the weak later poetry of the school of Machaut and the purely adventurous, unpsychological late prose romances. But its influence as a narrative form and source was immense. The nineteenth-century French critics who found the origin of the European novel in the *Roman de la Rose* and the northern French romances were broadly right.

CHRÉTIEN DE TROYES
(*fl.* 1170–82)
LVIII   *Lancelot*

Chrétien's *Lancelot (The Knight of the Cart)* is concerned entirely with the binding passion between Lancelot and Guinevere, and it emphasises throughout the irresistibility of their anti-rational, adulterous love. It was in an essay on this poem that *amour courtois* was first defined by Gaston Paris, so it is the classic of courtly love as defined by Lewis too, fulfilling the requirements of his definition to an unparalleled degree. It is thought to have been written about 1177, early in the great period of such writings. Chrétien holds to his theme with a fixity that gives power and compulsion to his narrative; Lewis, outraged perhaps by the 'revolting' passages of 'irreligion',[8] rather overstates the 'fantastic labours which Lancelot undergoes at the bidding of the queen' (p. 24), and I do not think it is true that 'the dark and tremendous suggestions of the Celtic myth that lurks in the background of his story . . . so far (for a modern reader) overshadow the love and adventure of the foreground' (p. 27). This poem has a consistency of theme and an interest far in excess of the other works of Chrétien, a consistency identified by Nitze as the *san* of the poem: 'it is Lancelot's constant striving to submit to the dictates of Guinevere, herself a sufferer in love's cause, even when they lower him in the estimation of others, that really constitutes the theme, the central idea – in a word, the *sens* of our romance'.[9] This constancy of purpose in the writer make *Lancelot* one of the greatest works of courtly and chivalric literature.

After a brief introduction in which the poet attributes to his lady, Marie of Champagne, the *san* and *matiere* of his story, the narrative begins with the arrival of a knight in full armour into Camelot on Ascension Thursday. The knight declares that he holds in his land (later revealed as Gorre) many people from Arthur's Kingdom (afterwards called Logres) whom he will release only if Arthur entrusts Guinevere to one of his knights who must fight with him for her. Kay announces that he will leave the court if this task is not granted him. Arthur sadly agrees, and Kay rides away with the queen, followed by several knights led by Gawain.

The pursuers soon come upon Kay's horse, riderless and bloody, and shortly afterwards they meet a knight on foot who asks for a horse which they give him. He rides off (his identity remaining undisclosed for half of the poem), and later on the knights find his horse dead amid signs of a battle. Gawain follows and soon sees the knight (Lancelot) on foot overtaking a cart driven by a dwarf. The dwarf urges Lancelot to climb on the cart (which is of the kind used to take criminals to the gallows) if he wishes to see Guinevere. (We are not told how Lancelot knows of the pursuit of the queen.) Lancelot hesitates for a moment before getting in, and the poet introduces the theme of the work:[10]

But common sense, which is inconsistent with love's dictates, bids him refrain from getting in, warning him and counselling him to do and undertake nothing for which he may reap shame and disgrace. Reason, which dares thus speak to him, reaches only his lips, but not his heart; but love is enclosed within his heart, bidding him and urging him to mount at once upon the cart. So he jumps in, since love will have it so, feeling no concern about the shame, since he is prompted by love's commands. (Everyman translation, pp. 274–5; lines 369–81)

Gawain and Lancelot spend the night in a town where three maidens receive them, repeatedly reproaching Lancelot for travelling in the cart. Next morning Lancelot sits by a window and sees the funeral procession of a knight going by, led by a tall knight who leads a fair lady by her horse's rein.

The knight at the window knew that it was the Queen. He continued to gaze at her attentively and with delight as long as she was visible. And when he could no longer see her, he was minded to throw himself out and break his body down below. And he would have let himself fall out had not my lord Gawain seen him, and drawn him back, saying: 'I beg you, sire, be quiet now. For God's sake, never think again of committing such a mad deed. It is wrong for you to despise your life.' 'He is perfectly right', the damsel says; 'for will not the news of his disgrace be known everywhere? Since he has been upon the cart, he has good reason to wish to die, for he would be better dead than alive. His life henceforth is sure to be one of shame, vexation, and unhappiness.' (p. 277; lines 564–86)

The two knights set off and meet a maiden who tells them that the tall knight is Meleagant, son of Bademagus, King of Gorre, who is taking Guinevere off to his land from which no foreigner returns. Two treacherous bridges lead there, the water-bridge which Gawain will take, and the sword-bridge which Lancelot is to look for. The friends part, Lancelot so deep in reverie that he hears no knight's challenge:

He of the cart is occupied with deep reflections, like one who has no strength or defence against love which holds him in its sway. His thoughts are such that he totally forgets himself, and he knows not whether he is alive or dead, forgetting even his own name, not knowing whether he is armed or not, or whither he is going or whence he came. Only one creature he has in mind, and for her his thought is so occupied that he neither sees nor hears aught else.[11] (p. 279; lines 715–28)

A little later, Lancelot is helped by a maiden who makes him promise to sleep with her. He keeps his promise, but without touching her, because

The knight has only one heart, and this one is really no longer his, but has been entrusted to someone else, so that he cannot bestow it elsewhere. Love, which holds all hearts beneath its sway, requires it to be lodged in a single place. All hearts? No, only those which it esteems. And he whom love deigns to control ought to prize himself the more. Love prized his heart so highly that it constrained it in a special manner, and made him so proud of this distinction that I am not inclined to find fault with him, if he lets alone what love forbids, and remains fixed where it desires. (p. 286; lines 1240–54)

The lady understands his love, and together they ride forth the next day.

She talks to him, but, not caring for her words, he pays no attention to what she says. He likes to think, but dislikes to talk. Love very often inflicts afresh the wound it has given him. Yet, he applied no poultice to the wound to cure it and make it comfortable, having no intention or desire to secure a poultice or to seek a physician, unless the wound becomes more painful. Yet there is one whose remedy he would gladly seek.[12] (p. 287; lines 1344–55)

Lancelot and the lady come across a beautiful comb which the lady recognises as Guinevere's. She keeps the comb and he keeps the hair, rejoicing in this love-token, Guinevere's tresses:

A hundred thousand times he raises them to his eyes and mouth, to his forehead and face: he manifests his joy in every way, considering himself rich and happy now. He lays them in his bosom near his heart, between the shirt and the flesh. He would not exchange them for a cartload of emeralds and carbuncles, nor does he think that any sore or illness can afflict him now; he holds in contempt essence of pearl, treacle, and the cure for pleurisy; even for St Martin and St James he has no need; for he has such confidence in this hair that he requires no other aid. (p. 287; lines 1475–90)

After a series of episodes in which Lancelot proves his excellence, including an encounter with a monk in a graveyard of beautiful tombs in which Lancelot lifts a stone which, according to its inscription, will only be lifted by the man who is to escape from Gorre, thereby releasing all the prisoners there, he comes to the sword-bridge which 'he passes over with great pain and agony, being wounded in the hands, knees and feet. But even this suffering is sweet to him: for Love, who conducts and leads him on, assuages and relieves the pain' (p. 309; lines 3124–9). He comes to the palace, from which the good king Bademagus and his evil son Meleagant watch his approach, and it is agreed that Meleagant and the injured Lancelot will fight for the queen next day. Guinevere is placed at a window from which she can watch the battle. When Lancelot tires in the course of it, a wise maiden learns the knight's name from the queen and tells him that the queen is watching. We too learn his name for the first time here. Lancelot fights with renewed vigour and is about to be victorious when Bademagus, in his son's interest, asks the queen to appeal to Lancelot to stop. She assents and Lancelot holds his hand immediately because 'the man who is a perfect lover is always obedient and quickly and gladly does his mistress' pleasure. So Lancelot was constrained to do his lady's will, for he loved more than Pyramus, if that were possible for any man to do'[13] (p. 318; lines 3816–22). It is agreed that the battle be resumed at Arthur's court in one year's time. When Lancelot approaches the queen, she rebuffs him, saying ' "Truly he has made poor use of his time. I shall never deny that I feel no gratitude towards him." Now Lancelot is dumbfounded; but he replies very humbly like a polished lover: "Lady, certainly I am grieved at this, but I dare not ask your reason." ' The queen leaves the room: 'And Lancelot followed her with his eyes and heart until she reached the door ... His eyes would gladly have followed her, had that been possible; but the heart, which is more lordly and masterful in its strength, went through the door after her, while the eyes remained behind weeping with the body' (p. 320; lines 3975–82 and 3988–98). Rumour tells Guinevere that Lancelot is dead, and she mourns bitterly the man 'in whose life she found her own' (p. 322), and whom she would wish to have held in her arms, 'yes, certainly, quite unclad, in order the better to enjoy him' (p. 323). Lancelot, for his part, reflects on the queen's hostility towards him:

"God! what could my crime have been? I think she must have known that I mounted upon the cart. I do not know what other cause she can have to blame me. This has been my undoing. If this is the reason of her hate, God! what harm could this crime do? Any one who would reproach me for such an act never knew what love is, for no one could mention anything which, if prompted by love, ought to be turned into a reproach. Rather, everything that one can do for his lady-love is to be regarded as a token of his love and courtesy. Yet, I did not do it for my 'lady-love'. I know not by what name to call her, whether 'lady-love', or not. I do not dare to call her by this name. But I think I know this much of love: that if she loved me, she ought not to esteem me less for this crime, but rather call me her true lover, inasmuch as I regarded it as an honour to do all love bade me do, even to mount upon a cart. She ought to ascribe this to love; and this is a certain proof that love thus tries his devotees and thus learns who is really his. But this service did not please my lady, as I discovered by her countenance. And yet her lover did for her that for which many have shamefully reproached and blamed him, though she was the cause of it; and many blame me for the part I have played, and have turned my sweetness into bitterness. In truth, such is the custom of those who know so little of love, that even honour they wash in shame. But whoever dips honour into shame, does not wash it, but rather sullies it. But they, who maltreat him so, are quite ignorant of love; and he, who fears not his commands, boasts himself very superior to him. For unquestionably he fares well who obeys the commands of love, and whatever he does is pardonable, but he is the coward who does not dare.' (p. 325; lines 4365–414)

The queen and the knight are reconciled, and she explains to him that her coldness towards him was because of his momentary hesitation, prompted by reason and common sense, in mounting the cart. They arrange a tryst and make love together:

And the queen extends her arms to him and, embracing him, presses him tightly against her bosom, drawing him into the bed beside her and showing him every possible satisfaction: her love and her heart go out to him. It is love that prompts her to treat him so; and if she feels great love for him, he feels a hundred thousand times as much for her. For there is no love at all in other hearts compared with what there is in his; in his heart love was so completely embodied that it was niggardly towards all other hearts ... Their sport is so agreeable and sweet, as they kiss and fondle each other, that in truth such a marvellous joy comes over them as was never heard or known. But their joy will not be revealed by me, for in a story it has no place. Yet, the most choice and delightful satisfaction was precisely that of which our story must not speak. That night Lancelot's joy and pleasure were very great. But, to his sorrow, day comes when he must leave his mistress' side. It cost him such pain to leave her that he suffered a real martyr's agony. His heart now stays where the Queen remains; he has not the power to lead it away, for it finds such pleasure in the Queen that it has no desire to leave her: so his body goes and his heart remains. He turns straight towards the window;[14] But enough of his body stays behind to spot and stain the sheets with the blood which has fallen from his fingers. (p. 329; lines 4672–719)

The rest of the romance is occupied with the treacherous hostility of Meleagant towards Lancelot, interrupted only by the tournament at which Lancelot proves his absolute obedience in love by doing badly in the fight when Guinevere sends him a command to do his worst (the most incredible of the 'fantastic labours' that Lewis protests at). We are told at the end that the last 967 lines of the poem were written by one 'Godefroi de Leigni, the clerk'. In the course of this section, at Lancelot's return to the court of Arthur where he had been believed dead, the queen's circumspect welcoming of him is explained:

She is so close to him that her body came near following her heart. Where is her heart, then? It was kissing and welcoming Lancelot. And why did the body conceal itself? Why is not her joy complete? Is it mingled with anger or hate? No, certainly, not at all; but it may be that the King or some of the others who are there, and who are watching what takes place, would have taken the whole situation in, if, while all were looking on, she had followed the dictates of her heart. If common-sense had not banished this mad impulse and rash desire, her heart would have been revealed and her folly would have been complete. Therefore reason closes up and binds her fond heart and her rash intent, and made it more reasonable, postponing the greeting until it shall see and espy a suitable and more private place where they would fare better than here and now. (p. 356; lines 6849–75)

This caution is in accordance with the requirements of secrecy in love, and also perhaps with the fragility of the woman's social situation (like Criseyde's); but the irony of Godefroi de Leigni's (he also has a fondness for quoting the proverbial wisdom of 'the rustic') giving Reason the last word over love serves only to underline the opposite in Chrétien's poem throughout which passionate love triumphs over reason and common sense.[15]

LIX

D'Amors ke m'ait tolut a moy
n'a li ne me veult retenir,
me plaing ensi, c'ades otroi
ke de moi faice son plaixir.
Et se ne me repuis tenir   5
ke ne m'en plaigne, et di por coi:
ke ceauls ki la traïxent voi
sovent a lor joie venir
et je mur por ma bone foy.

S'Amors, por essaucier sa loi,   10
veult ces anemis retenir,
de sen li vient, si com je croi,
c'as siens ne puet elle faillir.
Et jeu, ke ne m'en puis partir
de la belle a cui je souploi,   15
mon cuer, ki siens est, li envoi.
Maix de noiant la veul servir
se ceu li rent ke je li doi.

Dame, de ceu ke vostre sui,
dites moi se greit m'en saveis?   20
Nenil, se onkes vos conui,
ains vos poise quant vos m'aveis.
Et des ke vos ne me voleis,
dont seux je vostres per anui.
Maix se jai deveis de nullui   25
mercit avoir, dont me souffreis.
Ke je ne sai ameir autrui.

Onkes del bovraige ne bui
dont Tristans fut enpoisonneis,
maix plux me fait ameir ke lui   30
Amors et bone volenteis.
Se ne m'en doit savoir mal greit,

LIX

Thus do I complain of Love[16] who raised me to myself and does not want to keep me on: always I accept whatever his pleasure would do with me. Except that I cannot keep from complaining now, and I am saying why: it is that I see those who betray always come to their joy, and I die through my good faith.

If love wants to win over his enemies in order to exalt his rule, it is common sense, as I believe, that he cannot fail those who are his own. And I, who cannot part from the beautiful one to whom I bow, send her my heart which is hers. But to no purpose do I wish to serve her, if that which I give her belongs to her.

Lady, tell me concerning that heart which is yours, does it please you to know it is mine? No; if I know you at all, it depresses you, rather, how much you possess me. And since you do not want me, then I am yours as an annoyance to you. But if ever you choose to have pity on anyone, then let it be me, since I can love nobody else.

I never drank the potion with which Tristan was poisoned,[17] but Love and my good will cause me to love more than he. I am not obliged to suffer this grief since I am forced to it by nothing,

quant de riens esforciés n'en sui
fors de tant ke mes ieuls en crui
per cui seux en la voie entreis   35
dont ains n'issi ne ne recrui.

Cuers, se ma dame ne t'ait chier,
jai por ceu ne la guerpirais:
ades soies en son domgier
des k'enpris et comenciet l'ais.   40
Jai, mon veul, ne t'en partirais
ne por delai ne t'esmaier:
biens endoucist per delaier;
et quant plux desireit l'avrais,
plux serait douls a l'essaier.   45

Mercit trovaixe, el mien cuidier,
c'elle fuist en tout le conpas
del monde, lai ou je la quier,
maix je croi k'elle n'i est pais.
Onkes ne fine ne ne las   50
de ma doulce dame proier:
proi et reproi sens delaier
comme cil ki ne seit a gais
Amors servir, ne losengier.

BLONDEL DE NESLE[18]
(late twelfth century)

LX

Bien doit chanter qui fine Amors adreche
de joie avoir; mais pas ne m'en semont,
k'en moi ne truis ne joie ne leeche
par quoi je chant, je ne saroie dont.
Et nonporquant, se ces maus ne despont   5
k'entre ma dame et fine Amor me font,
bien puis morir: ja ne le saveront,
se par mon chant ne sevent la destrece
ou par mon vis dont la colors defont.

except that I believe my eyes. Through them I entered on the road that I have never left nor given up.

My heart, if my lady does not cherish you, never abandon her because of that. Always be in her power, because you have put yourself under it and begun this. Never, I wish, will you depart from her or be discouraged by delay. Good things are the sweeter for being delayed. And the more you have desired her, the more sweet will be the tasting.

In my opinion, I would have found pity if it existed anywhere in the world where I looked for it; but I think it does not exist. Never do I cease or stop beseeching you, my sweet lady; I pray and pray again without pause, since it is not for amusement or to flatter that I serve Love.

LX

Well should he sing whom *Fin Amour*[19] directs towards joy; but it does not summon me. For in myself I do not find joy or happiness to sing about, and I would not know what it was. And nevertheless, if these ills which my lady and *Fin Amour* between them do to me, do not cease, I may well die; and they will never know, if they do not recognise my distress through my song or my face whose colour pales.

Ne m'a rescos faintise ne perece   10
ke ma dame ne m'ait navré parfont
d'un doç regart, dont la plaie me bleche,
k'ele me fist as beaus ieus de son front:
n'em puis garir se mire ne m'i sont,
a l'aïe de son cuer ki confont   15
moi et le mien, dont plus l'aim en cest mont
k'a estre rois de la grignor hautece;
se Dieus m'en doint joie, ne guerredont!

Ja por dolor ke j'aie n'ert jus mise
ma volentés d'amer veraiement: 20
qu'il m'est a vis ke de loins l'ai aprise,
n'onques por çou n'amai mains loiaument.
Et si sai bien ke falir a sa gent
ne doit Amors, se droiture ne ment;
mais plus done dolor a un k'a cent.   25
Las, je sui cil qui plus grieve et justice:
mais c'est auques par mon comencement.

Que ja dolors mais pas ne fut asise
en cors ou cuers amast si loiaument:
mais de tel lieu m'est venue et tramise   30
dont je ne doi refuser le torment.
Bien fait Amors de moi a son talent,
et Esperance et ma dame, ensement,
molt m'engignent entre eles dochement:
ne sai se ja aront jor covoitise   35
de moi rendre mal guerredonement.

Molt fu Amors corageuse et hardie
quant ens mon cors vint mon cuer asalir;
et si sai bien k'ele n'i venist mie
s'ele quidast k'ele i dëust falir.   40
Mais tant conut volenté et desir
ke de mon cuer ne se vauront partir.
D'un doç regart fis verge a moi ferir:

Neither her indifference[20] nor her idleness saved me from being wounded deeply by a sweet look the injury from which pierces me, which she gave me from her brow's fair eyes. I cannot be saved if they are not my doctor, with the help of her heart which confounds me and my heart, so that I love her more than to be the king of the greatest eminence in this world. May God give me joy and reward!

Never because of the sorrow I undergo will my wish to love truly be lessened. Though I seem to have known this sorrow for a long time, I will never love less devotedly because of it. And I know well that Love should not fail his followers if he is not to fail in justice.[21] But he gives another sorrow to the person who has a hundred. Alas, I am the one he grieves and tries the most. But it is to some extent my own fault.

For never was sorrow placed in a body or heart that loved so devotedly. But it has come to me and been sent from such a place that I ought not to refuse the pain. Love disposes of me fittingly at his own whim, and Hope and my lady equally torment me much between them in a sweet way. I do not know if they intend ever to make me an ill reward.

Love showed great courage and foolhardiness when he came within my body to attack my heart. And I know well that he would not have come at all if he had thought that he should fail. But he recognised fully the wish and desire which would not be able to leave my heart. Out of a sweet look I made a rod to beat myself. But it is unfortunate that I saw it plucked from her

mais mar la vic en si beaus ieus coillie,
se ma dame l'a fait por moi traïr.   45

Por qui j'ai moi et tote riens guerpie,
car mi voloit a son oés retenir:
k'il n'est dolors d'Amors ne d'autre envie
qui mon voloir em pëust departir!
Se Loiautés valoit mieus de Traïr   50
et Amors velt ses biens a droit partir,
encoir porroie a grant bien avenir;
mais ens li est pitiés si endormie
que ne me velt ochirre ne garir.

GÂCE BRULÉ
(*d c.* 1220)[23]

LXI

Bien ait l'amor dont l'en cuide avoir joie
de bien amer et servir loiaument!
Mes je n'atent fors la mort de la moie,
que j'ai enpris d'amer si hautement.
Et si n'i voi fors mon definement,   5
se ma dame de moi pitié ne prent
ou Loiautez et Amor ne l'en proie.

S'il avenoit que si joene et si bloie
de si haut pris amast si bassement,
esperance de garison avroie   10
de ma doleur et des maus que je sent.
N'est pas ensi, ains est tout autrement:
car s'il avoit en moi valeurs tels cent,
si haute amor deservir ne porroie.

En Amors a si haute seignorie   15
qu'ele a povoir des povres enrichir;
pour ce atent sa merci et s'aïe.

beautiful eyes, if my lady gave the glance only to betray me.[22]

She for whom I have abandoned myself and everything else, may she wish to keep me for her use! For no sorrow from Love, nor envy of anyone else, could turn my desire from her. If devotion can avail more than treachery, and Love wishes to dispense his goods with justice, I may yet be able to come to a great good. But pity is so deep in slumber within him, that he is willing neither to kill me nor cure me.

LXI

Well may that love prosper through which one hopes to have the joy of successful love and serving loyally! But I expect nothing from mine except death, since I ask for love in such a lofty place. And so I see nothing in it but my end, if my lady does not take pity on me or if Devotion and Love do not ask it from her.[24]

If it could happen that one so young and so fair of such great distinction might love so lowly, I would have hope of salvation from my sorrow and from the ills I feel. But it is not so; it is entirely otherwise, for if there were in me a hundred times as much worth, I could not deserve such elevated love.

In Love there is such great nobility that it has the power to make the poor rich; so I look for its mercy and help. It can

Qu'el me puet fere en si haut point venir
que ja n'avrent povoir de moi nuisir
faus losengier qui pensent de traïr   20
loial amor: c'est lor ancesorie.

Douce dame, se j'ai dit par folie
nule chose dont maus doie venir,
ce fet Amors, qui si estroit me lie
que n'ai povoir de mon sens maintenir.   25
Dedenz son cors vueil ellire et choisir
le plus fin cuer, por loiaument servir,
dont onques fust haute heneur deservie.

Deservir! Deus, qui porroit en sa vie
si haute enprise achever ne fornir?   30
Je ne di pas que ce soie je mie.
Qu'Amors mi fet endurer et sentir,
a, ma dame, les maus dont je souspir,
dont riens ne m'est medecine a guerir
s'en bien amer ne recouroit m'amie.   35

LXII

Ire d'amors ke en mon cuer repaire
ne me lait tant ke de chanteir me taigne:
se me mervoil ke chanson en puis faire,
maix je ne sai dont l'ochoixon me vaigne.
Car li desirs et la grans volenteis   5
dont je seux si sospris et esgaireis
m'ont teil moneit — seu vos puis je bien dire—
c'a poene sai cognoistre joie d'ire.

Et nonporcant tous li cuers m'en esclaire
d'un douls espoir — Deux doinst ke il m'avaigne!   10
Moult doveroit a ma dame desplaire
se ceste amor m'ocist (bien l'en covaigne!):

make me come to such a high position that false flatterers will never have the power to injure me, those who want to betray loyal love, as is their established wont.

Sweet lady, if through folly I have said anything from which offence should result, Love is responsible who binds me so tightly that I am unable to keep my senses. Within him I want to elect and choose the finest heart in order to serve loyally, by which at one time high honour was merited.

To merit! God, who in all his life could achieve or carry out such a high enterprise? I am not in the least saying that I could. But Love makes me persist and feel (ah! my lady!) the ills from which I sigh, from which nothing can nurse me to recovery if my friend does not restore me to successful love.

LXII

The grief of love[25] which returns to my heart does not allow me to keep from singing. I am astonished that I can make a song out of it, but I do not know what theme may come to me. Because the desire and the great passion by which I am so crushed and distressed have brought me to a state (I can well assure you of this) where I can hardly distinguish joy from grief.

And yet all my heart is lighted by a sweet hope: God grant that it may be fulfilled! It ought to displease my lady much (well may she assent to this!) if this love should kill me. But she

mort m'ait ces cors, li gens, li aceneis,
et ces cleirs vis frexement coloreis,
sa grant biaulteis ou il n'ait riens ke dire.   15
Deus, por coi vout por moi tant escondire!

Loiauls amors (dont j'ai plux de cent paire)
m'ociront, voir, ains ke ma joie vaigne
ke tous jors m'est promisse por atraire,
maix je ne voi ke ma dame en sovaigne   20
ou Deus ait mis tant valors et bonteis:
maix envers moi c'est tant Orguels melleis
ke n'ai pooir de teil tort contredire,
pues ke mes cuers se veult por li ocire.

Ire me font celle gent de male aire   25
plux ke nuls mals ke por Amors soustaigne;
maix ne lor valt, ke jai ne poront faire
c'Amors ne m'ait et c'a cuer ne me taigne:
si loiaulment me seux a li doneis
ke sens morir n'en serai desevreis.   30
Nes c'om se puet vers Amors escondire,
ne puet on pais loiaul amie elire?

Tres grans amors me font folie faire,
s'ai grant paor ke longues ne me taigne—
ne je n'en puis mon coraige retraire: 35
ensi me plaist, coment k'il m'en avaigne.
Per teil raixon seux povres asezeis
quant ceu me plaist dont je seux plux greveis.
Et en chantant m'estuet jüeir et rire—
ains ne vi maix si decevant martyre!   40

Ha, cuens de Blois, vous qui fustes amez,
tiengne vous en et vous en remembrez:
car qui d'amer oste son cuer et tire,
aventure iert s'il grant honor desire.

herself has killed me: the fair and wise, her clear face freshly hued, her great beauty in which there is nothing to speak ill of. God, why does she want to reject me for so long?

Loyal love (of which I have a great abundance)[26] will kill me, certainly, before I reach my joy which every day is promised me as a bait. But I cannot see that my lady takes note of this, she in whom God has put so much worth and virtue. But Pride has warred so much against me that I am unable to protest at this crime, since my heart wants to die for her.

Some ill-natured people[27] cause me more grief than any ill I suffer through Love. But it will do them no good, for they will never be able to bring it about that Love will not aid me and keep me in his heart. So devotedly am I given to him that I will not be separated from him except by death. Just as a man cannot escape from Love, can he not choose a loyal friend either?

My very great love makes me behave foolishly, and I am greatly afraid that it will not support[28] me long. But I cannot hold back my heart: that is my pleasure, however it should turn out for me. By this reckoning, I am poor amid plenty, in that I am pleased by the thing by which I am most grieved. And in singing I must play and laugh. So did you ever see such a treacherous torture!

Ah, count of Blois,[29] you who were loved, be well-advised and take note: for he who withdraws his heart from love and takes it back, it will be a wonder if he longs for great honour.

CONON DE BÉTHUNE
(*died* 1224)[30]

LXIII

Ahi, Amors, com dure departie
me convenra faire de la millor
ki onques fust amee ne servie!
Dieus me ramaint a li par sa douçour
si voirement ke m'en part a dolor.   5
Las, k'ai je dit? Ja ne m'en part je mie:
se li cors va servir Nostre Signor,
li cuers remaint del tot en sa baillie.

Por li m'en vois sospirant en Surie,
car je ne doi faillir mon Creator: 10
ki li faura a cest besoing d'aïe,
saciés ke Il li faura a grignor.
Et saicent bien li grant et li menor
ke la doit on faire chevallerie
ou on conquiert paradis et honor   15
et pris et los, et l'amor de s'amie.

Dieus est assis en son saint iretaige:
ore i parra se cil le secorront
cui il jeta de la prison ombraige
quant il fu mors ens las Crois ke Turc ont.   20
Saichiés, chil sont trop honi ki n'iront
s'il n'ont poverte ou viellece ou malaige,
et cil ki sain et jone et riche sont
ne poevent pas demorer sans hontaige.

LXIII

Ah, Love,[31] what a sad parting must I make from the best one who was ever loved or served. May God in his benignity bring me back to her as surely as I now depart sorrowfully. Alas, what have I said? Really I am not leaving at all; if the body is going to serve Our Lord, the heart remains entirely under her rule.

Because of her I sigh as I go to Syria, because I must not fail my creator. The man who fails him in this need of help, you may be sure that God will fail him in greater. And may both great and humble know that it is there one must do deeds of chivalry by which Heaven and honour and esteem and praise are won, as well as the love of his lady.

God is under siege in his holy dwelling-place. Now it will be seen if those people will help him, those whom he released from the dark prison when he died on that Cross which the Infidels now possess. Know well, the people who will not go are greatly dishonoured, if they do not suffer from poverty or old age or illness. And those who are healthy and young and rich cannot hesitate without dishonour.

Tous li clergiés et li home d'eaige   25
qui ens ausmogne et ens biens fais morront,
partiront tot a cest pelerinaige
et les dames ki chastement vivront
et loiauté feront ceaus ki iront.
Et s'eles font, par mal consel, folaige,   30
as lasques gens et mauvais le feront,
car tot li boin iront en cest voiaige.

Ki chi ne velt avoir vie anuieuse,
si voist por Dieu morir liés et joieus,
ke cele mors est douce et savereuse   35
dont on conquiert le Resne presïeus;
ne ja de mort n'en i morra uns sels,
ains naisteront en vie glorïeuse.
Ki revenra, moult sera ëureus,
a tos jors mais en iert Honors s'espeuse.   40

Dieus, tant avons esté preus par huiseuse!
Or verra on ki a certes iert preus:
s'irons vengier la honte dolereuse
dont chascuns doit estre iriés et honteus.
Car a no tans est perdus li Sains Lieus   45
ou Dieus soffri por nos mort glorïeuse;
s'or i laissons nos anemis morteus,
a tos jors mais iert no vie honteuse.

All the clergy and the aged who die, having lived on charity and acts of generosity, will go on this pilgrimage,[32] every one, and the ladies who live chastely and keep faithful to those who go. And if, through ill-advisedness, they do commit folly, they will do so with cowardly and evil men, because all the good will go on this journey.

Those who do not want to have a dreary life, let them go to die for God, happy and joyful, because this death, by which the precious Kingdom is won, is sweet and pleasant. Not a single one dies or will die there, for they will be born into a glorious life. Those who do come back will be very happy, because they will be wedded to glory for all time.

God, how gallant we have been in idleness! Now it will appear who is really gallant. We go to avenge that sorrowful shame by which everyone should be grieved and ashamed. For in our time the Holy Place, where God underwent glorious death for us, has been lost. If we now leave it to our mortal enemies, the period of our life will be shameful to the end of time.

LXIV

Moult me semont Amors ke je m'envoise,
quant je plus doi de chanter estre cois:
mais j'ai plus grant talent ke je me coise,
por çou s'ai mis mon chanter en defois.
Ke mon langaige ont blasmé li François   5
et mes cançons, oiant les Champenois,
et la Contesse encoir, dont plus me poise.

La Roïne ne fist pas ke cortoise
ki me reprist, ele et ses fieus, li Rois:
encoir ne soit ma parole franchoise,   10
si la puet on bien entendre en franchois!
Ne chil ne sont bien apris ne cortois
s'il m'ont repris se j'ai dit mos d'Artois,
car je ne fui pas norris a Pontoise!

Dieus, ke ferai: dirai li mon coraige?   15
Li irai je dont s'amor demander?
Oïl, par Dieu, car tel sont li usaige
c'on n'i puet mais sans demant riens trover!
Et se jo sui outraigeus del trover,
ne s'en doit pas ma dame a moi irer,   20
mais vers Amors ki me font dire outraige.

LXIV

Love urges me greatly to rejoice, just when I should be most silent from song. But I have a greater desire to be silent, because I have given up my singing. This is because the French have attacked my language and my songs, in the presence of the Champenois and the countess herself, which is what pains me most.[33]

The Queen did not act courteously when she and her son the King criticised me. Even if my language is not French, it can perfectly well be understood in French. And they were not well-mannered or courteous when they blamed me for speaking words from Artois, because I was not brought up at Pontoise!

God, what will I do? Shall I declare my heart to her? Shall I then ask her for her love? Yes, by God, for such are manners now that one can never get anything without asking. And if I am excessive in my composing, my lady ought not to be angry with me but towards Love who makes me speak excess.

Le Roman de la Rose

The first 4,058 lines of this poem were written by Guillaume de Lorris (who died about 1237) probably about 1230. The continuation (4,059–21,780) was written by Jean de Meun, at some time around 1275. Guillaume's part is a lengthy allegorical presentation of the falling in love and the fate of a courtly lover. The continuation of Jean de Meun is a much more wide-ranging anatomy of love and matters related (sometimes loosely) to it, though the most influential modern critics[34] have tended to argue against the traditional view that the two parts of the poem are very different in spirit and subject. Gunn argues that de Meun's continuation is not a discursive, encyclopoedic work but a completion of de Lorris's original project of writing a poem in which 'l'art d'Amors est toute enclose' (38), with all necessary related rhetorical expansions. Whatever the differences between the two writers, it is certain that the poem as a whole is rooted in the situation of the courtly lover but presents his predicament in the course of its development from many points of view far removed from the exacting and narrow psychological world of the troubadours.

The poem begins with a reflection on the reliability of dreams and the narrator tells of a dream he had in which he entered the beautiful garden of *Deduit* (Mirth). There he meets Mirth himself, surrounded by friends, the most prominent of whom is the God of Love (865ff). The god stalks the dreamer as Idleness shows him around the garden. The dreamer looks into the well of Narcissus (a famous motif in the world of the introverted courtly lover, and mentioned by Bernard de Ventadorn);[35] it is decreed that whoever looks in it will fall in love with the next thing upon which his eye falls (as with the love potion in *Tristan* or the love-in-idleness flower in *A Midsummer Night's Dream*). As the dreamer's glance falls on a particular rosebud, Love's arrow pierces him through the heart. (Translations here are taken, with permission, from C. Dahlberg's version, Princeton N.J. (1971.)

LXV   *Guillaume de Lorris*

The God of Love, who had maintained his constant watch over me and had followed me with drawn bow, stopped near a fig tree, and when he saw that I had singled out the bud that pleased me more than did any of the others, he immediately took an arrow and, when the string was in the nock, drew the bow – a wondrously strong one – up to his ear and shot at me in such a way that with great force he sent the point through the eye and into my heart. Then a chill seized me, one from which I have, since that time, felt many a shiver, even beneath a warm fur-lined tunic. Pierced thus by the arrow, I fell straightway to the earth. My heart failed; it played me false. For a long time I lay there in swoon, and when I came out of it and had my senses and reason, I was very weak and thought that I had shed a great quantity of blood. But the point that pierced me drew no blood whatever; the wound was quite dry. I took the arrow in my two hands and began to pull hard at it, sighing as I pulled. I pulled so hard that I drew out the feathered shaft, but the barbed point called Beauty was so fixed inside my heart that it could not be withdrawn. It remains within; I still feel it, and yet no blood has ever come from there.

I was in great pain and anguish because of my doubled danger: I didn't know what to do, what to say, or where to find a physician for my wound, since I expected no remedy for it, either of herbs or roots. But my heart drew me towards the rosebud, for it longed for no other place. If I had had it in my power, it would have restored my life. Even the sight and scent alone were very soothing for my sorrows.

I began then to draw toward the bud with its sweet exhalations. Love selected another arrow, worked in gold. It was the second arrow and its name was Simplicity. It has caused many a man and woman all over the world to fall in love. When Love saw me approach, he did not threaten me, but shot me with the arrow that was made of neither iron nor steel so that the point entered my heart through my eye. No man born, I believe, will ever dislodge it from there, for I tried, without any great joy, to pull the shaft from me, but the point remained within. Now know for a truth that if I had been full of desire for the rosebud before, my wish was greater now. As my woes gave me greater distress, I had an increased desire to go away toward the little rose that smelled sweeter than violets. I would have done better to go farther away, but I could not refuse what my heart commanded. I had to go perforce, always where it aspired to be. But the bowman, who strove mightily and with great diligence to wound me, did not let me move without hurt in that direction. To madden me further, he caused the third arrow, called Courtesy, to fly to my heart. The wound was deep and wide, and I had to fall in a swoon beneath a branching olive tree. I lay there a long time without moving. When I was able to stir, I took the arrow and straightway removed the shaft from my side, but, no matter what I might do, I could not draw out the point. (1,681–776)

The dreamer then makes a courteous speech accepting Love's domination, and Love compliments him:

I replied simply: 'Sir, I surrender willingly, and I shall never defend myself against you. May it never please God for me even to think of ever resisting you, for to do so is neither right nor reasonable. You may do with me what you wish, hang me or kill me. I know very well that I cannot change things, for my life is in your hand. Only through your will can I live until tomorrow, and, since I shall never have joy and health from any other,[36] I await them from you. If your hand, which has wounded me, does give me a remedy, if you wish to make me your prisoner or if you do not deign to do so, I shall not count myself deceived. Know too that I feel no anger whatever. I have heard so much good spoken about you that I want to give my heart and body over to your service, to be used entirely at your discretion, for if I do your will I cannot complain of anything. I still believe that at some time I shall receive the mercy that I await, and under such conditions I submit myself prostrate before you."

With these words, I wanted to kiss his foot, but he took me by the hand and said, 'I love you very much and hold you in esteem for the way that you have replied here. Such a reply never came from a lowborn fellow with poor training.[37] Moreover, you have won so much that, for your benefit, I want you to do homage to me from now on: You will kiss me on my mouth, which no base fellow touches. I do not allow any common man, any butcher, touch it; anyone whom I take thus as my man must be courteous and open. Serving me is, without fail, painful and burdensome; but I do you a great honor, and you should be very glad – since Love carries the standard and banner of courtesy – that you have so good a master and a lord of such high renown. His bearing is so good, so sweet, open, and gentle, that no villainy, no wrong or evil training can dwell in anyone who is bent on serving and honoring him.'

Immediately, with joined hands, I became his man. And you may understand that I grew very proud when his mouth kissed mine; this gift gave me great joy. (1,898–958)

The God of Love then outlines to the dreamer the commandments of Love, continuing the religious parallel. The narrator/author introduces them:

The God of Love then charged me, word by word, with his commandments;[38] this romance portrays them well. Let him who wishes to love give his attention to it, for the romance improves from this point on. From now on one will do well to listen to it, if he is one who knows how to recount it, for the end of the dream is very beautiful, and its matter is new. I tell you that he who will hear the end of the dream can learn a great deal about the games of Love, provided that he wishes to wait while I tell the tale in French and explain the dream's significance. The truth, which is hidden, will be quite open to you when you hear me explain the dream, for it doesn't contain a lying word.

'First of all,' said Love, 'I wish and command that, if you do not want to commit a wrong against me, you must abandon villainy forever. I curse and excommunicate all those who love villainy. Since villainy makes them base, it is not right that I love it. A villain is cruel and pitiless; he does not understand the idea of service or friendship.

'Next, guard well against repeating anything about other people which should be kept quiet. Slandering is not a good characteristic. Take, for example, the seneschal Kay: in former days, he was hated on account of his jeers, and he had a bad reputation. Just as men praised Gawain, who was well trained, on account of his courtesy, so they blamed Kay because he was wicked and cruel, insolent and evil-tongued beyond all other knights.

'Be reasonable and easy to know, soft-spoken and just toward men of both high and low rank. Cultivate the habit, when you go along the streets, of being the first to greet other people; if someone greets you first, before you have opened your mouth, take care to return his greeting without delay.

'Next, take care not to utter dirty words or anything bawdy. You should never open your mouth to name anything base. I do not consider any man courteous who names anything that is filthy or ugly.

'Honor all women and exert yourself to serve them. If you hear any slanderer who goes around detracting women, take him to task and tell him to keep quiet. If you can, do something that is pleasing to ladies and girls, so that they will hear good reports told and retold about you. By this means you can rise in people's esteem.

'After all this, guard against pride, for pride, rightly understood and considered, is madness and sin. He who is tainted with pride cannot bend his heart to serve nor to make an entreaty. The proud man does the contrary of what a pure lover should do.

'He, however, who wants to take trouble for love must conduct himself with elegance. The man who seeks love is worth nothing without elegance. Elegance is not pride. One is worth more for being elegant, provided that he be empty of pride, so that he is neither foolish nor presumptuous. Outfit yourself beautifully, according to your income, in both dress and footwear. Beautiful garments and adornments improve a man a great deal. Therefore you should give your clothes to someone who knows how to do good tailoring, who will seat the seams well and make the sleeves fit properly. You should have fine laced shoes and small boots and get new ones often, and you must see that they are so close-fitting that the vulgar will go around arguing over the way you are going to get into or out of them. Deck yourself out with gloves, a belt, and a silk purse; if you are not rich enough to do so, then restrain yourself. You should, however, maintain yourself as beautifully as you can without ruining yourself. A chaplet of flowers that costs little, or of roses at Pentecost – everyone can have these, since great wealth is not required for them.[39]

'Allow no dirt on your person: wash your hands and scrub your teeth. If the least black shows under your fingernails, don't let it remain there. Sew your sleeves and comb your hair, but do not rouge or paint your face, for such a custom belongs only to ladies or to men of bad repute, who have had the misfortune to find a love contrary to Nature.

'Next, you should remember to keep a spirit of liveliness. Seek out joy and delight. Love cares nothing for a gloomy man. It's a courtly disease through which one laughs, plays, and has a good time. It is thus that lovers have hours of joy and hours of torment. At one hour they feel that the sickness of love is sweet, at another, bitter. The disease of love is very changeable. Now the lover is playful, now tormented, now desolated; at one hour he weeps and at another sings. If, then, you can produce some diverting entertainment by which you might be agreeable to people, I command you to do so. Everyone in all places should do what he knows suits him best, for such conduct brings praise, esteem, and gratitude.

'If you feel yourself active and light, don't resist the impulse to jump; if you are a good horseman, you should spur your mount over hill and dale; if you know how to break lances, you can gain great esteem from doing so; and if you are graceful at arms, you will be ten times loved for that quality. If you have a clear, sound voice and are urged to sing, you should not try to excuse yourself, for a beautiful song is very pleasing. Moreover, it is very advantageous for a young fellow to know how to play the viol, to flute, and to dance. By these means he can further himself a great deal.

'Don't let yourself be thought miserly, for such a reputation could be very troublesome. It is fitting for lovers to give more freely of what they have than do those vulgar, stupid simpletons. No man who doesn't like to give can ever know anything about love. If anyone wants to take pains in loving, he must certainly avoid avarice, for he who, for the sake of a glance or a pleasant smile, has given his heart away completely should certainly, after so rich a gift, give his possessions away without any reserve.

'Now I want to recall briefly what I have told you so that you will remember, for a speech is less difficult to retain when it is short. Whoever wants to make Love his master must be courteous and without pride; he should keep himself elegant and gay and be esteemed for his generosity.

'Next, I ordain that night and day, in a penitential spirit and without turning back, you place your thought on love, that you think of it always, without ceasing, and that you recall the sweet hour whose joy dwells so strongly in you. And in order that you may be a pure lover, I wish and command you to put your heart in a single place so that it be not divided, but whole and without deceit, for I do not like division. Whoever divides his heart among several places has a little bit of it everywhere. But I do not in the least fear him who puts his whole heart in one place; therefore I want you to do so. Take care, however, that you do not lend it, for if you had done so, I would think it a contemptible act; give it rather as a gift with full rights of possession, and you will have greater merit. The favor shown in lending something is soon returned and paid for, but the reward for something given as a gift should be great. Then give it fully and freely, and do so with an easy manner, for one must prize that which is given with a pleasant countenance. I would not give one pea for a gift that one gave in spite of himself.[40]

'When you have given your heart away, as I have been exhorting you to do, things will happen to you that are painful and hard for lovers to bear.' (2,057–268)

There follows a lengthy list of the things 'painful and hard for lovers to bear', the symptoms of being in love according to the courtly system, either genuinely felt or affected with care. Guillaume's tone here is very reminiscent of his masters, Ovid and Andreas. A lover will seek solitude and will become totally abstracted in company (we remember Lancelot in Chrétien's poem); he will remember that his sweetheart is far away (2,299) and reflect (like a troubadour or Dante):

'Oh God, how miserable I am when I do not go where my heart is! Why do I send my heart thus along? I think constantly of that place and see nothing of it. I cannot send my eyes after my heart, to accompany it; and if my eyes do not do so, I attach no value to the fact that they see. Must they be held here? No, they should rather go to visit what the heart so desires. I can indeed consider myself a sluggard when I am so far from my heart. God help me, I hold myself a fool. Now I shall go; no longer will I leave my heart. I shall never be at ease until I see some sign of it.' (2,301–17)

The lover will be filled with misery until he sees his love, but then the sight of her will exacerbate his pain. Afterwards he will wish he had spoken to her, and he will wander in the neighbourhood of her house. When she appears, he will forget what he was to say (an injunction of Andreas),[41] and he will be tormented and sleepness at night, dreaming she is with him and longing for the dawn (2,504). When he cannot bear it any longer, he will get up and go to the beloved's house so that she can hear his sighs. He will waste away. He must (like Ovid's pupil and Chrétien's Yvain)[42] befriend the servant girl of the house as an intermediary (2,557ff). The lover asks the god of Love how these hardships are to be endured, and the god explains how Hope sustains the lover's suit. Hope is aided in the matter by Sweet Thought (*Dous Pensers*), Sweet Talk (*Dous Parlers*) and Sweet Looks (*Dous Regars*). The god then urges the necessity of a confidante:

'Now I want you to seek out a wise and discreet companion, one to whom you can tell all your desires and reveal your whole heart. He will be a great help to you. When your troubles wring you with anguish, you will go to him for comfort, and the two of you will talk together about the beautiful lady who, with her beauty, her appearance, with her mere countenance, is stealing your heart. You will tell him your whole situation and will ask his advice on how you can do something which might be pleasing to your sweetheart. If he who is so much your friend has given his heart in good love, then the companionship will be worth more. It is quite right that he tell you in turn whether his sweetheart is a young girl or not, who she is and what her name is. And you will not fear that he will try to take your love away nor expose you. Rather will you keep good faith between you, you to him and he to you. Know that it is a very pleasant thing when one has a man to whom one dares to tell one's counsel and one's secrets. You will take this pleasure with great thanks and, when you have tried it, you will consider yourself well repaid. (2,686–716)

Love disappears, when he has outlined this programme to the lover, and the unfolding story expands the situation of the courtly lover allegorically: he is encouraged by Courtesy's son *Bel Acueil* and his friends *Franchise* and *Pitie*, and opposed by *Dangier, Malebouche* (a figure familiar as the *lauzengier* of the troubadours) and *Jalousie*.

Jean de Meun's continuation begins when the lover has succeeded in kissing the rose through Bel Acueil's help but then been desolated by Bel Acueil's imprisonment by Jalousie. *Raison* (who has already argued in Guillaume de Lorris's section that the lover should abjure Love, 2,971–3,098) urges flight from Love which she describes as Lust alone. The change of tone in the continuator is immediately evident as more witty and learned. The opening paradoxes of Love, found in Alain de l'Isle, become a popular motif amongst English writers, as (for instance) in Gower's Latin *Vox Clamantis* V, ii: [43]

LXVI   *Jean de Meun*

'Love is hateful peace and loving hate. It is disloyal loyalty and loyal disloyalty, fear that is completely confident and despairing hope. It is reason gone mad and reasonable madness, the sweet danger of drowning, a heavy burden easily handled. It is the treacherous Charybdis, repellent but attractive. It is a healthful languor and diseased health, a hunger satiated in the midst of abundance, a sufficiency always covetous. It is the thirst that is always drunk, a drunkenness intoxicated by its own thirst. False delight, joyous sorrow, enraged happiness, sweet ill, malicious sweetness, and a foul-smelling sweet perfume, love is a sin touched by pardon but a pardon stained by sin. It is suffering which is too joyous, a piteous cruelty, a movement without any certainty, a state of rest both too fixed and too movable. It is a spineless force, a strong weakness that moves all by its efforts. It is foolish sense, wise folly, a prosperity both sad and pleasant. It is the laugh filled with tears and weeping, and the repose always occupied by labor. Sweet hell and heaven of sorrow, it is the prison which solaces captivity. It is the springtime full of cold winter, the moth that refuses nothing but consumes everything from purple robes to homespun, for lovers are found beneath coarse clothing as well as in fine.

'There is no one, however high his lineage nor however wise he may be found, of such proved strength, bravery, or other good qualities, who may not be subjugated by the God of Love. The whole world travels that road. He is the god who turns them all from their road, if they are not those of genuinely evil life whom Genius excommunicates because they commit wrongs against Nature.[44] However, since I have nothing to do with these, I do not wish people to love with that love by which at the end they proclaim themselves unhappy and sorrowful wretches because the God of Love goes about making fools of them. But if indeed you wish to win through to the point where the God of Love will be unable to harm you, and to be cured of that madness, you can drink nothing better than the thought of fleeing from him. You can become happy in no other way. If you follow him, he will follow you; if you flee, he will flee.'

But Reason argued in vain, for when I had heard her through I replied: 'Lady, I flatter myself that I know no more than before of how I can extricate myself from love. There are so many contraries in this lesson that I can learn nothing from it; and yet I can repeat it well by heart, for my heart never forgot any of it; indeed, I can make a public lecture of the whole thing, but to me alone it means nothing. But since you have described love to me, and have praised and blamed it so much, I beg you to define it in such a way that I may better remember it, for I have never heard it defined.'

'Willingly,' she replied. 'Now listen carefully. Love, if I think right, is a sickness of thought that takes place between two persons of different sex when they are in close proximity and open to each other.[45] It arises among people from the burning desire, born of disordinate glances, to embrace and kiss each other and to have the solace of one another's body. A lover so burns and is so enraptured that he thinks of nothing else; he takes no account of bearing fruit, but strives only for delight.

'There are those of a certain kind who do not hold this love dear, but who always pretend to be pure lovers and do not deign to love *par amour*; thus they deceive ladies by promising them their hearts and souls and by swearing lies and fables to those whom they find guillible, until they have taken their pleasure with them. But such people are less deceived than the others; for it is always better, good master, to deceive than to be deceived, particularly in this battle, when one never knows where to seek the mean.

'But I know very well without divination that whoever lies with a woman ought to wish with all his might to continue his divine self and to maintain himself in his likeness in order that the succession of generations might never fail, since all such likenesses are subject to decay.[46] Nature wills, since father and mother disappear, that children rise up to continue the work of generation, and that one's life may be regained by means of another. For this purpose Nature has implanted delight in man because she wants the workman to take pleasure in his task in order that he might neither flee from it nor hate it, for there are many who would never make a move toward it if there were no delight to attract them. Thus Nature uses this subtle means of gaining her end.

'Now understand that no one who desires only his pleasure in love travels the right road or has a right intention. Do you know what they do who go seeking delight? They give themselves up, like serfs or foolish wretches, to the prince of all vices; to seek delight is the root of all evil, as Tully concludes in the book that he wrote *On Old Age*, which he praises and desires more than youth.'[47] (4,293–432)

From the first, then, Jean de Meun stresses the importance of Nature in love, and the significance of the fruitful sensual element in natural love. This is all seen as love in accordance with the design of God, and it is a view of love which L. T. Topsfield finds in the troubadour Marcabru (*fl.* 1130–50). Topsfield writes: '(The) conflict between Bernart (de Ventadorn)'s courtly view of love and Marcabru's idea of love as part of the natural order of life antedates by a century the contrast between the First and Second Parts of the *Roman de la Rose* by Guillaume de Lorris and Jean de Meung'[48] (*Troubadours and Love*, Cambridge University Press 1975, p. 120).

Reason goes on to expound the higher love, Friendship, and dwells on other virtues (whose connection with Love, argued by Gunn, is rather hard to accept), describing herself as a great lover of Socrates at the end of the wonderful description of the island of Fortune (lines 5,921–6,182). The next advisory figure, Ami, is a pragmatist of the school of Andreas and advises caution and even deceit in dealing with Malebouche (the Losengeor) and opposing love's enemies:

'It is good to appease Foul Mouth, for at any time men are accustomed to kiss the hand that they would wish burned. Would that the glutton were now in Tarsus, where he could slander all that he wanted, as long as he stole nothing from lovers! It is good to stop up Foul Mouth so that he may utter no blame or reproach. One has to trick Foul Mouth and his kin – may God never be their surety! – with fraud: one must serve them, caress, blandish and flatter them with ruse, adulation, and false simulation; one must bow to them and salute them. It is a very good idea to stroke a dog until one has passed by. His chatter would indeed be destroyed if he could be led to believe no more than that you had no desire to steal the bud that he has made safe from you. By this means you could triumph over him.' (7,377–98)

And if your eyes weep in front of them it will be a very great advantage for you. Weep; you will do a very wise thing. Kneel down before them with joined hands and, right on the spot, moisten your eyes with hot tears that run down your face so that they can easily see them falling; it is a very pitiable sight to see. Tears are not despicable, especially to men of pity.[49]

'And if you cannot weep, without delay take your saliva, or squeeze the juice of onions, or garlic, or take many other juices with which you may anoint your eyelids; if you do so, you will weep as many times as you want. Many tricksters have done so who afterward were pure lovers whom the ladies let hang in the snare that the men wanted to stretch for them, until, through their compassion, the ladies removed the rope from their necks.' (7,452–76)

All of this seems foreign to the theoretical spirit of helpless, spontaneous love. But it is an inevitable consequence of the codification of courtly love. The lover turns his back on it and the god of love returns to begin a war to release Bel Acueil. But even he accepts the services of Faus Semblant who intercedes for the lover with La Vielle (the duenna) who is guarding Bel Acueil. That is to say, the lover employs the tactics that he ostensibly rejected in Ami.

The Vielle (who is the inspiration for Chaucer's Wife of Bath and possibly, in part, for his Prioress) explains her theory of love, drawing upon Ovid's *Ars Amatoria* III with a closeness that is sometimes simply translation (for instance in her advice about beautiful deportment, 13,281–846). She finds fault with the God of love's commandments, rejecting the last two:

'Fair son, whoever wants to enjoy loving and its sweet ills which are so bitter must know the commandments of Love but must beware that he does not know love itself. I would tell you all the commandments here if I did not certainly see that, by nature, you have an overflowing measure of those that you should have. Well numbered, there are ten of them that you ought to know. But he who encumbers himself with the last two is a great fool; they are not worth a false penny. I allow you eight of them, but whoever follows Love in the other two wastes his study and becomes mad. One should not study them in a school. He who wants a lover to have a generous heart and to put love in only one place has given too evil a burden to lovers. It is a false text, false in the letter. In it, Love, the son of Venus, lies, and no man should believe him; whoever does will pay dearly, as you will see by the end of my sermon.

'Fair son, never be generous; and keep your heart in several places, never in one.[50] Don't give it, and don't lend it, but sell it very dearly and always to the highest bidder. See that he who buys it can never get a bargain: no matter how much he may give, never let him have anything in return; it were better if he were to burn or hang or maim himself. In all cases keep to these points: have your hands closed to giving and open to taking. Certainly, giving is great folly, except giving a little for attracting men when one plans to make them one's prey or when one expects such a return for the gift that one could not have sold it for more. I certainly allow you such giving. The gift is good where he who gives multiplies his gift and gains; he who is certain of his profit cannot repent of his gift. I can indeed consent to such a gift.' (13,011–60)

From here onwards, although the cause of the god of love is in theory victorious, the poem becomes less and less a courtly progress, so that by the end Genius warns against taking the original view of the garden too seriously. In the course of her absolution of Nature, she contrasts that garden with the heavenly garden of God (in terms inevitably suggestive of *Pearl* for the English reader):

If anyone wanted to draw a comparison between the lovely square garden, closed with the little barred wicket, where this lover saw the carol where Diversion dances with his people, and this fair park that I am describing, as wondrously fair as one could wish it, he would make a very great mistake if he did not draw the comparison as one would between a fable and the truth. Anyone who was inside this park or who only cast his eye within would dare to swear safely that the garden was nothing in comparison with this enclosure. This is not built in a square, but is so round and carefully made that no beryl or ball was ever so well rounded a shape. What do you want me to tell you? Let us speak of the things that the Lover saw at that time, both inside and outside, and in order not to tire ourselves, we will pass over them in a few words . . .

'For God's sake, my lords, take care. If anyone looks at the truth, the things contained here are trifles and bagatelles. There is nothing here that can be stable; whatever he saw is corruptible.[51] (20,279–302; 20,349–54)

The poet reverts without pleasure to the quest of the rose, and the poem ends with a description of the plucking of the rose in terms of obscene innuendo. So each part of the double ending, the religious and the realistic/'bourgeois', is at a considerable remove from the essentials of courtly love-suits.

Nevertheless, it is important to note the ending of the *Roman de la Rose* in a survey of courtly love writings in French for two reasons. First, it is where the development of the courtly tradition in the thirteenth century led to, not only in French but also in the German *dorfspoesie* and some Goliardic Latin poetry. Secondly, the tension between the 'school of Eblo',[52] the sensual poets who covered their pursuit of sexual conquest in refined terms, and the idealist love-poets, both secular and religious, was present at the heart of courtly love from the first. In expounding the implications of courtly writings, Jean de Meun inevitably exposed this ambivalence. Most importantly, because it was the most widely copied work of the Middle Ages, amongst writers as diverse as Dante, Chaucer, Langland and the late romance-writers, an understanding of the directions in which de Lorris and de Meun developed courtly theory and practice is essential for the reading of late medieval poetry.

NOTES

1   G. Paris, *Medieval French Literature* (London 1903), pp. 94ff. A. Jeanroy, in L. Petit de Julleville, *Histoire de la Langue et de la Littérature Française* (Paris 1900), pp. 366f, does point out that the earlier poets were purely derivative.

2   "Études sur les romans de la Table Ronde. Lancelot du Lac. II – La Conte de la Charrette" (*Romania* XII, 1883, pp. 459–534).

3   *Medieval French Literature*, p. 94.

4   G. Paris, in L. Petit de Julleville, *op. cit.* (note 1 above), vol. I, page m. C. Muscatine, *Chaucer and the French Tradition* (California University Press, Berkeley and Los Angeles 1957), pp. 58ff.

5   A. R. Press, *Anthology of Troubadour Lyric Poetry* (Edinburgh 1971), p. 74.

6   W. T. Pattison, *The Life and Works of the Troubadour Raimbaut d'Orange* (University of Minnesota Press, London 1952), p. 164. Note on lines 43–7 of "Non chant per auzel": 'Bernart de Ventadorn also calls him "Tristan l'amadors".')

7   *The Allegory of Love*, p. 127.

8   *Ibid.*, p. 29.

9   T. P. Cross and W. A. Nitze, *Lancelot and Guinevere* (University of Chicago 1930), p. 69.

10   English translation by W. W. Comfort, Everyman 1914. The excerpts here are taken from that translation, with kind permission.

11   This preoccupied abstraction of the lover is dwelt on in section 2 of *The Dove's Neck-Ring* (Nykl p. 15 and p. 19), amongst other places. See XXXV here.

12   For the common medical metaphor, cf. (for example) Blondel "Bien doit chanter" (LX here), *passim*; Gâce Brulé "Bien ait l'amor" (LXI here), lines 33–5; and *Le Roman de la Rose*, 1910–11.

13   Cf. *The Dove's Neck-Ring*, section 14 (Nykl p. 60) for this submissiveness, as well as the commandments of the god of love in Andreas (number 7, in Book I, dialogue 5. See XVII here).

14   Line 4,716, "He turns straight towards the window", is missed out by Comfort.

15   The subjugation of love by reason at the end may, of course, be a retraction, as at the end of *The Dove's Neck-Ring*, Andreas, Jean de Meun, *Decameron* and *The Canterbury Tales*. The tradition goes back to St Augustine's *Retractationum* (c. 426–7).

16   The six trouvère poems which follow use the texts published in Istvan Frank, *Trouvères et Minnesänger* (Universität des Saarlandes, Saarbrücken 1952), with the generous permission of the publishers. This book is quite invaluable for the full sense it gives of the close parallels in theme and terminology between the poets in Provençal,

northern French and German around the year 1200. Chrétien's few courtly lyrics are thought to date from the 1170s.

17   Chrétien's lost romance of Tristan also probably dates from the 1170s. For other references to Tristan in courtly poems, cf. Raimbaut d'Orange (died 1173) "Non chant per auzel" (XLVI here), 29–32, and the end of two poems of Bernart de Ventadorn, "Can vei la lauzeta mover" (XLV here), and "Lo rossinhols s'esbaudeya" (Press, p. 74).

18   Blondel wrote in Picardy in the late twelfth century. He is best known for the popular story concerning Richard I who is said to have been imprisoned in Germany on his return from the Holy Land in 1192. Blondel searched for the king and, as he rode beneath his prison wall, he sang a song which had been composed by him and Richard together. The king joined in from his cell and finished the song.

19   This song is full of the troubadours' technical vocabulary of love: "fine Amors", "joie", "faintise", "doc regart", "beaus ieus", "pities".

20   I. Frank, *op. cit.* p. 149, says that "faintise" is "faus semblant" (as in the *Roman de la Rose, passim*).

21   The assertion that Love ought not in justice to fail his own followers is a repeated one in the trouvères (cf. Chrétien's "D'Amors" (LIX here), 10ff).

22   Lines 43–5 are difficult; the sense is "the look from her eyes wounded me like a lance. The wound would have been suffered in a good cause if it had led to reciprocated love: but if it leads only to betrayal, it is unfortunate that my eyes met hers at all".

23   Gâce Brulé is often regarded, as by I. Frank, as the greatest of the *trouvères*. He was a knight of Champagne and one of the first northern imitators of the troubadours.

24   Although the terminology is that of the troubadours, here (as in the last stanza of the song of Blondel, LX above, or in the phrase "within Love's body" in line 26 here) the lover's situation is externalised into an allegorical framework like that of Guillaume de Lorris: Devotion and Love are active intercedents with the lady, for instance.

25   The opening line of this poem is attributed by Dante to "the King of Navarre" (Thibaut IV, 1201–53) in *De Vulgari Eloquentia* II, 6. The fact that Dante, who does not often cite the *trouvères*, knew it is evidence of its celebration. The opening lines, saying that Love makes the poet sing without giving him a theme ("ochoixon"), is an interesting rhetorical parallel to Chrétien's receiving of both *san* and *matiere* from Marie de Champagne (*Lancelot*, 26).

26   Literally, "of which I have over a hundred pairs": a commercial metaphor, as Frank says (p. 190).

27   The *malebouches* and the *lausengiers* of the troubadours.

28   Line 34: "taigne", meaning "hold", is awkward; the poet has just said that it is difficult to escape Love, so the fear that Love will *not* hold him

long follows rather violently. "Support" is not a normal sense of "tenir".

29 Either Thibaut V (1152–91) or Louis of Blois (1191–1205). I. Frank (footnote 4, page 190) reaches no definite conclusion.

30 Conon de Béthune came from Artois; hence his dialect (in LXIV, "Moult me semont"). He was noble, an ancestor of Sully. He took part in the late twelfth-century Crusades, and most of his ten songs (like "Ahi, Amors" here) are about them. He was regent of Empire in 1219 in the course of a prominent life in public affairs. His family was related through marriage to Philippe Auguste.

31 This poem is a *congé* to the poet's beloved on the occasion of his departure amongst the forces of Philippe Auguste and Richard I on the Third Crusade in January 1188. I. Frank (pp. 28–31) prints the poem parallel to a related one by Friedrich von Hausen, regarding the Conon poem as the earlier, probably written in 1188–9 (Frank, p. 144).

32 This idea of a Crusade at home, made by the virtuous who were unable to travel to the Holy Land, is an interesting one, in the light of the internal pilgrimage in *Piers Plowman*, for instance.

33 The victimisation of Conon because of his provincial language is probably a literary fiction.

34 Notably, A. M. F. Gunn, *The Mirror of Love* (Lubbock, Texas 1952) and J. V. Fleming, *The Roman de la Rose: a Study in Allegory and Iconography* (Princeton University Press 1969).

35 "Can vei la lauzeta mover" (XLV here), line 24. As in Bernart's stanza, Narcissus is an obvious figure for the lover who is concerned more with self-perfecting by love than with a description of the lady who inspires it. See note 24 to the Provençal section here.

36 The medical metaphor of the *trouvères* is very prominent in Guillaume de Lorris.

37 For the question of high birth as a qualification for loving (often denied in other poets), see M. Valency, *In Praise of Love* (London 1958), chapter 2, "The Knights", and Andreas (Parry, p. 35): "Character alone . . . is worthy of the crown of love".

38 Other lists of the commandments of Love are in Andreas I (Fifth Dialogue, XVII here) and II, chapter 8 (XXI here), and in Jean de Meun's section, lines 13,011ff (LXVI). Their variety is because they are based on the light-hearted advice of Ovid, as well as, more remotely, on the more solemn, philosophical definitions of the school of anatomists of love from the Arabs to the stilnovisti.

39 The curious, superficial side of the morality of the god of love is attributable to Ovid; see *Ars Amatoria* I, 513–21.

40 Note the nobler side of the god of love's injunctions. This demand that love should be whole-hearted, not partial, is clearly related to a

Christian tradition, founded perhaps on Revelation III, 15–6.

41 First Dialogue (Parry, p. 36).

42 *Ars Amatoria* I, 351ff (VI here). *Yvain*, 970ff.

43 *De Planctu Naturae*, verse v (*Patrologia Latina*, 210). An English version of the passage in Gower can be found in R. P. Miller, *Chaucer. Sources and Backgrounds* (Oxford University Press, New York 1977), p. 195.

44 *Le Roman de la Rose*, 19,527ff.

45 Reason now turns to Andreas's definition; see Parry, p. 28, Book I, chapter 1 (XIV here).

46 The obligation of furthering the species is a major part of Reason's argument and is the theme that Jean de Meun introduces to change the poem's priorities. See A. M. F. Gunn, *op. cit.*, Book IV, "The Fount of Generation" (pp. 203ff). The argument is drawn on extensively by the Wife of Bath.

47 Cicero, *De Senectute* XXI–XXIII.

48 *Troubadours and Love*, p. 120.

49 For the manipulation of tears, cf. Ovid, *Ars Amatoria* I, 659–62.

50 *Ars Amatoria* II, 387ff.

51 There is another total retraction here. Cf. note 15 above.

52 Cf. Bernart de Ventadorn, "Lo tems vai", 22–3ff for Eblo of Ventadour whose poems do not survive.

The Minnesänger

The *Minnelied* has a great deal in common with the poetry of the Provençal troubadours. The two genres are similar enough for Heinrich von Morungen to translate a troubadour poem more or less word for word into the corpus of *Minnelieder*.[1] German courtly poetry is said to have derived from the compositions of the Provençal poets and the Northern French *trouvères*: Gottfried von Strassburg suggests this derivativeness when, in the famous literary excursus in *Tristan*, 7, he credits Heinrich von Veldeke with 'having grafted the first slip on the tree of German poetry'.[2] Its greatest period, the *Blütezeit* of about 1180–1220, coincides with the later part of the troubadours' period of richest achievement. Istvan Frank's parallel presentation of troubadours, *trouvères* and *Minnesänger* (*Trouvères et Minnesänger*, Saarbrücken 1952) shows that there is considerable influence on the *Minnesang* from many Provençal poets of the mid twelfth century: Bernart de Ventadorn, Bertran de Born, Folquet de Marseilles, Peire Vidal and others. The *oeuvres* of both schools are similar, consisting of a central body of love poetry and some poetry of contemporary comment (the German *Sprüche* corresponding to the Provençal *sirventes*). The Crusades are a recurrent theme and setting, and the *congé* of leavetaking associated with them gains new emphasis in such poems as Friedrich von Hausen's 'Gelebte ich noch'. As in the Provençal lyric, and to an even greater degree, the love poems are founded in a highly conventional, almost unvarying situation in which the poet (here nearly always a knight in the convention) sings his love to an adored, exalted lady whose relationship to him is again that of feudal lord to votive follower. The form of the *Minnelied* is of great importance, and it increases in technical virtuosity of metre, rhyme and music throughout the period of the *Blütezeit*, culminating in the brilliant, over-conventional verses of Gottfried von Neifen. This virtuosity and musical richness (much of the evidence for which, again, has disappeared) is usually ascribed to troubadour influence. A further important similarity is the development in the poetry of fixed forms and vocabulary, many of them inherited from the troubadours: *dienst* (love-service); *lon* (the lady's reward); *hulde* (her mercy); the *merkaere* (censurer) and *lugenaere* (liar), both influenced by the Provençal *lauzengier* or Old French *losengeor*, according to Olive Sayce (*Poets of the Minnesang*, p. xiii); the *Hohe Minne* and *Niedere Minne* distinction; *Hoher Mut* perhaps corresponding to troubadour joi (see Dronke, *Medieval Latin and the Rise of the European Love Lyric*, p. 36); *rede* for *razo*; the important *tagelied* parallel to the *alba/aube*; the *wechsel* which has affinities with the Provençal *tenso* or *partimen*. The lady is remote and the votive becomes, or threatens to become, senseless or sleepless. Clearly there is enough in common here to warrant the postulating of a movement of courtly-love poetry throughout much of France and Germany in the chivalric age of the twelfth century.

Yet there are important differences between the German and Provençal schools, which can be overlooked in a survey which looks only for evidence of courtly love. Indeed the poems anthologised here, grouped around courtly love, tend to over-emphasise the similarities. The most important and most general difference is that, while in many of the most celebrated troubadour poems, concerned with such distinctions as that between the *trobar leu* and the *trobar clus*, there is a feeling that the theme of love is only a vehicle for the display of formal or intellectual brilliance in the writing, the poems of the *Minnesänger*, influenced also by the earlier, popular German tradition of the *trûtlied*, are rarely intellectual to the point of obscurity. We do not find, therefore, the explanatory Provençal *razo* which corresponds to the *ragione* in the cryptic poetry of the stilnovisti. The love-situation in the German poems is generally more naturalistic. So Heinrich von Morungen's *tagelied*, perhaps the greatest *Minnelied*, is descended from the alba of poets such as Guiraut de Borneil (e.g. L here), but is characterised by an emotional directness which is entirely foreign to the troubadour song. Another, more particular, difference is that many of the German poems are spoken by the woman, as is the case in many of the traditional popular German poems and in the Latin poetry of the Middle Ages. (Some similarities between such Latin poems as the eleventh-century 'Love-verses from Regensburg' and the later courtly-love poetry have been incontestably demonstrated by Dronke (pp. 221ff and 422ff), and these similarities are most strikingly with the German poetry.) Again, side by side with the terms and forms which the *Minnelied* shares with Provençal, there are many which it lacks: the *pastorela* is not found (the rough pastorals of the later *höfische dorfspoesie* of Neidhart von Reuental and his school are very different),[3] and there are no obvious correlatives to the well-worked notions of *mesura, conoissensa* and *devinalh*, nor to the distinctions between the various kinds of *trobar* or that between *sen* and *foudatz*. Although love of God vies (with inevitable success) with love of woman in poets such as Friedrich von Hausen, there is no suggestion of the transmutation of one love into the other hinted at by such troubadours as Arnaut Daniel and Montanhagol and brought to fullness in the Stilnovisti. The circumstances and, to a lesser extent, the writings of these German *ministeriales* have more in common, in some ways, with the Latin goliards than with the more patrician of the Provençal and Italian poets, with their intense and intellectualising compositions. The crusading songs and *sprüche* of the *Minnesänger* form a more significant proportion of their poetry than the rather remote and elegiac *sirventes* of the troubadours. Indeed the courtly flowering of the *Minne* lyric was a brief one, at the turn of the thirteenth century, and in the poetry of Neidhart, who derided the courtly manner in his *dorfspoesie*, the energetic German medieval lyric reverted to type. Even amongst the great *Minnesänger* of the *Blütezeit*, the principal part of the work of Hartmann von Aue, Wolfram von Eschenbach and Gottfried von Strassburg was in epic-romance, not in the short lyric poem that the title *Minnesänger* evokes, and Walther von der Vogelweide is often said to have outgrown 'the charmed circle of the Amour Cortois'. Only Meinloh von Sevelingen, Reinmar von Hagenau, Heinrich von Morungen and Gottfried von Neifen can be said to have composed their principal works in the courtly love lyric. And, though works such as *Tristan* are obviously of the first importance in the ideas of courtly love, the themes and conventions principally associated with it are to be sought in the shorter poems.

But this short-lived and circumscribed flowering of German lyric verse, perhaps because it drew for its energy upon several poetic traditions and kinds, includes some of the greatest short love poems of the Middle Ages. The earlier poetry of Der Kürenberc and Dietmar von Aist is the beginning of the introduction into the traditional German song of courtly elements. There is little point in trying to define too narrowly what exactly courtly elements are, but there can be no doubt that some poems of Dietmar already display some of the hallmarks of courtly love poetry. For instance the distant and unfulfilled love of the speaker (although in this case it is the lady) in Dietmar's poem included here, and the image of the falcon, are evocative of Provençal poetry. Meinloh's poem is unmistakably of the courtly love tradition. The great courtly poets are Reinmar and Heinrich von Morungen, and to the former is attributed a school of German courtly poetry which came into conflict (rather unsuccessfully in the following century) with the homely, anti-courtly erotic poetry of Neidhart and his followers. Already in Hartmann von Aue there is a lack of inspiration, combined with an excess of subtlety, which point the way to the contrived artificiality and weakness of the *meistergesang*.[5] But the greatest of these poems – Heinrich's 'Tagelied' (LXXIII here) and Wolfram's 'Sine klawen' (LXXXII) with its extraordinary opening – are in no way diminished by their conventionality. Perhaps the vigour of the best of this poetry comes not only from its roots in three literary traditions – French, German and Latin – but also from its association with the dramatic power and narrative strength of the epic-romances such as *Parsifal* and *Tristan*.[6] The repeated Tristan references in Raimbaut d'Orange and other troubadours indicate that the Arthurian epic-romances were an important inspiration for the shorter courtly love poetry, and the *Minnelieder* were very close to that centre in Hartmann, Gottfried and Wolfram, and in the Austrian *Nibelungenlied* (c. 1205).

Unless the contrary is stated, the German texts of the poems here are taken from *Poets of the Minnesang*, edited by Olive Sayce (Oxford University Press 1967), with the generous permission of the author and the publishers. Nouns were not initially capitalised in Medieval German, so here only those nouns are capitalised which occur commonly in the modern language (*Minnesänger* itself, for instance). Even words of that kind are left with lower-case initials when their context seems to tie them particularly to their medieval occurrence.

DIETMAR VON AIST
(*fl.* 1140–1170?)[7]

LXVII

Ez stuont ein frouwe alleine
und warte uber heide
und warte ir liebes,
so gesach sie valken fliegen.
"Sō wol dir, valke, daz du bist! 5
Du fliugest swar dir liep ist:
du erklusest dir in dem walde
einen boum der dir gevalle.
Alsō hān ouch ich getān:
ich erkōs mir selbe einen man, 10
den erwelton mīniu ougen.
Daz nident schoene vrouwen.
Owe wan lānt si mir mīn liep?
Joh engerte ich ir dekeiner trūtes niet."

LXVIII

"SLĀFEST du, friedel ziere?
Man wecket uns leider schiere:
ein vogellīn sō wol getān."
daz ist der linden an daz zwī gegān."

"Ich was vil sanfte entslāfen: 5
nu rüfestu king Wāfen.
Liep āne leit mac niht gesīn.
Swaz du gebiutest, daz leiste ich friundin mīn."

Diu frouwe begunde weinen.
"Du rītest und lāst mich eine. 10
Wenne wilt du wider her zuo mir?
Owē du füerest mīn fröide sament dir!"

LXVII

A lady[8] stood alone and looked across the heath, looking out for her beloved, when she saw some falcons flying. 'How free, falcon, are you! You fly wherever you want: you choose in the wood any tree you like. I too have done likewise: I chose a man myself; my eyes selected him. Fair ladies are envious of that. Ah, why will they not leave my lover to me? For I never hankered after the lover of any of them.'

LXVIII

'Are you asleep,[9] my handsome dear one? Sadly, we will soon be woken. A little bird will do that, which has alighted on the branch of the linden tree.'

'I was sleeping very softly; now you, beloved, call the alarm. Love without grief cannot be. Whatever you bid, my dear friend, I will do.'

The lady began to weep. 'You will ride off and leave me alone. When will you come again here to me? Alas, you bear my happiness along with you.'

MEINLOH VON SEVELINGEN
(late twelfth century)[10]

LXIX

Dō ich dich loben hōrte,   dō het ich dich gerne erkant.
durch dīne tugende manige   fuor ich ie welende, unz ich dich
vant.
daz ich dich nu gesehen hān,   daz enwirret dir niet.
er ist vil wol getiuret,   den du wilt, vrowe, haben liep.
du bist der besten eine,   des muoz man dir von schulden
jehen. 5

sō wol den dīnen ougen!
die kunnen swen si wellen   an vil güetelīchen sehen.

HEINRICH VON VELDEKE
(*fl.* 1170–90)[11]

LXX

Tristrant mūste āne sīnen danc
stāde sīn der koninginnen,
want poisūn heme dār tū dwanc
mēre dan dī cracht der minnen.
des sal mich dī gūde danc   5
weten dat ich nīne gedranc
sulic pīment ende ich sī minne
bat dan hē, ende mach dat sīn.
wale gedāne, valsches āne,
lāt mich wesen dīn   10
ende wis dū mīn.

LXIX

When I heard you praised, I longed to get to know you. Because of your many excellences, I searched for you continually and I found you. The fact that I have seen you does not reduce your charm in the least. The man that you, lady, choose to hold dear is very greatly enhanced. You are imcomparable even among the best: that must be said of you by right. Blessed be your eyes! They can look most graciously wherever they wish.

LXX

Tristan, without intending it, had to be constant to the queen, because a potion compelled him to it more than the power of love. So my lady should feel grateful to me that I never drank any such wine and I love her better than he, if that can be. Beautiful lady without deceit, let me be yours, and you be mine.

FRIEDRICH VON HAUSEN
(died 1190)[12]

LXXI

In mīnem troume ich sach
ein harte schoene wīp
die naht unz an den tac;
do erwachet ich ē zīt.
dō wart si mir benomen,   5
daz ichn weiz wā si sī,
von der mir fröide kom.
daz tuont mir dougen mīn:
der wolte ich āne sīn.

LXXII

Gelebte ich noch die lieben zīt
    daz ich daz lant solt aber schouwen,
dar inne al mīn fröude līt
    nu lange an einer schoenen frouwen,
sō gesaehe mīnen līp   5
    niemer weder man noch wīp
    getrūren noch gewinnen rouwen.
mich dūhte nu vil manigez guot,
    dā von ē swaere was mīn muot.

Ich wānde ir ē vil verre sīn   10
    dāa ich nu vil nāhe wāre.
alrērste hāt das herze mīn
    von der frömde grōze swāre.
ez tuot wol sīne triuwe schīn.
    waere ich iender umb den Rīn,   15
    sō friesche ich līhte ein ander māre,
des ich doch leider nie vernam
    sīt daz ich über die berge quam.

LXXI

In my dream I saw a very beautiful woman, all night until the daytime. When I awoke she left. When she was taken from me, I did not know where she was gone, she from whom my joy came. My eyes did this to me: I would rather be without them.

LXXII

If I should live[13] until that blessed day when I could once more see that land in which all my joy has lain for a long time now with a lovely lady, then no one, man or woman, would see sorrow or grief triumphant in me. Very many things would then seem good to me, things because of which my mind has ever been grieving.

I thought she was very far away before, in a place where now I would be very near. For the first time my heart has great distress because of absence. Its loyalty is fully shown in this. If I were somewhere around the Rhine, I might perhaps then hear another story which I have never heard, alas!' since I came across the mountains.[14]

HEINRICH VON MORUNGEN
(died 1222)[15]

LXXIII

Owē, sol aber mir iemer mē
geliuhten dur die naht
noch wīzer danne ein snē
ir līp vil wol geslaht?
der trouc diu ougen mīn.   5
ich wānde, ez solde sīn
des liehten mānen schīn.
    dō tagete ez.

'Owē, sol aber er iemer mē
den morgen hie betagen,   10
als uns diu naht engē,
daz wir niht dürfen klagen?
"owē, nu ist ez tac,"
als er mit klage pflac,
do er jungest bī mir lac.   15
    dō tagete ez.

Owē, sī kuste āne zal
in deme slāfe mich:
dō vielen hin ze tal
ir trehene nider sich.   20
iedoch getrōste ich sie,
daz si ir weinen lie
und mich al umbevie.
    dō tagete ez.

'Owē, daz er sō dicke sich   25
bī mir ersehen hāt!
als er endahte mich,
sō wolte er sunder wāt
mīn arme schouwen blōz.
ez was ein wunder grōz   30
daz in des nie verdrōz.
    dō tagete ez.'

LXXIII

Alas,[16] will her very shapely body, whiter even than the snow, never more again shine through the night for me? It tricked my eyes: I thought it must be the shining of the bright moon. Then it dawned.

Alas, will he ever again be here as the morning dawns, so that, when the night leaves us, we need no longer grieve, 'alas now it is day', as he was wont to do with misery when he lay by me most recently. Then it dawned.

Alas, she kissed me in her sleep times without number. Then her tears fell down to the depths; yet I comforted her so that she left her crying and embraced me without reserve. Then it dawned.

Alas, that he has looked upon me so often! When he uncovered me, he wanted to see my poor self naked without clothes. It was a great wonder that he never wearied of it. Then it dawned.

LXXIV

Ez tuot vil wē,   swer herzeclīche minnet
an sō hōher stat   dā sīn dienest gar versmāht.
sīn tumber wān   vil lützel dran gewinnet,
swer sō vil geklaget   dā'z ze herzen niht engāt.
er ist vil wīs   swer sich sō wol versinnet   5
daz er dienet dā   dā man dienest wol enpfāt
und sich dar lāt   dā man sīn genāde hāt.

Ich bedarf vil wol   daz ich genāde vinde,
wan ich habe ein wīp   ob der sunnen mir erkorn.
daz ist ein nōt   die ich niemer überwinde,   10
[sine] gesehe mich ane   als si tete hie bevorn.
si ist mir liep   gewest dā her von kinde,
wan ich wart durch si   und durch anders niht geborn:
ist ir daz zorn,   weiz got, sō bin ich verlorn.

Wā ist nu hin   mīn liehter morgensterne?   15
wē waz hilfet mich   daz mīn sunne ist ūf gegān?
si ist mir ze hōch   und ouch ein teil ze verne
gegen mittem tage   unde wil dā lange stān.
ich gelebte noch   den lieben ābent gerne,
daz si sich her nider   mir ze trōste wolte lān,   20
wand ich mich hān   gar verkapfet ūf ir wān.

LXXV

Von den elben wirt entsēn vil manic man:
sō bin ich von grōzer liebe entsēn
von der besten die ie man ze vriunt gewan.
wil si aber mich dar umbe vēn,
und ze unstaten stēn,   mac si danne rechen sich   5
und tuo des ich si bite: sō vreut si sō sēre mich,
daz mīn līp vor wunnen muoz zergēn.

LXXIV

Great is his misery, whoever puts heartfelt love[17] in such a high place that his service is entirely unpleasing. His foolish hope wins very little thereby, he who makes so many complaints where it makes no impression on the heart. He is very wise who knows himself so well that he serves where service is well received and entrusts himself where mercy is to be had.

I have very great need that I should find mercy, since I have chosen for myself a lady beyond the sun. It is a pain which I will never overcome if she does not look upon me again as she did formerly. She has been my love from childhood on, since for her sake and no-one else's was I born. If that angers her, God knows, I am lost.

Where has my bright morning-star gone now? Alas, what does it help me that my sun has risen up? She is too high for me, and a little too far at her zenith; and there she is determined to remain for a long time. Still, I would gladly greet the dear evening, when she might be willing to let herself down here to console me, for I have utterly stared my eyes out waiting for her.

LXXV

Very many a man is bewitched by the elf;[18] in the same way I am enchanted with great love by the best lady that ever a man won as his lover. But if for that reason she wants to attack me and become hostile, then she can revenge herself by doing what I ask. So exceedingly she would then fill me with happiness that my being would dissolve in joy.

Si gebiutet und ist in dem herzen mīn
frowe und hērer danne ich selbe sī.
hei wan müeste ich ir alsō gewaltic sīn   10
daz si mir mit triuwen wēre bī
ganzer tage drī   und eteslīche naht!
sō verlür ich niht den līp und al die maht.
jā ist si leider vor mir al ze vrī.

Mich enzündet ir vil liehter ougen schīn   15
same daz viur den dürren zunder tuot,
und ir fremeden krenket mir daz herze mīn
same daz wazzer die vil heize gluot;
und ir hōher muot,   ir schōne, ir werdecheit,
und daz wunder daz man von ir tugenden seit,   20
daz wirt mir vil übel oder līhte guot.

Swenne ir liehten ougen sō verkērent sich
daz si mir al dur mīn herze sēn,
swer dā entzwischen danne gēt und irret mich,
dem müeze al sīn wunne gar zergēn.   25
ich muoz vor ir stēn   und warten der frouwen mīn
reht alsō des tages diu kleinen vogellīn:
wenne sol mir iemer liep geschēn?

LXXVI

Mir ist geschehen als einem kindelīne,
daz sīn schoenez bilde in einem glase gesach
unde greif dar nāch sīn selbes schīne
sō vil biz daz ez den spiegel gar zerbrach.
dō wart al sīn wunne ein leitlich ungemach.   5
alsō dāhte ich iemēr frō ze sīne,
dō ich gesach die lieben frouwen mīne,
von der mir bī liebe leides vil geschach.

Minne, diu der werlde ir frōide mēret,
seht, diu brāhte in troumes wīs die frouqen mīn   10

She is in command and more the ruling lady and lord in my heart than I am myself. Oh, if only she could be so much in my control that for three whole days and a few nights she might be by me unfailingly! Then I would not lose my life and all my strength. Unhappily she is indeed all too free of me.

The brightness of her eyes has kindled me to a great radiance just as fire does to the dry tinder, and her aloofness ruins my heart as the water does to the fire blazing up. And her noble heart, her beauty and her worth and the miracle that is seen in her excellence: these will do me much evil or little good.

When her bright eyes turn so that she can see my heart, right through me, whoever then comes between and obstructs me, may all his joy utterly perish![19] I must stand at her command and wait for my lady, just as the small birds await the day. When will love ever befall me?

LXXVI

I have had the same experience[20] as a little child who sees his handsome reflexion in a mirror and grabs at his own image in it, with the result that it shatters the mirror entirely. Then all his delight is turned to grievous distress. So too I always thought I would be joyful, when I saw my lovely lady, through whom, as well as love, much sorrow has befallen me.

Behold love, which increases the world's joy and which brought my lady in the form of a dream when my body was

dā mīn līp an slāfen was gekēret
und ersach sich an der besten wunne sīn.
dō sach ich ir werden tugende, ir liehten schīn,
schōne und für alle wīp gehēret;
niwan daz ein lützel was versēret   15
ir vil fröiden rīchez [rōtez] mündelīn.

Grōze angest hān ich des gewunnen,
daz verblīchen süle ir mündelīn sō rōt.
des hān ich nu niuwer klage begunnen,
sīt mīn herze sich ze solcher swēre bōt,   20
daz ich durch mīn ouge schouwe solche nōt,
sam ein kint daz wīsheit unversunnen
sīnen schaten ersach in einem brunnen
und den minnen muose unz an sīnen tōt.

Hōher wīp von tugenden und von sinne,   25
die enkan der himel niender ummevān,
sō die guoten die ich vor ungewinne
vremden muoz und immer doch an ir bestān.
ōwē leider, jō wānde ichs ein ende hān,
ir vil winneclīchen werden minne: 30
nu bin ich vil kūme an dem beginne:
des ist hin mīn wunne und ouch mīn gerender wān.

REINMAR VON HAGENAU
(died, probably young, before 1210)[22]

LXXVII

Ich hān ir vil manic jār
gelebt, und si mir selden einen tac.
da von gewinne ich noch daz hār
daz man in wīzer varwe sehen mac.
ir gewaltes wirde ich grā.   5
si möhte sichs gelouben unde zurnde anderswa.

given up to sleep, lost in gazing upon its greatest delight. Then I saw her noble perfections, her bright radiance, beautiful and exalted above all other ladies, except that her very delightful, noble, red small mouth was slightly impaired.

I have taken great anguish from the fact that her small mouth, so red, should thus grow pale. Because of that I have now begun a new lament, since my heart was committed to such grief that I saw with my eyes such a distressful thing, just like a child, innocent of wisdom, who saw his reflection in a fountain and had to love it until his death.[21]

Heaven can nowhere encompass ladies higher in perfections and mind than the lady whom I, in my misfortune, must always keep apart from and yet must always cling to. Alas, sadly I thought that I had attained the goal of her very joyful, noble love; now I am come right back to the beginning. So my joy is vanished and my yearning hope as well.

LXXVII

I have lived for her for very many years,[23] and she never a single day for me. As a result of this I am getting this hair which can be seen to be of a white colour. I am becoming grey under her power. Surely she could stop this and vent her anger somewhere else?

Waenet si daz ich den muot
von ir gescheide umb alse līhten zorn?
obe si mir ein leit getuot,
sō bin ich doch ūf anders niht geborn   10
wan daz ich des trōstes lebe
wie ich ir gediene und si mir swaere ein ende gebe.

LXXVIII

"Sage, daz ich dirs iemer lōne,
hāst du den vil lieben man gesehen?
ist ez wār und lebet er schōne
als si sagent und ich dich hoere jehen?"
"Vrowe, ich sach in. Er ist frō;   5
sīn herze stāt, ob irz gebietent, iemer hō."

"Ich verbiute im vröude niemer.
lāze eht eine rede; sō tuot er wol:
des bit ich in hiute und iemer:
demst alsō daz manz versagen sol."   10
"Frowe, nu verredent iuch niht.
er sprichet, allez daz geschehen sol daz geschiht."

"Hāt aber er gelobt, geselle,
daz er niemer mē gesinge liet,
ezn sī ob ich ins biten welle?"   15
"Vrowe, ez was sīn muot do ich von im schiet.
ouch mugent irz wol hān vernomen."
"Owē, gebiute ichz nu, daz mac ze schaden komen.

"Ist ab daz ichs niene gebiute,
sō verliuse ich mīne saelde an ime   20
und verfluochent mich die liute,
daz ich al der werlte ir vröude nime.
alrest gāt mir sorge zuo.
owē, nunweiz ich obe ichz lāze od ob ichz tuo.

Does she think that I can give her up, then, just because of a little temper? Even if she causes me suffering, I am nevertheless born for nothing but to live with the hope of serving her and of her bringing an end to my distress.

LXXVIII

'Say, and I will reward you for ever, whether you have seen that most beloved man? Is it true that he lives as happily as they say and as I have heard you claim?' *'Lady, I saw him. He is joyful. His spirits are always high, if you command that.'*

'I will never begrudge him joy. But let him just give up one kind of song; that would be a good thing for him to do. I ask that of him today and always. Such it is that it should be stopped.' *'Lady, do not now speak so wrongly. He speaks, saying everything that he ought to say.'*

'But has he declared, comrade, that he will never sing me a song, except if I wish to ask him for it?' *'Lady, that was his intention when I left him. You too must certainly have heard that.'* 'Alas, if I now make a command, it may lead to offence.

'But if thus I ask for nothing at all, I will lose by that the bliss I get from him, and the people will curse me utterly, saying that I take joy away from the whole world. This above all causes me sorrow. Alas, I do not know whether to leave it or do it!

"Daz wir wīp niht mugen gewinnen   25
friunt mit rede, si enwellen dannoch mē,
daz müet mich. in wil niht minnen.
staeten wīben tuot unstaete wē.
waere ich, des ich niene bin,
unstaete, lieze er danne mich, sō lieze ich in."   30

       LXXIX
Ich wil allez gāhen
zuo der liebe die ich hān.
So ist ez niender nāhen
daz sich ende noch mīn wān.
Doch versuoche ichz alle tage   5
und diene ir sō dazs āne ir danc
     mit fröiden muoz erwenden kumber den ich trage.

Mich betwanc ein maere
daz ich von ir hōrte sagen,
wies ein vrouwe waere   10
diu sich schōne kunde tragen.
Daz versuochte ich unde ist wār.
Ir kunde nie kein wīp geschaden
     (daz ist wol kleine) alsō grōz als umbe ein hār.

Swaz in allen landen   15
mir ze liebe mac geschehen,
daz stāt in ir handen:
anders niemen wil ichs jehen.
Si ist mīn ōsterlīcher tac,
und hāns in mīnem herzen liep: 20
     daz weiz er wol dem nieman niht geliegen mac.

'It annoys me that we women cannot win a friend by conversation without them wanting more. I will not love him. Inconstancy is painful to constant women; but if I were inconstant (which I certainly am not) and he then left me, I would likewise leave him.'

LXXIX

I will hurry resolutely[24] to the love I have; yet my hope of speaking to her is by no means near. Still every day I try and serve her, so that in spite of herself she must change the misery I endure into joy.

A report that I heard made of her took my notice: that she was a woman who behaved as befits a lady. I tried this out, and it is true. No woman could ever vilify her nature as much as by a hair (and that is very little).

Whatever in the way of happiness may befall me anywhere stands in her hands; of nobody else will I say this. She is my Easter day, and deep in my heart I love her. He to whom no one can lie at all knows this well.

LXXX *From* **'Waz ich nu niuwer maere sage'**
(Sayce, pp. 80–1, lines 19–27)

Sō wol dir, wīp, wie reine ein nam!
wie sanfte er doch z'erkennen und ze nennen ist!
ez wart nie niht sō lobesam,
swā duz an rehte güete kērest, sō du bist.
dīn lop mit rede nieman volenden kan.   5
swes du mit triuwen phligest, wol im, der ist ein saelic man
und mac vil gerne leben.
du gīst al der welte hōhen muot:
wanne maht och mir ein wenic fröide geben?

LXXXI *From* **'Der lange sueze kumber min'**
(Sayce, pp. 81–3, lines 37–45)

Ein rede der liute tuot mir wē:
dā enkan ich niht gedulteclīchen zuo gebāren.
nu tuont siz alle deste mē:
si frāgent mich ze vil von mīner frowen jāren,
und sprechent, welher tage si sī,   5
dur daz ich ir sō lange bin   gewesen mit triuwen bī.
si sprechent daz ez möhte mich verdriezen.
nu lā daz aller beste wīp
ir zühteloser vrāge mich geniezen.

LXXX

Blessed be you, lady![25] How excellent a name! How pleasing it is both to hear and to say! There was never anything so praiseworthy as you are, if you set yourself to strict virtue. Nobody can accomplish your praise with words. Whoever you truly care for, he is certainly a happy man and can live most joyfully. You give to the whole world an elevated spirit. When can a little joy be given to me too?

LXXXI

One thing the people say pains me;[26] then I cannot comport myself with patience. Now they do it all the more: they ask me how old my lady is and they say this, asking how many days it is now that I have been in her ambit faithfully for so long. They say it in order to annoy me. Now may the best of all ladies let me gain benefit from their discourteous inquiry.

WOLFRAM VON ESCHENBACH[27]
(*c.* 1170–1220)

LXXXII

'Sīne klāwen   durh die wolken sint geslagen,
er stīget ūf mit grōzer kraft,
ich sih in grāwen   tägelīch als er wil tagen,
den tac, der im geselleschaft
erwenden wil, dem werden man,   5
den ich mit sorgen īn bi naht verliez.
ich bringe in hinnen, ob ich kan.
sīn vil manigiu tugent mich daz leisten hiez.'

'Wahtaer, du singest   daz mir manige frōide nimt
unde mēret mīne klage.   10
maere du bringest,   der mich leider niht gezimt,
immer morgens gegen dem tage.
diu solt du mir verswīgen gar.
daz gebiut ich den triuwen dīn:
des lōn ich dir als ich getar.   15
sō belībet hie der geselle mīn.'

'Er muoz et hinnen   balde und āne sūmen sich:
nu gip im urloup, süezez wīp.
lāze in minnen   her nāch sō verholne dich,
daz er behalte ēre und den līp.   20
er gap sich mīner triuwe alsō,
daz ich in braehte ouch wider dan.
ez ist nu tac; naht was ez, dō
mit drucken an die brust dīn kus mir in an gewan.'

'Swaz dir gevalle,   wahtaer, sinc, und lā den hie,   25
der minne brāhte und minne enphienc.
von dīnem schalle   ist er und ich erschrocken ie:
sō ninder der morgenstern ūf gienc
ūf in, der her nāch minne ist komen,
noch ninder lūhte tages licht,   30
du hāst in dicke mir benomen
von blanken armen, und ūz herzen nicht.'

LXXXII

(*Watchman*:) 'Its claws[28] have fought through the sky, it rises up with great power. I see turning to grey, the colour of day, when dawn is about to break, the day which will deprive of companionship the excellent man that I let in with such difficulty. I will lead him away safely if I can. His very many virtues prompted me to do this.'

(*Lady*:) 'Watchman, you sing to such purpose that you take away my many joys and increase my sorrow. You bring tidings which little please me every morning at the approach of day. You should keep it completely secret from me. I command that of your loyalty. I will reward you for this when I can, provided that my companion can stay here.'

(*Watchman*:) 'He must be away from here quickly and without delay. Now give him a farewell kiss, sweet lady. After this let him be in love with you so secretly that he maintain both honour and life. He put himself in my trust in such a way that I should bring him away again as well. Now it is day; it was the night when with embrace you took him from me to your breast with your kiss.'

(*Lady*:) 'Whatever you please, watchman, sing; and leave him here who brought and received love. He and I have always been startled by your clamour. When the morning-star had not by any means risen up upon him who came here for love, when not the least daylight gleamed, you have often taken him from me, out of my white arms, but not out of my heart.'

Von den blicken,   die der tac tet durh diu glas,
und dō [der] wahtaere warnen sanc,
si muose erschricken   durch den der dā bī ir was.   35
ir brüstelīn an brust si dwanc.
der riter ellens niht vergaz
(des wold in wenden wahtaers dōn):
urloup nāhe und nāher baz
mit kusse und anders gab in minne lōn.   40

LXXIII

Der helden minne ir klage
du sunge ie gen dem tage,
daz sūre nāch dem süezen,
swer minne und wīplich grüezen
alsō enpfienc,   5
daz si sich nuosen scheiden:
swaz du dō riete in beiden,
dō ūf gienc
der morgensterne, wahtaere, swīc,
dā von niht [langer] sinc.   10

Swer pfliget oder ir gepflac
daz er bi lieben wībe lac
den merkern unverborgen,
der darf niht durh den morgen
dannen streben,   15
er mac des tages erbeiten:
man darf in niht ūz leiten
ūf sin leben.
ein offen süeze wirtes wīp
kan solhe minne geben.   20

Because of the rays which the day made through the glass, and because the watchman sang his warning, she had to be concerned for him who was with her. Her small breasts she pressed against his chest. The knight did not forget the prowess that the watchman's song wanted to change in him.[29] The reward of love sealed their parting, in ever closer embrace, with kiss and more besides.[30]

LXXXIII

Always towards day you sang a dirge for hidden love,[31] the sour after the sweet. Whoever thus received love and womanly greeting, they had to part. Whatever then you advised the two of them when the morning-star rose up, watchman, be silent now; of that sing no longer.

The man who is, or has been, accustomed to lie by his beloved lady unconcealed from slanderers, he has no need to strive to get away because of the morning.[32] He can wait for day. He need not be led out at the risk of his life. A husband's overt, sweet wife can give such love.

HARTMANN VON AUE[33]
(*c.* 1165–post 1210)

LXXXIV

Ich var mit iuwern hulden, herren unde māge:
liut unde lant die müezen saelic sīn.
ez ist unnōt daz ieman mīner verte vrāge:
ich sage wol für wār die reise [mīn].
mich vienc diu Minne und lie mich varn ūf mīne sicherheit.   5
nu hāt si mir enboten bī ir liebe daz ich var.
ez ist unwendic: ich muoz endelīchen dar:
wie kūme ich braeche mīne triuwe und mīnen eit!

Sich rüemet maniger waz er dur die Minne taete:
wā sint die werc? die rede hoere ich wol.   10
doch saehe ich gern daz si ir eteslīchen baete
daz er ir diente als ich ir dienen sol.
ez ist geminnet, der sich dur die Minne ellenden muoz.
nū seht wie si mich ūz mīner zungen ziuhet über mer.
und lebte mīn her, Salatin und al sīn her   15
dien braehten mich von Vranken niemer einen fuoz.

Ir minnesinger, iu muoz ofte misselingen:
daz iu den schaden tuot, daz ist der wān.
ich wil mich rüemen, ich mac wol von minne singen,
sīt mich diu Minne hāt und ich si hān.   20
daz ich dā wil, seht daz wil alse gerne haben mich;
sō müezt aber ir verliesen underwīlent wānes vil:
ir ringent umbe liep daz iuwer niht enwil:
wan müget ir armen minnen solhe minne als ich?

LXXXIV

Lords and kinsmen, I am going, by your leave.[34] May the people and the land be happy! There is no need for anyone to ask about my going; I am saying clearly what the reason for my journey is. Love captured me and let me go on my security. Now she has commanded me, by the love I owe her, to set off. It is unavoidable; I must do it at last. I can hardly break my pledge and my oath.

Many a man boasts of what he would do for Love. So where are his actions? I hear his claims well enough; but I would like to see him serve at her command as I am accustomed to serve her. The man who must go into exile because of Love is truly in its sway. Now see how she drags me away across the sea from my native land. If my lord were alive,[35] Saladin could never with all his army pull me a foot's distance from the land of the Germans.

Poets of love, often you must fail. That which is your vain hope does injury to you. I want to boast of myself that I certainly make songs from love, since Love has me and I have her. So observe that what I want wants just as keenly to have me. But sometimes you must lose much of your vain hope, as you strive for love that does not want to be yours. Why can you, poor things, not love a love such as mine?

LXXXV

Maniger grüezet mich alsō
(der gruoz tuot mich ze māze frō),
'Hartman, gēn wir schouwen
ritterlīche frouwen.'
mac er mich mit gemache lān   5
und īle er zuo den frowen gān!
bī frowen triuwe ich niht vervān,
wan daz ich müede vor in stān.

Ze frowen habe ich einen sin:
als si mir sint als bin ich in;   10
wand ich mac baz vertrīben
die zīt mit armen wīben.
swar ich kum dā ist ir vil,
dā vinde ich die diu mich dā wil;
diu ist ouch mīnes herzen spil: 15
waz touc mir ein ze hōhez zil?

In mīner tōrheit mir geschach
daz ich zuo zeiner frowen sprach
'frowe, ich tān mīne sinne
gewant an iuwer minne.'   20
dō wart ich twerhes an gesehen;
des wil ich, des sī iu bejehen,
ir wīp in solher māze spehen
diu mir des niht enlānt geschehen.

LXXXV

Many a man greets me thus (only moderately does the greeting give me joy): 'Hartman, let us go in knightly fashion to look at ladies'. He is welcome to leave me and to hurry off to go to the ladies! From ladies I expect to gain nothing, except to stand in weariness before them.

Towards ladies I have a tactic: as they are to me, so am I to them. For I can pass the time better with a simple woman. Wherever I come where there are many of them, there I find one who will oblige me then. That is delight for my heart as well. What use to me is too high a goal?

In my foolishness, it happened to me that I said to a certain lady, 'Madam, I have lost my mind for love of you'. I was looked upon askanse. Since then, I declare to you that I will choose myself a woman of such a kind as will not show me denial.

WALTHER VON DER VOGELWEIDE
(*c.* 1170–*c.* 1230)[37]

LXXXVI

Sō die bluomen ūz dem grase dringent,
same si lachen gegen der spilden sunnen,
in einem meien an dem morgen fruo,
und diu kleinen vogellin wol singent
in ir besten wise, die si kunnen,   5
waz wünne mac sich dā gelīchen zuo?
Ez ist wol halb ein himelrīche.
Suln wir sprechen, waz sich deme gelīche,
sō sage ich, waz mir dicke baz
in minen ougen hāt getān,   10
    und taete ouch noch, gesaehe ich daz.

Swā ein edeliu schoene frouwe reine,
wol gekleidet unde wol gebunden,
dur kurzewile zuo vil liuten gāt,
hovelīchen hōhgemuot, niht eine,   15
umbe sehende ein wēnic under stunden,
alsam der sunne gegen den sternen stāt,—
der meie bringe uns al sīn wunder,
waz ist dā sō wünnecliches under,
als ir vil minneclicher līp?   20
wir lāzen alle bluomen stān
    und kapfen an daz werde wīp.

Nū wol dan, welt ir die wārheit schouwen!
Gān wir zuo des meien hōhgezīte!
Der ist mit aller sīner krefte komen.   25
Seht an in und seht an schoene frouwen,
wederz dā daz ander überstrīte:
daz bezzer spil, ob ich daz hān genomen.
Owē der mich dā welen hieze,
deich daz eine dur daz ander lieze,   30
wie rehte schiere ich danne kür!
Hēr Meie, ir müeset merze sīn,
    ē ich mīn frouwen dā verlür!

LXXXVI

As the flowers[38] thrust up through the grass as if they laugh at the dazzling sun, in May in the morning early, and the little birds sing well in the best melody they know, what joy can be compared with this? It is certainly half Paradise. But if we are talking about what can be compared with it, I will tell you what often has more affected my eyes, and would still now too if I saw it.

When a noble, fair and excellent lady, well-dressed and well-coiffured, goes for amusement amongst a throng of people, courtly and fine-tempered, not alone, looking round a little now and then, she stands like the sun in relation to the stars. Although May brings us all his wonders, which among them is as joyful as her most beautiful person? We stop looking at the flowers and gaze at the worthy lady.

So come then, whoever wishes to see the proof of this. Let us go to the May festival. He has come with all strength. Look at him and look at beautiful ladies, to see which of the two surpasses the other, whether I have chosen the better delight. Ah, if there I had to choose among them, even though I had to leave one of them in favour of the other, how very quickly I would then choose! Sir May, you would have to be March before I would abandon my lady in such a case.[39]

GOTTFRIED VON STRASSBURG[40]
Tristan
(*c.* 1210)

The first extract is the literary excursus in *Tristan*[41] (lines 4,619–4,818). In beginning his account of the nobility of the robing of Tristan for his investiture, Gottfried wishes for the eloquence in description of his predecessors and contemporaries in German poetry whom he proceeds to catalogue:

LXXXVII

Ah, how Hartmann of Aue dyes and adorns his tales through and through with words and sense, both outside and within! How eloquently he establishes his story's meaning! How clear and transparent his crystal words both are and ever must remain! Gently they approach and fawn on a man, and captivate right minds. Those who esteem fine language with due sympathy and judgement will allow the man of Aue his garland and his laurels.

But if some friend of the hare, high-skipping and far-browsing,[42] seeks out Poetry's heath with dicing terms, and, lacking our general assent, aspires to the laurel wreath, let him leave us to adhere to our opinion that we too must have a hand in the choosing. For we who help to gather the flowers with which that twig of honour is entwined to make a floral wreath, we wish to know *why* he asks. Since if anyone lays claim to it, let him leap up and add his flowers! We shall judge from them if they grace it so well that we should take it from the poet of Aue and confer the laurel on him. But since none has yet come who has a better claim, then in God's name let us leave it as it is! We shall not allow anyone to wear it whose words are not well-laved, and his diction smooth and even; so that if someone approaches at the trot, well-poised and with an upright seat, he will not stumble there. Inventors of wild tales, hired hunters after stories, who cheat with chains and dupe dull minds, who turn rubbish into gold for children and from magic boxes pour pearls of dust! – these give us shade with a bare staff, not with the green leaves and twigs and boughs of May. Their shade never soothes a stranger's eyes. To speak the truth, no pleasurable emotion comes from it, there is nothing in it to delight the heart. Their poetry is not such that a noble heart can laugh with it. Those same story-hunters have to send commentaries with their tales: one cannot understand them as one hears and sees them. But we for our part have not the leisure to seek the gloss in books of the black art.

But there are other 'dyers'. Bligger of Steinach's words are delightful. Ladies worked them with silk and gold on their embroidery-frames – one could trim them with fringes from Byzantium! He has a magic gift of words. And I fancy his limpid invention was wondrously spun by the fairies and cleansed and refined in their well – for he is surely inspired by the fairies! Thus his tongue, which bears a harp,[43] has two utter felicities: words and inspiration. These two between them harp out their tales with rare excellence. See what marvels of verbal ingenuity this master of words traces meanwhile on his tapestry, how deftly he throws couplets like knives, or glues them together as if they had grown there. I even believe he has books and letters tied on for wings, for – if only you will look – his words ride the air like eagles!

Whom else can I single out? There are and have been many, inspired and eloquent. Heinrich of Veldeke had every poetic gift. How well he sang of love! How finely he trimmed his invention! I imagine he had his insight from Pegasus' spring, from which all wisdom comes. I have never seen Heinrich myself; but I hear the best (those who were masters in his day and since) voice their opinion and accord him the glory of having grafted the first slip on the tree of German poetry. From this have sprouted branches whence the blossoms came from which they drew the cunning of their masterly inventions. And now this skill has spread its boughs so far and has been so diversely trained that all who are now writing break blossoms and sprays to their hearts' content, in words and melodies.

'Nightingales' there are many, but I shall not speak of them, since they do not belong to this company. Thus I shall say no more of them than what I must always say – they are adepts at their tasks and sing their sweet summer songs most excellently. Their voices are clear and pleasing, they raise our spirits and gladden our hearts within us. The world would be full of apathy and live as if on sufferance but for this sweet bird-song, which time and again brings back to any who has loved, things both pleasant and good, and varied emotions that soothe a noble heart. When this sweet bird-song begins to tell us of its joy it awakens intimate feelings that give rise to tender thoughts.

'Oh, do tell us about the Nightingales!'

They all know their calling and can all express their pining so well in words and song. So who is to bear the banner, now that their lady marshal, the Nightingale of Hagenau,[44] who bore the master-secret of all music sealed in her tongue, has fallen thus silent to the world? I often think of her – I mean her sweet and lovely music – and wonder where she acquired such a store and whence she received her wondrously flexible airs. I should think that Orpheus' tongue, which had power over all music, sounded through her mouth.

But since she is no longer with us, give us some advice! Let some kind man offer an opinion here. Who is to lead the charming bevy, who is to marshal this retinue? I think I shall find the one who must bear the banner! Their mistress is well able to do so, the Nightingale of Vogelweide! How she carols over the heath in her high clear voice! What marvels she performs! How deftly she sings in organon! How she varies her singing from one compass to another (in that mode, I mean, which has come down to us from Cithaeron, on whose slopes and in whose caves the Goddess of Love holds sway)! She is Mistress of the Chamber there at court – let her be their leader! She will marshal them admirably, she knows where to seek Love's melody. May she and her company sing with such success that they bring their sad love-plaints to a joyful consummation, and may I live to see it![45]

When Tristan and Isolde have drunk the love-potion, meant for Isolde and Mark and which will bind them in love for ever, the joy of their love is described and followed by a reflection on the nature of love by the poet (lines 12,161–415).

LXXXVIII

That night, as the lovely woman lay brooding and pining for her darling, there came stealing into her cabin her lover and her physician – Tristan and Love. Love the physician led Tristan, her sick one, by the hand: and there, too, she found her other patient, Isolde. She quickly took both sufferers and gave him to her, her to him, to be each other's remedy. Who else could have severed them from the ill which they shared but Union, the knot that joined their senses? Love the Ensnarer knit their two hearts together by the toils of her sweetness with such consummate skill and such marvellous strength that in all their days the bond was never loosed.

A long discourse on Love wearies well-bred minds. But a short discourse on worthy love gratifies good minds.[46]

However little I have suffered the sweet torment in my time, the gentle pain that wounds our hearts so agreeably, something tells me (and I am well inclined to believe it) that these two lovers were in a happy and contented mood at having got out of their way Love's enemy, cursed Surveillance, that veritable plague of Love! I have thought much about the pair of them, and do so now and ever shall. When I spread Longing and Affection as a scroll before my inward eye and inquire into their natures, my yearning grows, and my comrade, Desire, grows too, as if he would mount to the clouds! When I consider in detail the unending marvels that a man would find in love if he but knew where to seek them, and the joy there would be in love for those who would practise it sincerely, then, all at once, my heart grows larger than Setmunt[47] and I pity Love from my heart when I see that almost everybody today clings and holds fast to her, and yet none gives her her due. We all desire our amorous fancies and wish to keep company with Love. No, Love is not such as we make her for one another in the spurious way we do! We do not look facts in the face: we sow seed of deadly nightshade and wish it to bear lilies and roses! Believe me, this is impossible. We can only garner what has been put into the ground, and accept what the seed bears us. We must mow and reap as we have sown. We cultivate Love with guile and deceit and with minds as bitter as gall, and we then seek joy of body and soul in her! But, instead, she bears only pain and evil and poison-berries and weeds, just as her soil was sown. And when this yields bitter sorrow, festers in our hearts and there destroys us, we accuse Love of the crime and say she is to blame whose fault it never was. We all sow seeds of perfidy — then let us reap sorrow and shame. If the sorrow should chance to hurt us, let us think of that beforehand; let us sow better and better, and we shall reap accordingly. We who have a mind for the world (whether this be good or bad), how we abuse the days which we squander in Love's name, finding nothing but the self-same crop that we sowed in her — failure and disaster. We do not find the good that each of us desires, and which we are all denied; I mean steadfast friendship in love, which never fails to comfort us and bears roses as well as thorns and solace as well as trouble. In such friendship joy always lurks among the woes; however often it is clouded, it will bring forth gladness in the end. Nowadays no one finds such steadfast affection, so ill do we prepare the soil.

They are right who say that 'Love is hounded to the ends of the earth'. All that we have is the bare word, only the name remains to us: and this we have so hackneyed, so abused, and so debased, that the poor, tired thing is ashamed of her own name and is disgusted at the word. She heartily loathes and despises herself. Shorn of all honour and dignity she sneaks begging from house to house, shamefully lugging a patchwork sack in which she keeps what she can grab or steal and, denying it to her own mouth, hawks it in the streets. For shame! It is we who are the cause of this traffic. We do such things to her and yet protest our innocence. Love, mistress of all hearts, the noble, the incomparable, is for sale in the open market. What shameful dues our dominion has extorted from her! We have set a false stone in our ring and now we deceive ourselves with it. What a wretched sort of deception, when a man so lies to his friends that he dupes himself. False lovers and love-cheats as we are, how vainly our days slip by, seeing that we so seldom bring our suffering to a joyful consummation! How we dissipate our lives without either profit or pleasure!

Yet we are heartened by something that does not really concern us; for when there is a good love-story, when we tell in poetry of those who lived once upon a time, many hundreds of years ago, our hearts are warmed within us and we are so full of this happy chance that there can be none who is loyal and true and free of guile towards his lover that would not wish to create such bliss in his own heart for himself, except that the selfsame thing from which it all takes rise, I mean heartfelt Fidelity, lies beneath our feet in misery all the time. In vain does she address us – we look the other way and without a thought tread the sweet thing underfoot. We have shamefully trampled upon her. Were we to seek her where she lies, we should at first not know where to look. Good and rewarding as fidelity between lovers would be, why have we no liking for it? One look, one tender glance from the eyes of one's beloved will surely quench a myriad pangs of body and of soul. One kiss from one's darling's lips that comes stealing from the depths of her heart – how it banishes love's cares!

I know that Tristan and Isolde, that eager pair, rid each other of a host of ills and sorrows when they reached the goal of their desire. The yearning that fetters thoughts was stilled. Whenever the occasion suited they had their fill of what lovers long for. When opportunity offered, they paid and exacted willing tribute from Love and from each other with faithful hearts. During that voyage they were in ecstasy. Now that their shyness was over they gloried and revelled in their intimacy, and this was wise and sensible. For lovers who hide their feelings, having once revealed them, who set a watch on their modesty and so turn strangers in love, are robbers of themselves. The more they veil themselves the more they despoil themselves and adulterate joy with sorrow. This pair of lovers did not play the prude: they were free and familiar with looks and speech.

And so they passed the voyage in a life of rapture, yet not altogether scatheless, for they were haunted by fear of the future. They dreaded beforehand what actually came to pass and what in days to come was to rob them of much pleasure and face them with many hazards – I mean that fair Isolde was to be given to one to whom she did not wish to be given. And another cause for sorrow tormented them – Isolde's lost virginity. They were deeply troubled about this and it made them very wretched. Yet such cares were easily borne, for they freely had their will together many, many times.[48]

NOTES

1   Here Nos. LVII and LXXVI.
2   A. T. Hatto's translation, Penguin (1960), p. 106.
3   It might be noted in passing that the reaction towards a more 'naturalistic', sensual kind of love poetry in the *dorfspoesie* parallels the development of the 'bourgeois' tradition in northern France, particularly evident in Jean de Meun. See n. 4 to the northern French section above.
4   Here in the words of M. F. Richey, *Essays on Medieval German Poetry* (Oxford 1969), p. 77.
5   This reliance upon rule-governed formalism, often lacking in inspiration, is a major part of the subject of Wagner's *Die Meistersinger von Nürnberg*, where the originality of Walther is the exception to the rule. Further, the parallel between the *merkaere* there and the Provençal *lauzengier* is striking.
6   See the poem by Von Veldeke, LXX here.
7   Nothing is known of Dietmar, beyond the existence of thirty-seven stophes under his name. He is generally said to belong to an earlier period of native German love-song, the *trûtlied*, before the development of the Provençal-influenced *Minne*. The German texts of the two poems by Dietmar here are taken, with kind permission, from *The Penguin Book of German Verse*, edited by Leonard Forster (1957), pp. 10–11.
8   The fact that the speaker is the lady in many of the German poems, such as this one, associates them with earlier Latin and German poetry rather than with the troubadours.
9   This *tagelied* is in a form which reached great heights of accomplishment amongst the *Minnesänger*, as in the famous examples by Heinrich von Morungen (LXXIII) and Wolfram von Eschenbach (LXXXII) below. Obviously it is related to the Latin and Provençal *alba*, but it is a form so widely attested that no direct influence need be inferred. The poem is a *wechsel* between a man and a woman, distantly related to the Provençal *tenso* or *partimen*, though the lady rarely has a voice there.
10 Meinloh is said to be a transitional poet, having elements both of the primitive *trûtlied* and of the *Minnesang* influenced by the European tradition of Courtly Love poetry. In this poem, striking 'courtly' features are the suggestions of love from afar in the first half, and of the love-inspiring properties of the eyes.
11 Von Veldeke came from the Netherlands, and his work was believed by Sievers to be a composite oeuvre of several poets. He is clearly related to the traditions of Provence and France, as the reference to Tristan here suggests, even if his love is a matter of *blîdscap*, 'happiness', rather than the elevating sentiments of the troubadours.
12 Von Hausen is the first *Minnesänger* whose work corresponds closely to that of the troubadours and *trouvères*, and he corresponds to some

of them in life-style too, as a crusader like Conon de Béthune. He was an aristocrat and politician from the Rhineland who died in a fall from his horse in the course of a battle against the Turks during the Third Crusade, led by Barbarossa. He campaigned in Italy in 1186 and 1187. His poems lack nature openings and their concern is nearly always hopeless love (as in both poems here), although he wrote three Crusading poems in which God triumphs over the lady's love, as in Conon and Folquet de Marseilles.

13 This poem of love from afar may have been written from the Crusades or from Italy (see preceding note), although a literal absence need not be supposed in poets of the period. The text is taken from *Deutscher Minnesang*, Reclam, Stuttgart 1954, p. 36.

14 Crossing the mountains, perhaps the Alps, does suggest that the poem might have been written from Italy.

15 Von Morungen is generally regarded as the greatest of the poets of courtly love amongst the Germans (assuming Von der Vogelweide to have been in reaction against that school). He enjoyed the same kind of celebration amongst followers as the troubadours did in the *vidas*, and he is the subject of a fifteenth-century ballad, 'Vom edlen Moringer'. Only twenty-three of his poems survive, mostly in celebration of a mistress as remote as the lady of the troubadours, whom he calls 'hohe Minne'. He came from Thuringia and seems to have been influenced by Latin and Provençal predecessors.

16 This famous *tagelied* (alba) is one of the most admired poems of the *Minne*, although its untechnical language is not typical of Von Morungen. As a *wechsel* with a lady's part, it goes back more, perhaps, to German influences. In any case, it has an understated naturalism unparalleled in the poetry of the period.

17 The connexions of this poem with the main courtly tradition hardly needs underlining: common themes are *dienst* (love-service), *genade* (mercy) and such terms as *minnet*, *not* and *liep* itself. But into this technical framework there is incorporated the sustained metaphor of the sun in the last stanza.

18 The opening of this poem presents love as an enchantment, evoking the theme of the lover as an inspired madman amongst the troubadours. This idea is continued in the theme of possession by the lady, and her lack of captivation by the poet, in the second stanza. Her nobility and bright eyes in stanza three are universal themes of courtly love.

19 The malediction upon the man who obstructs love is familiar, related to Ovid's attitude to the doorkeeper in *Amores* I, vi (X here). The birds awaiting the day are the celebrants of love, from Jaufre Rudel to Petrarch.

20 This poem is printed by Istvan Frank, *Trouvères et Minnesänger*, pp. 112–15, parallel with the last poem in the Provençal section (LVII) here. The first stanzas are identical, and stanza three of the German

corresponds closely in its ideas to stanza two of the Provençal. Olive Sayce (*op. cit.*, p. 229) notes parallels to the associating of the mirror and the dream as symbols of impermanence in Wolfram's *Parsifal*, lines 20–4 and in Walther von der Vogelweide (Sayce L/K 122.24). She believes that the troubadour poem was the model for Von Morungen.

21   Narcissus is a likely symbol for the introverted love of the courtly lover. Cf. line 14 of the parallel poem (LVII here), and n. 24 in the Provençal section, to XLV, Bernart de Ventadorn's "Can vei la lauzeta", line 24.

22   Reinmar (also referred to as 'der Alte' or 'Her Reinmar') was probably born in Alsace but he was a Viennese Court poet. He was greatly admired in his own time; when he died, his art was lamented by Walther von der Vogelweide, and Gottfried von Strassburg called him 'the nightingale of Hagenouwe', saying that the chief place, formerly occupied by him, will now be taken by Walther (see LXXXVII here). He is the most archetypal courtly lover of the *Minnesänger*, almost always tinged with melancholy, and he is not as much admired nowadays as in the era of courtly love. His great theme is *Minnedienst*, chivalric service, and it is always clear that fulfilment would destroy the ennobling power of that service. With him more than any other *Minnesänger* is associated a school of courtly song, against which the 'bourgeois' school of Neidhart reacted in the following century. Reinmar probably went on a Crusade in 1197–8, and one of his poems is a very explicit crusading song, 'Des tages to ich daz kriuze nam' (See M. F. Richey, *Medieval German Lyrics*, Edinburgh and London 1958, p. 55).

23   The texts of the first two poems by Reinmar are taken, with permission, from the edition of C. Von Kraus (Munich 1918–20), published in *Abhandlungen der Bayerischen Akademie der Wissenschaften, Phil.-hist. Klasse*, XXX.

24   The German text of this poem is taken, with permission, from *The Penguin Book of German Verse*, pp. 18–19. Line 19, 'She is my Easter-day', is much quoted.

25   The first line of this strophe is quoted by Walther von der Vogelweide in his elegy for Reinmar, 'Owē daz wīsheit und jugent' (See Sayce, pp. 106–7), line 12.

26   This strophe is notable for an English reader because of its assertion of the impropriety of enquiring about the lady's age, inviting comparison with a famous and apparently irrelevant remark by the narrator of *Troilus and Criseyde*: 'But trewely, I kan nat telle hir age' (V, 826).

27   Wolfram was the author of three epics, *Parsifal*, *Willehalm* and *Titurel*; eight short poems of his survive too. *Parsifal* is thought to date from the first decade of the thirteenth century, and the other two epics are incomplete. The Provençal watchman is introduced by him into German poetry, and he is a very important figure in the first poem

here. Wolfram plays a rôle of nobility and selflessness in love in Wagner's *Tannhäuser*.

28 Wolfram is celebrated as a composer of the *tagelied*, which is the form of five of his eight shorter poems. This one is the most famous, admired in particular for the extraordinarily imaginative personification of the dawn in its opening.

29 That is, the watchman wants to deprive the knight of his prowess in love, though the word *ellen* belongs primarily to martial prowess. The conflicts of the knight's martial duties and his attendance upon the lady is a major theme in Wolfram; see Appendix 1 in Richey, *Essays on Medieval German Poetry*, 'Wolfram von Eschenbach and the paradox of the Chivalrous Life'. (The essays in the appendices, concerned with the epics, are the part of this book that is of greatest critical interest.)

30 I have taken the translation of the difficult last two lines from Sayce's edition, p. 123.

31 The message of this poem seems to be that there is no need for the watchman to call a warning and a halt to the love of married lovers. The poem is an extremely important piece of contrary evidence in the argument about the definitiveness of adultery as an aspect of courtly love. For more such evidence, see the article by A. R. Press referred to in note 22 to the Latin section here.

32 The suggestion here may be that, once the lovers who previously had to be on their guard against the *gilos* have got married, they are at peace. This would imply that the *gilos* is not always the husband but sometimes the guardian: Arnaut's *oncle*, perhaps in LIII here.

33 Hartmann is one of the great epic poets of the *Blütezeit*, the author of *Erec* and *Iwein*, both adapted from Chrétien, and the story *Der Arme Heinrich*, as well as the treatise of love, *Das Büchlein*, and a number of *Minnelieder*. He was involved in a Crusade, in either 1189–90 or 1197. His poems are generally of *hohe Minne* but the second one included here is a famous instance of the *niedere Minne*. He wrote three crusading songs. He is sometimes contrasted with Walther, in that Hartmann is a relatively late and slightly decadent poet of the *Minne* and an exponent of the kind of poetry against which Walther is said to have reacted to creative purpose.

34 This crusading song has as its theme Lovelace's 'I could not love thee, Dear, so much, / Loved I not honour more', an often-pressed excuse for the crusader. But the exchanges between Yvain and Laudine in *Yvain*, for example, show that the conflict between the two prowesses, the amorous and the martial, was an important theme in the romances.

35 This puzzling clause may mean 'if the love of my lady were directed towards me', with a suggestion perhaps of the feudal masculine form for the loved lady, as in Provençal *midons* and in Rust'haveli.

36 This poem of *niedere Minne* needs to be borne in mind before Hartmann is dismissed as a decadent poet of the *Minne*. It seems to be an anticipation of the reactions against that poetry in Neidhart von

Reuenthal.

37 Walther is generally thought to be the greatest lyric poet in Middle High German. His work is usually divided into three periods: the first of conventional poems of the *Minne*, inspired perhaps by Dietmar; the second of spontaneous love-poetry, with more accent on nature as an element than is usual in courtly love poetry; and the third (and greatest) a religious kind of poetry of the *hohe Minne*, containing the vitality of the *niedere Minne*. The latter distinction, inspired by but not corresponding to the Provençal distinction between the *trobar ric* and *trobar leu*, was first noted as a critical principle by Walther. Over a hundred of his poems survive, many of them of great metrical and musical brilliance. In his virtuosity and unaccepting reflection of the poetry of his predecessors, he reminds the reader of English of Dunbar.

38 The German text of this poem is taken, with kind permission, from *The Penguin Book of German Verse*, pp. 19–20.

39 The idea, perhaps, is that May would have to have the harshness and vigour of March before he could compel the poet away from his lady.

40 We know nothing of the life of Gottfried. The poem is dedicated to one Dieterich, but we do not know who he was. Gottfried seems to have used Thomas's *Tristan* as his source, and only five-sixths of the poem is complete. The excerpts from the poem here are taken from A. T. Hatto's admirable translation (Penguin 1960), with the permission of the publishers. The importance of Tristan as a central figure in courtly love means that Gottfried's poem brings the German poetry of his age into the mainstream of that tradition.

41 Immediately before the point at which Tristan is made co-regent by King Mark, when the poet feels perhaps that his subject will demand great poetic strength as he turns to his principal theme, Gottfried reviews the great poets of his time.

42 The friend of the hare is Wolfram von Eschenbach whom Gottfried clearly dislikes.

43 A reference apparently to his family arms. Only a few undistinguished lyrics by this poet survive. Gottfried's lines clearly suggest some longer narrative, but no trace of it survives.

44 Reinmar: only this reference connects him with Hagenau in Alsace; his known life is otherwise confined to Vienna.

45 Translation by Hatto, Penguin, pp. 105–7.

46 The worthiness of discussion of love is widely asserted in courtly writing. There are a number of other traditional features in this passage, such as the curse of surveillance.

47 Setmunt has not been explained. The general theme of the sentence, that true love is not as noble as it was in the olden days, is already a lament of the early troubadours and is familiar in English in Malory's comparison of true love to summer (*Works*, ed. E. Vinaver, Oxford University Press, London 1971, pp. 648–9).

48 Hatto's translation, Penguin, pp. 201–4.

The Stilnovisti

The most impressive product of troubadour courtly-love poetry, and the most extreme in refinement, was the school of poetry in Tuscany which Bonagiunta of Lucca calls 'the sweet new style' (*il dolce stil nuovo*)[1] in *Purgatorio* XXIV, 57 (XCVII here). There is a clear tradition from the troubadours to these poets: Dante invents some elegant lines of Provençal for Arnaut Daniel in *Purgatorio* XXVI (XCVIII here); Sordello, who is assigned a distinguished place in *Purgatorio*, wrote in Provençal in preference to his native Mantuan Italian; and Bonagiunta here, as well as Guinicelli in *Purgatorio* XXVI, testifies to the influence of Provençal. Guinicelli points out Arnaut Daniel as 'the better poet' in the vernacular literature (*Purgatorio* XXVI, 117), saying that Tuscan poets such as Guittone d'Arezzo were mistaken in regarding Guiraut de Borneil as the greatest troubadour. Arnaut's superiority to Guiraut seems to be accounted for by the quality in the *stil nuovo* which Bonagiunta says that he and Guittone and the Notary (the Sicilian Jacopo da Lentino) lacked. It seems, then, that the Stilnovisti saw themselves as descended from the Provençal *trobar clus* (obscure poetry), represented by Arnaut, rather than the 'easy style' followed by the Sicilians and the other thirteenth-century Italian poets. Petrarch, indeed, was to turn the tradition away from the extreme scholasticism and intellectualism of the Stilnovisti, back into the relatively more tractable line of the Sicilians and the earlier *poesia cortese toscana*.

But these poets are of enormous significance and interest in the development of courtly-love literature. By them the conventional settings of troubadour love-poetry (lady, suppliant lover, jealous husband, tale-bearer) are internalised and presented in philosophical dress: the love-battle becomes a *psychomachia*.[2] This is a development which, refined though it is, seems almost inevitable in poetry which concentrates so entirely on the suppliant lover and his state of mind. The undifferentiated lady of the troubadours was merely the object which provoked the passion that became the subject of the poetry. Poetry that perpetually examined the lover's (or poet's) state of mind in the same conventional terms was limited both in expression and sensibility. But the Stilnovisti, by their extreme, often ingenious intellectuality, gave a new meaning and life, if a short and austere one, to the tradition.

The philosophical terms in which these poets presented the love-situation were used to resolve many of the ageless paradoxes raised by troubadour poetry, in particular the problem of the *dolce dolor* of love (usually associated exclusively with Petrarch nowadays): the lover's joy is accompanied by a pain that, at least figuratively, causes his death. The Stilnovisti presented the sorrows connected with earthly love as the product of a kind of alienation from heavenly love. By philosophical scrutiny of the nature of love, they found its ideal form, and its first cause, in God. So they developed the 'angelicised' ladies, Giovanna, Selvaggia and Beatrice (who were to some extent suggested by the angel-similes of the later troubadours such as Montanhagol and Guittone). Human love was explained and justified philosophically by reference to divine love. Dante is the culmination of this tradition, particularly in the *Vita Nuova*, although its way of presenting human love in relation to divine reaches its highest point at the end of *Paradiso*. As later Tuscan poets, such as Onesto da Bologna, show, there is no room for development past this point. The intellectual argument, developed by the *trobar clus* and carried on by the Italians, was concluded by Dante.

The quality which Dante claims for the *stil nuovo*, and which Bonagiunta in *Purgatorio* apparently understands it to have by distinction from previous poetry like his own, is something like 'sincerity'; Dante says, 'I am one who, when love speaks to me, take note of what he says, and proceed to express it in the way that he dictates within me' (*Purgatorio* XXIV, 52–4). The philosophical doctrine underlying this is a highly complex one, and the fact that Bonagiunta immediately understands what his own relative shortcoming was, is in part a literary fiction. Furthermore, the claim that he follows the dictates of inner love may appear surprising in a writer of poems characterised by such apparently worked and unspontaneous ingenuity. But what Dante is claiming is that the process is a natural and inevitable one, once the physiology and psychology of the matter is understood. The image of the lady was apprehended by the sensitive soul, and its imaginative form was then apprehended as an idea by the rational soul. This apprehension of the idea of love led naturally to love of God.[3] It was this *natural* progression that the poetic predecessors, working in purely conventional images, failed to understand and express in their poetry. And since this was conformity with the highest truth, it could be seen as a deeper realism or sincerity, as distinct from artificiality.

Upon first acquaintance, the poetry of the Stilnovisti is rather forbidding, suffering from the same narrowness of imagery that characterises much strictly philosophical poetry, in this case compounded by the limited range of imagery of courtly poetry (eyes, heart, mind, whiteness, arrows). It has to a higher degree the intellectuality of, say, the English Metaphysical poets, but without their arresting originality in the use of images. This is the criticism of the poetry already made by Onesto in 'Mente ed Umile' (CIV here). Some of the poetry (notoriously, Cavalcanti's 'Donna me prega', XCIV here, has remained to some extent incomprehensible. But, once even the rudiments of the underlying philosophical/ physiological system is understood, most of the best of the poetry has many of the same positive qualities of wit as the school of Donne.[4] It is, moreover, a natural product of the courtly love tradition in which the Stilnovisti were well-versed, as is shown by the episode of Paolo and Francesca, a conventional classic of the *genre* with its absent jealous husband and its Arthurian phrase. Nor must the extent to which Petrarch, the father of later European love-poetry, turned away from this poetry by overstated; much of the mentality implied in the words 'Petrarchan' and 'Petrarchism' is founded in the Stilnovisti. And, finally, it is important to bear in mind that this poetry, searchingly intellectual as it was, was available to writers of the age of Chaucer. Awareness of this fact should dispel any disposition to think of later medieval poetry as necessarily inchoate, metrically, morally or intellectually.

GUIDO GUINICELLI

LXXXIX   **Canzone:** *Al Cor Gentil*[5]

Al cor gentil rempaira sempre amore
Come l'ausello in selva a la verdura;
    Ne fe' amor anti che gentil core,
Ne gentil core anti ch'amor, natura.
    Ch'adesso con' fu'l sole   5
Si tosto lo splendore fu lucente,
Ne fu davanti'l sole;
E prende amore in gentilezza loco
Cosi propriamente
Come calore in clarita di foco.   10

    Foco d'amore in gentil cor s'aprende
Come vertute in petra preziosa,
    Che da la stella valor no i discende
Anti che'l sol la faccia gentil cosa;
    Poi che n'ha tratto fore   15
Per sua forza lo sol cio che li e vile,
Stella li da valore:
Cosi lo cor ch'e fatto da natura
Asletto, pur, gentile,
Donna a guisa di stella lo'nnamora.   20

    Amor per tal ragion sta'n cor gentile
Per qual lo foco in cima del doplero.
  Splendeli al su' diletto, clar, sottile;
No li stari' altra guisa, tant' e fero.
    Cosi prava natura   25
Recontra amor come fa l'aigua il foco
Caldo, per la freddura.
Amore in gentil cor prende rivera
Per suo consimel loco
Com' adamas del ferro in la minera.   30

LXXXIX

To the noble heart love always comes back, as the bird does into the greenness of the wood. Nature[6] did not make love before the noble heart, nor the noble heart before love. As soon as the sun came to exist, so did its shining radiance; nor did that exist before the sun. And love takes its place in nobility of heart as inevitably as heat in the radiance of fire.

The fire of love catches flame in the noble heart as does its special quality in a precious stone,[7] which does not come to it from its star before the sun makes the star a noble thing. After the sun by its strength has drawn out from it whatever in it is ignoble, the star gives it its special quality. Similarly a woman, like a star, infuses with love the heart which by nature is made unmarked, pure and well-disposed.

By the same token[8] love stands in the noble heart as does the flame on the top of a torch. It shines freely, with a clear and pure light: it is so disposed and cannot be otherwise. An ignoble nature opposes love, as water through its coldness opposes the hot fire. Love dwells in the noble heart as its sympathetic place, as diamond in the mine settles in steel.

Fere lo sol lo fango tutto'l giorno;
Vile reman, ne'l sol perde calore.
   Dis' omo alter, 'Gentil per sclatta torno':
Lui sembla al fango, al sol gentil valore.
   Che non de dar om fe   35
Che gentilezza sia for di coraggio
In degnita d'ere'
Sed a vertute non ha gentil core,
Com' aigua porta raggio
E'l ciel riten le stelle e lo splendore.   40

   Splende'n la'ntelligenzia del cielo
Deo criator piu che ('n) nostr'occhi'l sole:
   Ella intende suo fattor oltra'l cielo,
E'l ciel volgiando, a Lui obedir tole.
   E con' segue, al primero,   45
Del giusto Deo beato compimento,
Cosi dar dovria, al vero,
La bella donna, poi che ('n) gli occhi splende
Del suo gentil, talento
Che mai di lei obedir non si disprende.   50

   Donna, Deo mi dira, 'Che presomisti?',
Siando l'alma mia a lui davanti.
   'Lo ciel passasti e'nfin a Me venisti
E desti in vano amor Me per semblanti;
   Ch'a Me conven le laude   55
E a la reina del regname degno,
Per cui cessa onne fraude.'
Dir li poro, 'Tenne d'angel sembianza
Che fosse del Tuo regno;
Non me fu fallo, s'in lei posi amanza'.   60

The sun shines on the mud all day: it remains worthless, nor does the sun lose its radiance. The proud man says, 'I am noble by family';[9] he is like the mud, and nobility of heart like the sun. A man must by no means believe that nobility in the dignity of ancestry is divorced from natural excellence. If he does not have a noble heart disposed to virtue, he will receive the ray merely like water, and the sky will keep the stars and the radiance.

God the creator shines upon the intelligence of the sky[10] more than the sun into our eyes. The intelligence apprehends her creator above the sky and makes to obey him, turning the heaven. And just as the happy fulfilling of the will of just God follows instantaneously from this, so indeed the beautiful lady, as soon as she shines upon the eyes of the noble man, must fulfil the desire which never wavered from obeying her.

Lady, God[11] will say to me when my soul is standing before him, 'How dare you! You travelled beyond the sky and came to me, only to regard me as a parallel for your worldly love. Praise is for me and for the queen of that worthy realm where all dissimulation ends.' I shall be able to say to him, 'She was like an angel who was of your kingdom; it was not a fault in me to place my love in her'.

XC   *Dolente, Lasso*[12]

Dolente, lasso, già non m'asecuro,
ché tu m'assali, Amore, e mi combatti:
diritto al tuo rincontro in pie' non duro,
ché mantenente a terra mi dibatti,

come lo trono che fere lo muro   5
e'l vento li arbor' per li forti tratti.
Dice lo core agli occhi: 'Per voi moro',
e li occhi dice al cor: 'Tu n'hai desfatti'.

Apparve luce, che rendé splendore,
che passao per li occhi e'l cor ferìo,   10
ond'io ne sono a tal condizïone:

ciò furo li belli occhi pien' d'amore,
che me feriro al cor d'uno disio
come si fere augello di bolzone.

GUIDO CAVALCANTI
(*c.* 1255–1300)[15]

XCI   *Biltà di Donna*

Biltà di donna e di saccente core
e cavalieri armati che sien genti;
cantar d'augelli e ragionar d'amore;
adorni legni 'n mar forte correnti;

aria serena quand' apar l'albore   5
e bianca neve scender senza venti;
rivera d'acqua e prato d'ogni fiore;
oro, argento, azzuro 'n ornamenti:

ciò passa la beltate e la valenza
de la mia donna e'l su' gentil coraggio,   10
sì che rasembla vile a chi ciò guarda;

XC

Sorrowing, alas, I cannot feel stable now that you, Love, attack me and oppose me. Directly opposed to you, I cannot stand up, but straightaway you strike me to the ground, like the thunderbolt[13] that strikes the wall or the wind that strikes the trees with fierce buffets. The heart says to the eyes, 'I die because of you,' and the eyes to the heart, 'You have killed us'. A light appeared giving off a ray that passed through the eyes and struck the heart;[14] and I am in this state because of it. These were the beautiful eyes full of love, that struck me to the heart with desire as a bird is pierced by an arrow.

XCI

Beauty of woman and of a wise heart, and noble knights in arms; the song of birds and discussion of love; splendid ships in a fast-flowing sea; the quiet air when dawn comes and white snow falling without winds; a full river and a meadow with every flower; gold, silver and lapis lazuli in ornaments: all this is surpassed by the beauty and the worth and the noble nature of my lady, and it bears a poor resemblance for the onlooker.

e tanto più d'ogn' altr' ha canoscenza,
quanto lo ciel de la terra è maggio.
A simil di natura ben non tarda.

XCII

Chi è questa che ven, ch'ogn'om la mira,
che fa tremar di chiaritate l'are
e mena seco Amor, sì che parlare
null' omo pote, ma ciascun sospira?

O Deo, che sembra quando il occhi gira,   5
dical' Amor, ch'i' nol savria contare:
cotanto d'umiltà donna mi pare,
ch'ogn'altra ver' di lei i' la chiam' ira.

Non si poria contar la sua piagenza,
ch'a le' s'inchin' ogni gentil vertute,   10
e la beltate per sua dea la mostra.

Non fu sì alta già la mente nostra
e non si pose 'n noi tanta salute,
che propriamente n'aviàn canoscenza.

XCIII

Perch'i' no spero di tornar giammai,
ballatetta, in Toscana,
va' tu, leggera e piana,
dritt' a la donna mia,
che per sua cortesia   5
ti farà molto onore.

Tu porterai novelle di sospiri
piene di dogli' e di molta paura;
ma guarda che persona non ti miri
che sia nemica di gentil natura: 10
ché certo per la mia disaventura

And she exceeds in noble insight anybody else by as much as the sky is greater than the earth. The good does not hold back from what is like it in nature.[16]

XCII

Who is she that comes[17] so that every man stares at her, and who makes the air shimmer with brightness, and who brings Love with her so that no man can speak but each of them is sighing?

Oh God, let Love describe what she looks like when she looks around, because I could not recount it. She seems to me to be a woman of modesty to such an extent that every other lady beside her I call anger.

Her pleasingness could not be described because every noble quality bows towards her, and beauty points to her as its goddess.

Never yet has our intellect been so elevated, nor have we so much grace in us that we can have a proper understanding of her.

XCIII

Because I do not hope[18] to return ever again to Tuscany, little song, you go lightly and gently straight to my lady who will show you great honour because of her graciousness.

You will carry news of sighs, full of sorrow and of great fear; but be careful that noone should see you who is hostile to a noble nature. For you would certainly be challenged, to my

tu saresti contesa,
tanto da lei ripresa
che mi sarebbe angoscia;
dopo la morte, poscia,   15
pianto e novel dolore.

    Tu senti, ballatetta, che la morte
mi stringe sì, che vita m'abbandona;
    e senti come 'l cor si sbatte forte
per quel che ciascun spirito ragiona.   20
    Tanto è distrutta già la mia persona,
ch'i' non posso soffrire:
se tu mi vuoi servire,
mena l'anima teco
(molto di ciò ti preco)   25
quando uscirà del core.

    Deh, ballatetta mia, a la tu' amistate
quest'anima che trema raccomando:
    menala teco, nella sua pietate,
a quella bella donna a cu'ti mando.   30
    Deh, ballatetta, dille sospirando,
quando le se' presente:
'Questa vostra servente
vien per istar con voi,
partita da colui   35
che fu servo d'Amore'.

    Tu, voce sbigottita e deboletta
ch'esci piangendo de lo cor dolente,
    coll'anima e con questa ballatetta
va' ragionando della strutta mente.   40
    Voi troverete una donna piacente,
di sì dolce intelletto
che vi sarà diletto
starle davanti ognora.
Anim', e tu l'adora   45
sempre, nel su'valore.

misfortune, and reprimanded by her in a way that would be torture to me: then, after death, tears and fresh sorrow!

You know, little song, that death wrings me so that the life is leaving me; and you feel how my heart is battered fiercely by what every spirit in me says. Already so much of me is destroyed that I cannot bear more. If you want to be of use to me, take my soul with you when it leaves my heart: deeply I implore this of you.

Ah, little song, to your friendship I commit this trembling soul. Take it, in its anguish, with you to the beautiful lady to whom I am sending you. Ah, little song, sighing tell her when you are in her presence, 'This, your servant, comes to stay with you, divided from him who was Love's servant.'

You, dismayed and feeble voice that comes out in tears from the sorrowing heart, go with the soul and with this little song, describing my emaciated mind. You will find a gracious woman of such a sweet understanding that it will be bliss for you to stay by her always. And soul, adore her in her worthiness for ever!

XCIV

Donna me prega, – per ch'eo voglio dire
d'un accidente – che sovente – è fero
ed è sì altero – ch'è chiamato amore:
   sì chi lo nega – possa 'l ver sentire!
Ed a presente – conoscente – chero,   5
perch' io no spero – ch'om di basso core
   a tal ragione porti canoscenza:
ché senza – natural dimostramento
non ho talento – di voler provare
là dove posa, e chi lo fa creare,   10
   e qual sia sua vertute e sua potenza,
l'essenza – poi e ciascun suo movimento,
e 'l piacimento – che 'l fa dire amare,
e s'omo per veder lo pò mostrare.

   In quella parte – dove sta memora   15
prende suo stato, – sì formato, – come
diaffan da lume, – d'una scuritate
   la qual da Marte – vène, e fa demora;
elli è creato – ed ha sensato – nome,
d'alma costume – e di cor volontate.   20
   Vèn da veduta forma che s'intende,
che prende – nel possibile intelletto,
come in subietto, – loco e dimoranza.
In quella parte mai non ha possanza
   perché da qualitate non descende: 25
resplende – in sé perpetüal effetto;
non ha diletto – ma consideranza;
sì che non pote largir simiglianza.

   Non è vertute, – ma da quella véne
ch'è perfezione – (ché si pone – tale),   30
non razionale, – ma che sente, dico;
   for di salute – giudicar mantene,
ché la 'ntenzione – per ragione – vale:

XCIV

A lady has asked me,[19] so I assent, to speak about a certain quality which often is inhuman and is so overbearing that is called love. Even he who denies it can feel the truth. And for the present I address an initiate in it, because I do not hope that a man of base heart can bear knowledge in such reasoning. So, without demonstration by the laws of Physics,[20] I have not the inclination to desire to show where it dwells, and who creates it, and what its natural worth and force may be, its essential nature and again each motion started by it, and its satisfaction: what it means to love, and if man can demonstrate that it is visible.

In that region where memory is, it takes its residence, given being in the same way that a transparent thing comes from light, cast by the dark shadow of Mars, and then exists. It is created and has a real name, with a form from the soul and a will of the heart. It proceeds from a seen form which becomes intelligible and takes its place and dwelling in the possible intellect, as in its subject.[21] In that place it can never be in act because it does not derive from a quality, but in itself it reflects the eternal impression. It takes no joy itself, but is thought, so that it cannot produce an image itself.

It is not a faculty,[22] but proceeds from that which is its perfecting and so defines it: not the rational but the senstive faculty. It makes judgment outside what is reliable because its resolve triumphs over reason; it discriminates badly, in which discerne male – in cui è vizio amico.

Di sua potenza segue spesso morte,   35
se forte – la vertù fosse impedita,
la quale aita – la contraria via:
non perché oppost' a naturale sia;
    ma quanto che da buon perfetto tort'è
per sorte, – non pò dire om ch'aggia vita,   40
ché stabilita – non ha segnoria.
A simil pò valer quand' on l'oblia.

L'essere è quando – lo voler è tanto
ch'oltra misura – di natura – torna,
poi non s'adorna – di riposo mai.   45
    Move, cangiando – color, riso in pianto,
e la figura – con paura – storna;
poco soggiorna; – ancor di lui vedrai
    che 'n gente di valor lo più si trova.
La nova – qualità move sospiri,   50
e vol ch'om miri – 'n non formato loco,
destandos' ira la qual manda foco
    (imaginar nol pote om che nol prova),
né mova – già però ch'a lui si tiri,
e non si giri – per trovarvi gioco: 55
né cert' ha mente gran saver né poco.

De simil tragge – complessione sguardo
che fa parere – lo piacere – certo:
non pò coverto – star, quand' è sì giunto.
    Non già selvagge – le bieltà son dardo,   60
chè tal volere – per temere – è sperto:
consiegue merto – spirito ch'è punto.
    E non si pò conoscer per lo viso:
compriso – bianco in tale obietto cade;
e, chi ben aude, – forma non si vede: 65
dunqu' elli meno, che da lei procede.
    For di colore, d'essere diviso,

way it is a friendly evil. From its influence death follows often, if its action is ever blocked – that action that helps the opposite of death.[23] This is not because it is opposed to what is natural but because a man, in as much as he is by some chance turned aside from his proper fulfilment, cannot be said to possess his life when he has no control over his security. When a man forgets it, it has the same effect.

The essence of love[24] is when the will is so great that it responds past all natural measure, and then never avails of any rest. It acts by changing colour, changing smile to tears, and out of fear it distorts the appearance of its object; it does not stay long; also you will see of it that among people of worth it is most to be found. That new quality prompts sighs, and it desires a man to stare into the shapeless distance, rousing a passion that sends out fire (a man who has not experienced it cannot imagine it), and he does not move because already he is drawn to it, and he does not turn aside to find relief. Neither does his mind have great knowledge or little.

From a similar temperament[25] to its own it draws a look which makes its fulfilment seem certain. When it is united thus, it cannot be hidden. Its beauties are not indeed a spear for the shy backwoodsmen, because such desire is banished by fear. Reward will follow the spirit pierced by it. And it cannot be seen in the face, in the way that the whiteness it has inheres in such an object.[26] And, to the person who understands this well, it is not seen as a form. Therefore that which follows it leads it. Empty of colour, of divided essence, set in deep obscurity, it

assiso – 'n mezzo scuro, luce rade.
For d'ogne fraude – dico, degno in fede,
che solo di costui nasce mercede.   70

    Tu puoi sicuramente gir, canzone,
là 've ti piace, ch'io t'ho sì adornata
ch'assai laudata – sarà tua ragione
da le persone – c'hanno intendimento:
di star con l'altre tu non hai talento.   75

XCV

Pegli occhi fere un spirito sottile,
che fa 'n la mente spirito destare,
dal qual si move spirito d'amare,
ch'ogn'altro spiritel[lo] fa gentile.

Sentir non pò di lu' spirito vile,   5
di cotanta vertù spirito appare:
quest' è lo spiritel che fa tremare,
lo spiritel che fa la donna umìle.

E poi da questo spirito si move
un altro dolce spirito soave,   10
che sieg[u]e un spiritello di mercede:

lo quale spiritel spiriti piove,
ché di ciascuno spirit' ha la chiave,
per forza d'uno spirito che 'l vede.

erases light. Empty of all deceit, I say, made worthy by my faith, that reward comes from it alone.

You can go confidently, my song, wherever you want, for I have dressed you up in such a way that your message will be greatly praised by people of understanding. You have no wish to stand amongst the others.

XCV

A fine spirit[27] strikes through the eyes, and it causes a spirit to kindle in the mind by which a spirit of love is roused so that every other spirit becomes noble.

With that it is not possible to have any sense of a base spirit, of such worth does that spirit seem. This is that small spirit that causes trembling, the spirit that makes the lady modest.

And then from this spirit there arises another sweet, gentle spirit which a spirit of mercy follows:

that spirit then rains spirits, because it has the key of every spirit, through the power of a spirit which it sees.

DANTE ALIGHIERI
(1265–1321)

XCVI

'Siede la terra dove nata fui
  su la marina dove 'l Po discende
  per aver pace co' seguaci sui.

Amor, ch' al cor gentil ratto s' apprende,   100
  prese costui de la bella persona
  che mi fu tolta; e 'l modo ancor m' offende.

Amor, ch' a amato amar perdona,
  mi prese del costui piacer sí forte,
  che, come vedi, ancor non m' abbandona.   105

Amor condusse noi ad una morte:
  Caina attende chi a vita ci spense.'
  Queste parole da lor ci fur porte.

Quand' io intesi quell' anime offense,
  chinai 'l viso, e tanto il tenni basso,   110
  fin che 'l poeta mi disse: 'Che pense?'

Quando rispuosi, cominciai: 'Oh lasso,
  quanti dolci pensier, quanto disío
  menò costoro al doloroso passo!'

Poi mi rivolsi a loro e parla' io,   115
  e comminciai: 'Francesca, i tuoi martíri
  a lacrimar mi fanno tristo e pio.

Ma dimmi: al tempo de' dolci sospiri,
  a che e come concedette amore
  che conosceste i dubbiosi desiri?'   120

E quella a me: 'Nessun maggier dolore
  che ricordarsi del tempo felice
  ne la miseria; e ciò sa 'l tuo dottore.

Ma s' a conoscer la prima radice
  del nostro amor tu hai cotanto affetto,   125
  farò come colui che piange e dice.

Noi leggevamo un giorno per diletto

XCVI

'The place where I[28] was born lies on the coast where the Po with its tributaries flows down to have its rest. Love, which is soon felt in the noble heart,[29] took hold of him, towards that beautiful body which was taken from me at death. And I still regret the manner of it.[30] Love, which does not allow anyone who is loved not to love in return, so strongly enamoured me of him that, as you can see, it still has not left me. Love led us to a single death; Caina[31] is waiting for the man who banished us from life.' These words were borne to us from them. When I had heard these injured souls, I lowered my face and kept it so low that in the end the poet said to me 'What are you thinking?' When I replied, I began: 'Alas, how many sweet thoughts and how much yearning led those two to this sorrowful situation!' Then I turned back to them and spoke, beginning: 'Francesca, your sufferings make me weep, sorry and sympathetic. But tell me: at the time of the sweet sighs, by what means and how did love relent so that you recognised the affections which are in doubt?' And she said to me: 'There is no greater unhappiness than to recall a time of joy in misery;[32] and this your teacher there knows. But if you have such great eagerness to know of the first rooting of our love, I will act as one who weeps and tells.

One day, for pleasure, we were reading about Lancelot,[33]

di Lancialotto come amor lo strinse:
soli eravamo e sanza alcun sospetto
Per piú fiate li occhi ci sospinse   130
quella lettura, e scolorocci il viso;
ma solo un punto fu quel che ci vinse.
Quando leggemmo il disiato riso
esser baciato da cotanto amante,
questi, che mai da me non fia diviso,   135
la bocca mi baciò tutto tremante.
Galeotto fu il libro e chi lo scrisse:
quel giorno piú non vi leggemmo avante.'
Mentre che l' uno spirto questo disse,
l' altro piangea sí, che di pietade   140
io venni men cosí com' io morisse;
e caddi come corpo morto cade.
(*Inferno* V, 97–142)

XCVII
'Ma dì s' i' veggio qui colui che fore
trasse le nove rime, cominciando   50
'*Donne ch'avete intelletto d'amore*'.'
E io a lui: 'I' mi son un, che quando
Amor mi spira, noto, e a quel modo
ch'e' ditta dentro vo significando'
'O frate, issa vegg' io' diss'elli 'il nodo   55
che 'l Notaro e Guittone e me ritenne
di qua dal dolce stil novo ch' i' odo!
Io veggio ben come le vostre penne
di retro al dittator sen vanno strette,
che delle nostre certo non avvenne;   60
e qual più a riguardare oltre si mette,
non vede più dall'uno all'altro stilo';
e, quasi contentato, si tacette.
(*Purgatorio* XXIV, 49–63)

how love oppressed him. We were alone and without the least suspicion. Many times that reading moved our eyes to meet and changed our complexions. But one single point was the one that overcame us. When we read how the desired smile was kissed by so great a lover, this man (who will never be separated from me), all trembling, kissed my mouth. The book was a Pandar,[34] and whoever wrote it. That day we read no further from it.' While one spirit said this, the other wept so much that I collapsed out of pity, as if I had died; and I fell as a dead body falls.

XCVII

'But tell me,[35] do I see here the one who in the world outside composed the new lines, beginning 'Ladies who have a knowledge of love'?' And I said to him: 'I am one who, when love inspires me, register it, and proceed to set it out in the same form as he dictates within'. 'Oh brother', he said, 'now I understand the problem that restricted the Notary and Guittone and me from achieving the sweet new style that I hear now.[36] I understand well how your pens follow strictly behind love as he dictates, which certainly was not the case with ours. And whoever sets about looking further into the matter will not see any better what distinguishes one style from the other'. And he fell silent, as though contented.

XCVIII

Ed elli a me: 'Tu lasci tal vestigio,
    per quel ch' i' odo, in me e tanto chiaro,
    che Letè nol può torre nè far bigio.

Ma se le tue parole or ver giuraro,
    dimmi che è cagion per che dimostri   110
    nel dire e nel guardare avermi caro.'

E io a lui: 'Li dolci detti vostri,
    che, quanto durerà l'uso moderno,
    faranno cari ancora i loro incostri'.

'O frate,' disse, 'questi ch' io ti cerno   115
    col dito', e additò un spirto innanzi,
    'fu miglior fabbro del parlar materno.

Versi d'amore e prose di romanzi
    soverchiò tutti; e lascia dir li stolti
    che quel di Lemosì credon ch'avanzi.   120

A voce più ch'al ver drizzan li volti,
    e cosi ferman sua oppinīone
    prima ch'arte o ragion per lor s'ascolti.

Cosi fer molti antichi di Guittone,
    di grido in grido pur lui dando pregio,   125
    fin che l'ha vinto il ver con più persone.

Or se tu hai sì ampio privilegio,
    che licito ti sia l'andare al chiostro
    nel quale è Cristo abate del collegio,

falli per me un dir d'un paternostro,   130
    quanto bisogna a noi di questo mondo,
    dove poter peccar non è più nostro.'

Poi, forse per dar luogo altrui secondo
    che presso avea, disparve per lo foco,
    come per l'acqua il pesce andando al fondo.   135

Io mi feci al mostrato innanzi un poco,
    e dissi ch'al suo nome il mio disire
    apparecchiava grazioso loco.

El cominciò liberamente a dire:

XCVIII

And he[37] said to me: 'With what I hear, you are making so great and so clear an impression on me that Lethe cannot expunge it or cloud it. But, if your words now declared the truth, tell me what the reason is why you show in your speech and looking that you hold me in affection.' And I said to him: 'Your sweet poems which, as long as the modern style will prevail, will keep their very ink precious all the time'. 'Oh brother', he said, 'this man I am showing you with my finger' (and he pointed to a spirit in front of him) 'was a better craftsman of his native tongue. He surpassed everyone in verses of love and stories of romance: and let the fools who think the man from Limoges was better say so.[38] They turn their faces to reputation rather than to the truth, and so they establish their opinion before skill or reason is consulted by them. In the past many people did the same with Guittone, shout after shout giving him the crown, until finally the truth has triumphed with most people. Now, if you have the great privilege to be allowed to go to the sanctuary in which Christ is the abbot of the fraternity, say an 'Our father' for me in so far as we in this realm need it, where the capacity to sin is no longer ours.' Then, maybe to make room for someone behind him who was pushing, he disappeared in the flames, like a fish going through the water to the depths. I approached a little the one he had pointed out and said that my desire was making ready a welcoming place for his name. And freely he began to say[39] 'So

'Tan m'abellis vostre cortes deman,   140
   qu' ieu no me puesc ni voill a vos cobrire.
Ieu sui Arnaut, que plor e vau cantan;
   consiros vei la passada folor,
   e vei jausen lo joi qu'esper, denan.
Ara vos prec, per aquella valor   145
   que vos guida al som de l'escalina,
   sovenha vos a temps de ma dolor!'
Poi s'ascose nel foco che li affina.
(*Purgatorio* XXVI, 106–48)

XCIX

Donne ch'avete intelletto d'amore,
i' vo' con voi de la mia donna dire,
non perch'io creda sua laude finire,
ma ragionar per isfogar la mente.

   Io dico che pensando il suo valore,   5
Amor sì dolce mi si fa sentire,
che s'io allora non perdessi ardire,
farei parlando innamorar la gente.

   E io non vo' parlar sì altamente,
ch'io divenisse per temenza vile;   10
ma tratterò del suo stato gentile
a respetto di lei leggeramente,
donne e donzelle amorose, con vui,
ché non è cosa da parlarne altrui.

   Angelo clama in divino intelletto   15
e dice: 'Sire, nel mondo si vede
maraviglia ne l'atto che procede
d'un'anima che 'nfin qua su risplende.'

   Lo cielo, che non have altro difetto
che d'aver lei, al suo segnor la chiede,   20
e ciascun santo ne grida merzede.

much your courteous request pleases me that I am not able or anxious to hide my identity from you. I am Arnaut who weeps and goes along singing. In reflexion I see my past madness[40] and rejoicing I see in front of me the day that I hope for. Now I beg you, by that worth that leads you to the top of the stairway, remember sometimes my sorrow.' Then he hid himself in the fire that purifies them.

XCIX

Ladies who have a knowledge of love,[41] I want to speak to you about my lady, not because I believe that I can fulfil her praise so much as to expound in order to relieve my mind. I assert that, when I think of her worth, such sweet Love makes itself felt in me that, if I did not lose my daring then, by speaking I would make the whole race in love with her. And I am not going to speak with such ambition that I will become unnerved through fear at it. But I will speak of her noble nature too lightly for her qualities, to you, ladies and girls of love, for it is not a thing to speak to anyone else about.

An angel[42] calls out in the divine mind and says: 'Lord, there is visible on earth a marvel in act which emanates from a mind which shines out as far as this height.' The heaven, which has no other defect except to lack her, asks for her from its Lord, and everyone of the blessed cries to him for this reward. Pity

Sola Pietà nostra parte difende,
   che parla Dio, che id madonna intende:
'Dilett miei, or sofferite in pace
che vostra spene sia quanto me piace   25
là 'v'è alcun che perder lei s'attende,
e che dirà ne lo inferno: "O mal nati,
io vidi la speranza de' beati".'

   Madonna è disïata in sommo cielo:
or vòi di sua virtù farvi savere.   30
Dico, qual vuol gentil donna parere
vada con lei, che quando va per via,
   gitta nei cor villani Amore un gelo,
per che onne lor pensero agghiaccia e pere;
e qual soffrisse di starla a vedere   35
diverria nobil cosa, o si morria.
   E quando trova alcun che degno sia
di veder lei, quei prova sua vertute,
ché li avvien, ciò che li dona, in salute,
e sì l'umilia, ch'ogni offesa oblia.   40
Ancor l'ha Dio per maggior grazia dato
che non pò mal finir chi l'ha parlato.

   Dice di lei Amor: 'Cosa mortale
come esser pò sì adorna e sì pura?'
Poi la reguarda, e fra se stesso giura   45
che Dio ne 'ntenda di far cosa nova.
   Color di perle ha quasi, in forma quale
convene a donna aver, non for misura.
ella è quanto de ben pò far natura;
per essemplo di lei bieltà si prova.   50
   De li occhi suoi, come ch'ella li mova,
escono spirti d'amore inflammati,
che feron li occhi a qual che allor la guati,
e passan sì che 'l cor ciascun retrova:
voi le vedete Amor pinto nel viso,   55
là 've non pote alcun mirarla fiso.

alone takes our part, with the result that God, who is drawn towards my lady, says: 'My beloved ones, now accept peacefully that what you hope for should be, for as long as I wish it, in that place where there is someone[43] who is waiting to lose her, and who will say in the hell of her loss: 'Oh wretched people, I have seen the hope of the blessed'.'

My lady is desired in heaven on high. Now I want to make you feel her worth. I say that any lady who wants to appear noble should follow her, for when she goes along the way, Love casts a chill over mean hearts[44] so that every thought of theirs freezes and perishes. And whoever succeeded in standing his ground to look at her would turn into something noble, or else would die. And when she finds someone who might be worthy to look at her, he proves her worth, in that whatever she gives to him turns to his advantage, and makes him so humble that he forgets every indignity. Again, God has given her a larger grace so that nobody who has spoken to her can end badly.

Love says of her: 'How can something mortal be so excellent and pure?' Then he looks at her and swears to himself that God purposes to make a new phenomenon in her. Her colour has the quality of a pearl, in a way such as is fitting for a lady to have, not beyond measure. She contains as much of what is good as Nature can make. Beauty is tested with her as the paradigm. From her eyes, however she turns them, there issue forth spirits inflamed with love which strike the eyes of whoever may then be gazing at her and pass through so that each one finds a heart. You see Love depicted in her face, there where no one can gaze fixedly.

   Canzone, io so che tu girai parlando
a donne assai, quand'io t'avrò avanzata.
Or t'ammonisco, perch'io t'ho allevata
per figliuola d'Amor giovane e piana,   60
   che là 've giugni tu diche pregando:
'Insegnatemi gir, ch'io son mandata
a quella di cui laude so' adornata.'
E se non vuoli andar sì come vana,
   non restare ove sia gente villana: 65
ingegnati, se puoi, d'esser palese
solo con donne o con omo cortese,
che ti merranno là per via tostana.
Tu troverai Amor con esso lei;
raccomandami a lui come tu dei.   70

   C

Amore e 'l cor gentil sono una cosa,
sì come il saggio in suo dittare pone,
e così esser l'un sanza l'altro osa
com'alma razional sanza ragione.

Falli natura quand'è amorosa,   5
Amor per sire e 'l cor per sua magione,
dentro la qual dormendo si riposa
tal volta poca e tal lunga stagione.

Bieltate appare in saggia donna pui,
che piace a li occhi sì, che dentro al core   10
nasce un disio de la cosa piacente;

e tanto dura talora in costui,
che fa svegliar lo spirito d'Amore.
E simil face in donna omo valente.

Song, I know that you will go around talking to many ladies when I have sent you out. Now I urge you (because I have reared you as a young and unpretentious daughter of Love), that wherever you arrive you should say in petition: 'Teach me where to turn, because I am directed to her with whose praise I am embellished'. And if you do not wish to go to no purpose, do not stay where the people are ignoble.[45] Bring it about, if you can, that you are revealed only to courteous ladies and men who will direct you by a quick way. You will find Love with the lady herself; commend me to him as you should.

C

Love and the noble heart are the same thing,[46] as the wise man posits in his writing; and the one can exist without the other only as the rational soul without reason.

Nature makes them when it is amorous, with Love as the lord and the heart as his habitation within which he rests in sleep,[47] sometimes for a little while and sometimes for a long period.

Then there appears in a wise woman beauty that pleases the eyes so that a desire for the attractive thing takes root within the heart.

And sometimes it endures in the heart long enough to awaken the spirit of Love. And a worthy man achieves the same reaction in a woman.

CI

Al poco giorno e al gran cerchio d'ombra
son giunto, lasso, ed al bianchir de' colli,
quando si perde lo color ne l'erba:
e 'l mio disio però non cangia il verde,
sì è barbato ne la dura petra   5
che parla e sente come fosse donna.

Similemente questa nova donna
si sta gelata come neve a l'ombra;
chè non la move, se non come petra,
il dolce tempo che riscalda i colli,   10
e che li fa tornar di bianco in verde
perché li copre di fioretti e d'erba.

Quand'ella ha in testa una ghirlanda d'erba,
trae de la mente nostra ogn'altra donna;
perché si mischia il crespo giallo e 'l verde   15
sì bel, ch'Amor li viene a stare a l'ombra,
che m'ha serrato intra piccioli colli
più forte assai che la calcina petra.

La sua bellezza ha più vertù che petra,
e 'l colpo suo non può sanar per erba;   20
ch'io son fuggito per piani e per colli,
per potere scampar da cotal donna;
e dal suo lume non mi può far ombia
poggio né muro mai né fronda verde.

Io l'ho veduta già vestita a verde,   25
sì fatta ch'ella avrebbe messo in petra
l'amor ch'io porto pur a la sua ombra:
ond'io l'ho chesta in un bel prato d'erba,
innamorata com'anco fu donna,
e chiuso intorno d'altissimi colli.   30

CI

To the short day[48] and to the large ring of shadow I have arrived, alas!, and to the whitening of the hills when the colour is lost by the grass. And still my desire does not change its greenness, so well-rooted is it in the hard rock that speaks and feels as if it were a woman.

Likewise, this young lady stands frozen like snow in shadow, so that the sweet season moves her no more than if she were rock – the season that warms the hills anew and makes them turn from white to green because it covers them with flowers and grass.

When she has on her head a garland of grass, she eradicates from our mind every other woman, because the yellow curl and the green assort so beautifully that Love comes there to dwell in the shade: he who has imprisoned me among small hills much more securely than its mortar binds the rock.

Her beauty has more force than rock, and her blow cannot be cured by herbs. So I have fled through plains and hills to be able to escape from such a woman. And neither hill nor wall nor green grass can ever make for me shade from her light.

Once I saw her dressed in green, in such a form that she would have given to stone the love that I bear for her very shadow. And I have longed for her in a beautiful meadow of grass, closed round by highest hills, as deeply in love as any woman ever was.

Ma ben ritorneranno i fiumi a' colli,
prima che questo legno molle e verde
s'infiammi, come suol far bella donna,
di me; che mi torrei dormire in petra
tutto il mio tempo e gir pascendo l'erba,   35
sol per veder do' suoi panni fanno ombra.

Quandunque i colli fanno più nera ombra,
sotto un bel verde la giovane donna
la fa sparer, com'uom petra sott'erba.

CII

Amor che ne la mente mi ragiona
de la mia donna disïosamente,
move cose di lei meco sovente,
che lo 'ntelletto sovr'esse disvia.
   Lo suo parlar sì dolcemente sona,   5
che l'anima ch'ascolta e che lo sente
dice: 'Oh me lassa, ch'io non son possente
di dir quel ch'odo de la donna mia!'
   E certo e'mi conven lasciare in pria,
s'io vo' trattar di quel ch'odo di lei,   10
ciò che lo mio intelletto non comprende;
e di quel che s'intende
gran parte, perché dirlo non savrei.
Però, se le mie rime avran difetto
ch'entreran ne la loda di costei,   15
di ciò si biasmi il debole intelletto
e 'l parlar nostro, che non ha valore
di ritrar tutto ciò che dice Amore.

   Non vede il sol, che tutto 'l mondo gira,
cosa tanto gentil, quanto in quell'ora   20
che luce ne la parte ove dimora
la donna, di cui dire Amor mi face.
   Ogni Intelletto di là su la mira,

But certainly the rivers will go back to the hills before this damp and green wood catches fire, as beautiful woman is wont to do for me. I would bring myself to sleep on the rock all my life, and go around feeding on grass, just to see where her clothes make a shadow.

Whenever the hills make the darkest shadow the young woman makes it disappear under a beautiful green, as rock is under the grass.

CII

Love, which speaks devotedly of my lady in my mind,[49] often puts to me such things about her that my understanding is set astray under them. His speaking sounds so sweet that the soul which listens and hears him says: 'Oh alas, that I am not able to put in words what I hear about my lady!' And indeed, if I want to recount what I hear about her, first it is necessary for me to abandon what my understanding does not encompass, as well as a considerable part of what it does grasp because I would not know how to say it. So, if my poems which venture on her praise have a deficiency, let the blame for that fall on a weak understanding and on our ability to speak which does not have the strength to recount everything that Love says.

The sun which travels around the whole world sees nothing as noble as in the hour when it shines on the region where that lady lives of whom Love forces me to speak. Every intelligence

e quella gente che qui s'innamora
ne' lor pensieri la truovano ancora,   25
quando Amor fa sentir de la sua pace.
    Suo esser tanto a Quei che lel dà piace,
che 'nfonde sempre in lei la sua vertute
oltre 'l dimando di nostra natura.
La sua anima pura,   30
che riceve da lui questa salute,
lo manifesta in quel ch'ella conduce:
ché 'n suc bellezze son cose vedute
che li occhi di color dov'ella luce
ne mandan messi al cor pien di desiri,   35
che prendon aire e diventan sospiri.

    In lei discende la virtù divina
sì come face in angelo che 'l vede;
e qual donna gentil questo non crede,
vada con lei e miri li atti sui.   40
    Quivi dov'ella parla, si dichina
un spirito da ciel, che reca fede
come l'alto valor ch'ella possiede
è oltre quel che si conviene a nui.
    Li atti soavi ch'ella mostra altrui   45
vanno chiamando Amor ciascuno a prova
in quella voce che lo fa sentire.
Di costei si può dire:
gentile è in donna ciò che in lei si trova,
e bello è tanto quanto lei simiglia.   50
E puossi dir che 'l suo aspetto giova
a consentir ciò che par maraviglia;
onde la nostra fede è aiutata:
però fu tal da etterno ordinata.

    Cose appariscon ne lo suo aspetto   55
che mostran de' piacer di Paradiso,
dico ne li occhi e nel suo dolce riso,

from above gazes upon her, and those people who are in love in this world find her always in their thoughts, when Love makes them feel his peace. Her existence pleases so much Him who gives it to her that he always inundates her with his power beyond the requirement of our nature. Her pure soul, which receives this grace from him, manifests that origin in whatever she controls; because in her charms are seen such things that the eyes of those on whom she shines send to the heart messages about them, full of desire, which take breath and turn into sighs.

The divine power descends upon her as it does on to an angel that sees it. And whatever noble lady does not believe this, let her attend her and regard her actions. Wherever she speaks, a spirit descends from the sky to announce as an article of faith that the high virtue she possesses is beyond what is appropriate for human kind. The acts of grace that she performs towards others go calling Love, each of them, in evidence in a voice that he cannot fail to hear. It can be said of her that nobility is in a woman that which is found in her, and a woman is beautiful in as much as she resembles her. And it can be said that her appearance avails to gain consent for that which seems a miracle. By that our faith is helped, and for this reason she was pre-ordained from eternity.

Things are evident in her appearance that show the delights of Paradise; I mean in her eyes and her sweet smile, for Love

che le vi reca Amor com'a suo loco.
    Elle soverchian lo nostro intelletto,
come raggio di sole un frale viso: 60
e perch'io non le posso mirar fiso,
mi conven contentar di dirne poco.
    Sua bieltà piove fiammelle di foco,
animate d'un spirito gentile
ch'è creatore d'ogni pensier bono;   65
e rompon come trono
l'innati vizii che fanno altrui vile.
Però qual donna sente sua bieltate
biasmar per non parer queta e umile,
miri costei ch'è essemplo d'umiltate!   70
Questa è colei ch'umilia ogni perverso:
costei pensò chi mosse l'universo.

    Canzone, e'par che tu parli contraro
al dir d'una sorella che tu hai;
ché questa donna, che tanto umil fai,   75
ella la chiama fera e disdegnosa.
    Tu sai che 'l ciel sempr'è lucente e chiaro,
e quanto in sé non si turba già mai;
ma li nostri occhi per cagioni assai
chiaman la stella talor tenebrosa.   80
    Così, quand'ella la chiama orgogliosa,
non considera lei secondo il vero,
ma pur secondo quel ch'a lei parea:
ché l'anima temea,
e teme ancora, sì che mi par fero   85
quantunqu'io veggio là 'v'ella mi senta.
Così ti scusa, se ti fa mestero;
e quando pòi, a lei ti rappresenta:
dirai: 'Madonna, s'ello v'è a grato,
io parlerò di voi in ciascun lato.'   90

leads them there as his own place. They surpass our understanding, as the ray of sun defeats weak sight.[50] And since I am not able to stare fixedly on them, I must be satisfied with saying little of them. Her beauty pours down flames of fire, vivified by a noble spirit which is the instigator of every good thought. And they smash like a thunderbolt the inborn evils that make someone base. So whatever woman feels her beauty to be culpable in not seeming peaceful and modest, let her look at this lady who is the model of humility. She is the one who restores to modesty every aberration: he who put the universe in motion thought of her.

My song, it seems that you are speaking in contradiction of one of your sisters,[51] because this lady, whom you make so humble, she calls fierce and disdainful. You know that the sky is always bright and clear and how it is never overcast by itself; but our eyes for many reasons sometimes declare that the star is darkened. So, when your sister calls her proud, she does not regard her according to the truth, but only according to how she seemed to her. My soul was afraid (and it still is) so that whatever I see where she looks upon me seems to me to be fearsome. Excuse yourself in this way, if you need to; and when you can, present yourself to her. You will say: 'My lady, if this pleases you, I will speak of you on every side'.

CINO DA PISTOIA
(1270–1336/7)[52]

CIII

Poi ch'i' fu', Dante, dal mio natal sito
fatto per greve essilio pellegrino
e lontanato dal piacer piu fino
che mai formasse il Piacer infinito,

io son piangendo per lo mondo gito   5
sdegnato del morir come meschino;
e s'ho trovato a lui simil vicino,
dett'ho che questi m'ha lo cor ferito.

Ne de le prime braccia dispietate,
onde 'l fermato disperar m'assolve,   10
son mosso perch' aiuto non aspetti;

ch'un piacer sempre me lega ed involve,
il qual conven che a simil di beltate
in molte donne sparte mi diletti.

ONESTO DA BOLOGNA
(*c.* 1240–1301/3)[54]

CIV   *A Messer Cino da Pistoia*

Mente ed umíle e piò de mille sporte
   piene de spirti e 'l vostro ondar sognando
   me fan considerar che d'altra sorte
   no se po' trar raxon de vo', rimando.
No so chi 'l ve fa fare, o vita o morte,   5
   che per lo vostro çir filosofando
   avete stanco qualunqu' è piò forte
   ch'ode vostro bel dire imaginando.
Ed ancor pare a zaschun molto grave
   vostro parlare in terzo con altrui   10
   e 'n quarto raxonando cum vo' stessi.
Ver quel de l'omo ogne pondo è soave;
   canzar dunqua manera fa per vui,
   se no ch'e' porò dir: 'Ben sete bessi'.

CIII

Since, Dante, I was made a pilgrim[53] away from my birthplace by grievous exile, and distanced from the finest delight that the infinite Delight ever gave form to,

I have wandered grieving around the world, scorned as a nobody even by death. And if I have come across a delight near me that was like that one, I have said that it was the new one that pierced my heart.

Not that I have moved from the first merciless arms from which my strongly-rooted despair frees me, because I am not looking for help;

But it is the same delight that always binds and holds me, and it is inevitable that I will rejoice at a reminder of her beauty in many various women.

CIV   *To Cino da Pistoia*

'Mind' and 'humble' and over a thousand baskets full of spirits, and your sleepwalking make me feel that it is not possible in any way to drag sense out of you when you are writing poetry. I don't know what it is, love or death, that makes you tire out with your philosophical mien even the strongest listener to your lovely and fanciful composing. Another thing: everyone finds very tedious your talking to someone else in a threesome and in a quartet with yourself. The truth is that every other human burden is relatively light, compared with singing in the way you do: except, of course, that one can say 'You are great fools'.

NOTES

1 Though the term was apparently invented by the late Provençal troubadour Montanhagol, according to Boase (*Origin and Meaning*, p. 33).

2 It also becomes a *psychomachia* in Guillaume de Lorris, of course.

3 For a very coherent exposition of this process, see M. Valency, *In Praise of Love*, chapter 8, 'The New Style'.

4 T. A. Kirby, *Chaucer's Troilus*, p. 82, compares Cavalcanti with Donne and Eliot, adding that 'the comparison is not entirely accurate since Cavalcanti is so much superior to both in poetry as well as philosophy'.

5 Guido Guinicelli (*c.* 1230–*c.* 1276) of the Principi family of Bologna is regarded as the founder of the poetic school of the *dolce stil nuovo*, said by Oderisi in *Purgatorio* XI, 97–8 to have been surpassed by Guido Cavalcanti, and met by Dante in *Purgatorio* XXVI. *Al cor gentil* is Guinicelli's most celebrated poem and, along with Cavalcanti's *Donna me prega* (XCIV here) and Dante's *Donne ch'avete intelletto d'amore* (XCIX here), the most copied and commented upon of the stilnovisti poems. The qualities of the noble heart Guinicelli inherits from the troubadours, and observations on it are found everywhere in late medieval literature (Boccaccio, Petrarch and Chaucer's repeated 'Pittee renneth soone in gentil herte'). The poems by Guinicelli and Cavalcanti here are taken, with kind permission, from *Poeti del Duecento*, a cura di G. Contini (Ricciardi, Milano–Napoli, 1960), Tom. 2.

6 The inevitability of the movement of love into the noble heart is the principal theme of all the imagery of the poem; *nature* itself causes this movement.

7 This stanza combines the teaching of Lapidaries, that the quality of precious stone came to it from its own particular star, with the Aristotelian doctrine (transmitted through Averroes and Aquinas principally) of act and potency. See W. D. Ross, *Aristotle* (2nd ed., London 1930), pp. 176–8. As the sun refines the stone, nature refines the heart, making it noble (*gentil*) and in potency to receive the activity of love from the lady who is its star. The procedure is typical of the allying of courtly-love imagery with philosophy by these poets. But compare the imagery in Ibn Hazm (XXXIII here).

8 *Ragion*, as in the history of the word 'reason' in English, means both 'the power of Reason' and 'explanation'. The flame on the taper is a particularly apt simile, since it seems to be escaping from it and rising above it while at the same time depending on it for its existence, just as rational love is prompted initially by the observation of the material lady in the sensitive soul. Like the *Minnesängers' rede*, the poetic use of the word is descended from the *razo* in Provençal.

9   The champions of the noble heart, from the troubadours onwards, constantly stressed the fact that this nobility was not to be assumed in those who were noble by birth. See Valency, *In Praise of Love*, chapter 2, 'The Knights'.

10 The intelligences of the heavens bring to pass the will of God by perceiving him, since this mediacy is the *raison d'être* of their nature; likewise, as soon as the lady is seen by the eyes, the desire of the heart is fulfilled. Although their sense is clear, the syntax of lines 45–50 is difficult, and translation is necessarily rather loose.

11 The love of the lady in the sensitive soul ought to have led to an apprehension of the idea of love in the rational soul whose only fit object is God. Guinicelli, for the purposes of his amatory poem, is ignoring the implications of the philosophical structure he is drawing on, to say that the lady (the angelic intelligence which acted as the stimulus to his love) was so suggestive of the divine that it was no shame for the idea of love to take her as its object. The ending is a sophistry, for poetic affect. The classic exposition of the doctrine of 'angelicisation' is C. S. Singleton's *An Essay on the Vita Nuora*, Harvard University Press 1949). Cf. 'deification' in Kirby's *Chaucer's Troilus*, pp. 76ff.

12 Although the sonnet was already the commonest form among the stilnovisti in Guinicelli's time, it was still new, first attested in, and perhaps invented by, 'the Notary' (*Purgatorio* XXIV, 56: XCVII here), Iacopo da Lentino of the Sicilian school of the first half of the thirteenth century.

13 Battering by thunder and wind is a favourite image in Guinicelli.

14 These lines are a concise statement of the physiological circumstances that gave rise to the lover's condition, according to the troubadours and stilnovisti. See G. Holmes, *Dante* ('Past Master' Series, Oxford University Press 1980), p. 8.

15 Guido Cavalcanti (*c.* 1255–1300) of Florence, the son of Cavalcante Cavalcanti (see *Inferno* X), is the most difficult and philosophical of the poets of the new style, as Boccaccio's description of him in the ninth story of the sixth day of *Decameron* suggests: he was 'one of the greatest logicians in the world and the best natural philosopher' and he surpassed all other men in everything 'appropriate to a noble man (*gentile*)'. He is the Guido who is said by the miniaturist Oderisi to have supplanted Guinicelli in the glory of literature (*Purgatorio* XI, 97–8). The *Vita Nuova* is dedicated to him, and he is referred to there as Dante's first friend. There are several references to him in the *Divina Commedia*, though he does not appear there. He is said to have held Virgil in disdain (*Inferno* X, 63), implying perhaps a preference for philosophy to poetry.

16 This rather dry statement of the philosophical basis of this elegant poem is a reminder of the intellectual framework of Cavalcanti's

writing.

17   An echo of the opening of the Marian *magnificat*, taken from the Song of Songs VI, 10: 'Who is she that cometh forth as the morning rising, fair as the moon, bright as the sun, terrible as an army set in array?' (Douay version). The association of the beloved lady with grace (*salute*, line 13), the Blessed Virgin and God is evident here, as in the Marian liturgy and associations in the medieval secular lyric. For *salute*, see C. S. Singleton, *op. cit.*, pp. 4ff.

18   Though the occasion of this famous poem is no longer thought to have been a literal exile from Tuscany in the course of which the poet contracted a mortal illness, it is nevertheless one of Cavalcanti's least remote poems. Cf. opening of T. S. Eliot's *Ash Wednesday*. The address to the song is a familiar device, from the troubadours onwards.

19   Cavalcanti's most famous poem, generally thought to be the most intellectually demanding of all medieval love poems. If its length and difficulty do not immediately commend themselves to the reader of lyric love poetry, it is nevertheless of great importance as one of the culminating points of the rarefied examination of love from the point of view of philosophy – a process extending back to Andreas, the troubadours and the Arabs. It must be emphasised that, although the existence and nature of love are argued in the same way as those of God in Thomist theology, the subject of the poem is strictly love itself, presented as a negative passion (at least up to line 56) and hence less identifiable with love of God than is usual in the courtly poets. The poem belongs to the tradition of love definitions, evidenced elsewhere in this book in *The Dove's Neck-Ring* (XXXII here) and Andreas (XIV here). Love is defined as an 'accidente', that is an aspect of something else and not a substantial thing in its own right. See W. D. Ross, *op. cit.*, p. 45.

20   I.e. 'I shall demonstrate these things by arguments drawn from Natural Philosophy, not from Moral Philosophy'. For Cavalcanti as natural philospher, see quotation from *Decameron* in note 15 above. The poem goes on to consider love under each of the headings of lines 10–14: 'where it dwells', lines 15ff; 'who creates it', 29–31; 'what its natural worth and force may be', 32–42; 'its essential nature', 43–5; 'each motion started by it, and its satisfaction', 46ff.; 'what it means to love', 50–62; and whether or not it is visible, 63–70.

21   For this technical use of the terms of Aristotelian philosophy, such as 'subject', see the Introduction to this section, p. 259, and Ross, pp. 148–53. There has been much argument about the subject of 'non ha' in line 24, which can be either 'Amore' or 'veduta forma'. If the 'seen form' is the subject, the lines must mean that the beloved object (such as the lady) is taken in by the beholder to the possible intellect but can only reflect the divine plan there. This clearly falls short of the

'angelicisation'/'deification' of the lady. If 'Love' is the subject, the sentence is a restatement of the accidental, inactive nature of Love. The former is perhaps to be preferred; the view of love in the poem as a whole might suggest an explicit denial to love of grace-giving, godlike qualities.

22 Turning to the question raised in line 11, Love is said to be not itself a faculty of the soul but to be only an aspect of the lower, sensitive (as opposed to the rational) faculty. This further reductive assertion could confine love to a sensation experienced by animals as well as men, as something sexual, not rational. Cf. Ross, pp. 129–30.

23 The paradox of love is that, although its objective is the extension of life by generation, in man it often achieves the opposite, death in the soul, because it does not conduce to his proper, i.e. rational, fulfilment. These contradictory views of love are a major concern of Cavalcanti's older contemporary, Jean de Meun, in the views presented by the god of love, Nature, Reason and La Vielle in the continuation of *Le Roman de la Rose*.

24 In defining the essence of love (as required in line 12), Cavalcanti lists the qualities of the courtly lover familiar from Chrétien's *Lancelot* and the troubadours: love causes paleness, sighs and abstraction; it is ephemeral and found among people of worth.

25 *Similis simili gaudet*, etc. For the application of this proverbial wisdom to love, cf. note 14 to the Georgian–Arabic section here (*The Dove's Neck-Ring*, Nykl, p. 7). Another traditional Latin proverb, *similia similibus curantur*, the basis of homoeopathic medicine, applies very aptly to the description of love as ill-health, only curable by the beloved, amongst the Arabs and the courtly writers.

26 This assertion of the whiteness of its subject has been said to be in contradiction with 'for di colore' in line 67. One solution has been to interpret these lines: 'love is not itself visible in the face in the way that paleness is'. But the paradox is not surprising in view of the very raising of the question whether love is visible. Compare the parallel paradox in line 65, 'forma non si vede' in the light of line 21, 'veduta forma'. Contini (*op. cit.*, Tom. II, p. 528) contrasts the definition of Andreas (see XIV here).

27 This poem is a parody of the rarefied spirits that are aroused in the lover by love, eloquently taking the terminological refinements of Cavalcanti's school to a logical absurdity. Cf. CIV here by Onesto.

28 The text of the passage from *Inferno* is taken, with kind permission, from the edition of S. A. Barbi (Firenze 1921). Shortly after Dante and Virgil have seen Tristan (V, 67), amongst those damned for love they meet Francesca, the daughter of Guido da Polenta, and her lover Paolo, the younger brother of her deformed husband Gianciotto Malatesta of Rimini (*c.* 1275). Gianciotto discovered the lovers together and stabbed them to death.

29   Cf. LXXXIX here, 'Al cor gentil' and the note to it (5 above).

30   According to some versions of the story, Francesca was married to the deformed Gianciotto by a ruse through which Paolo was shown to her in her husband's place. Hence, perhaps, 'the manner of it' here.

31   Caina was the area of *Inferno* to which those who had killed a relative were assigned. See Canto XXXII. It is, of course, named after Cain, the first killer of the kind.

32   Boethius, *De Consolatione Philosophiae* II, Prosa IV, 4. Virgil is said to know the truth of this in particular, perhaps, because after a lifetime of poetic distinction he is confined to Limbo in the afterlife (line 123).

33   Dante's familiarity with Arthurian romance is shown in *De Vulgari Eloquentia* I, x, 12–20, and Lancelot is referred to in the *Convivio* IV, xxviii, 8. Paget Toynbee (*A Dictionary of Proper Names and Notable Matters in the Works of Dante*, revised C. S. Singleton, Oxford University Press 1968, p. 380) suggests that Dante probably knew the story of the amours of Lancelot and Guinevere either from Chrétien or from the thirteenth-century prose *Lancelot*. It is more likely to be the latter, since Gallehault does not bring the lovers together in Chrétien. See line 137 below.

34   See previous note.

35   The texts of the excerpts from *Purgatorio* are taken, with kind permission, from the edition of G. Vandelli (Milano 1968). The speaker in the first passage is Bonagiunta da Lucca, encountered amongst the gluttons in the sixth circle of *Purgatorio*. Bonagiunta is mentioned in *De Vulgari Eloquentia* I, xiii and he is known to have been still living in 1296. He was one of the transmitters of the Sicilian school of poetry to the Tuscans.

36   The stilnovisti take their title from this line; but see note 1 above.

37   The speaker is Guido Guinicelli, encountered amongst the lustful in the seventh circle of *Purgatorio*. See note 5 above.

38   The better craftsman indicated is Arnaut Daniel, and 'he of Limoges' is thought to be Guiraut de Borneil. For both, see Provençal section here. These lines should not be taken to show lack of admiration for Guiraut in Dante; the references to him in *De Vulgari Eloquentia* attest the contrary. See n. 35 in the Provençal section.

39   Dante's ability to write Provençal poetry was a common accomplishment amongst the thirteenth-century Italian lyric poets who followed the troubadours. See Sordello in the Provençal section. above. A famous poem by the Provençal troubadour Folquet de Marseilles opens with the words 'Tant m'abellis'.

40   Arnaut's madness (as in lines 43–5 of 'En cest sonet', LII here) as a faithful follower of love was legendary.

41   The texts of the four poems by Dante which follow, and of Cino's sonnet, are taken with permission from *Dante's Lyric Poetry*, ed. K. Foster and P. Boyde (Oxford University Press 1967). 'Donne

ch'avete' is in *Vita Nuova* XIX, and it is the poem referred to by Bonagiunta in *Purgatorio* XXIV, 51 (XCVII here). It is the first *canzone* of the five in the *Vita Nuova*, and it comes at a very important stage of the work, when Dante, who previously has longed for Beatrice's greeting, is denied that greeting and sees that that denial is an essential stage in the upward development of his love. He therefore devotes himself for the future, not to winning his lady's favour, but to working her praise. This poem is the first example of this. (See *Vita Nuova*, translated by Barbara Reynolds, Penguin, London 1969, p. 54.) Charles Singleton argues that this solves the troubadours' dilemma and argument about whether *fin amor* was aimed at consummation or not (*An Essay on the Vita Nuova*, pp. 87ff).

42 In his commentary on the poem in the *Vita Nuova*, Dante divides the poem into three sections. The second, concerned with his lady's high reputation in Heaven as on Earth, begins here (Penguin, p. 58).

43 Dante himself, to whom Beatrice's death would be his Hell.

44 The *cor villani* is clearly of the heritage of the cognate words in Provençal: *villanejar*, etc. To modify the view that the *Vita Nuova* is an altogether new world (argued by Singleton, for example) one could compare Bernart de Ventadorn's 'Non es meravelha', (XLIV here) lines 9–10.

45 This address to the song might be compared with the end of *Donna me prega* (XCIV here).

46 *Vita Nuova* XX. Dante says he was asked for a definition of love, given in this poem, by a friend of his who had read 'Donne ch'avete' (Penguin, p. 59). The *saggio* of line 2 is Guinicelli, and the *dittare* is 'Al cor gentil'.

47 Dante's philosphical glossing of the poem (Penguin, p. 60) says that the first part shows love to be a potentiality in the heart that is made actual by the beauty of the wise woman (line 9). See note 7 on 'Al cor gentil' above.

48 For the sestina form, of Arnaut's 'Lo ferm voler', (LIII here). For an interesting discussion of the requirements of rhyme and assonance in the sestina, see Foster and Boyde, *Dante's Lyric Poetry*, vol. 2, pp. 78–9.

49 Dante says in *Convivio* III that the lady in this poem represents Philosophy. The *Convivio*, in general, glosses the poems of Philosophy in the same way as the *Vita Nuova* glosses the love poems. But there is a much less absolute distinction than this implies between the two kinds of poetry, since the latter is always the metaphor at least for the former, and Dante uses the term 'Amore' in a sense that embraces both. This poem is sung to Dante by Casella in *Purgatorio* II, 112, suggesting perhaps that this was one of the poems of Dante that Casella set to music.

50 For the image of the sun too bright for the eyes, cf. *Paradiso* XXX, 25,

and Petrarch *Canzoniere* XIX, translated by Wyatt as 'Some fowles there be that have so perfaict sight'.

51 Dante more than once refers to his poems as each other's sisters. The reference here (we learn from *Convivio* III, ix, 1) is to the canzone 'Voi che savete ragionar d'Amore' (Foster–Boyde, p. 104), which complains of this 'disdainful lady' (line 3).

52 Cino was a writer and teacher of law who taught Petrarch (who wrote a sonnet on his death). He was one of those who replied to Dante's challenge to expound his poem 'A ciascun' alma presa e gentil core' (see *Vita Nuova* III), and he wrote many exchanges of sonnets of the kind that were popular in the second half of the thirteenth century amongst the Italian poets (an extension, perhaps, of the Provençal *tenso* or *partimen*); hence Dante's observation that Cino is caught on every 'little hook' that tempts him to write an answering sonnet ('Io mi credea', line 6: Foster–Boyde, p. 202). Dante asks why Cino is so faithless and mercurial in love, and this poem is the reply. Clearly, the whole tradition has close affinities with Andreas's arguments about particular love-cases, especially in *De Arte* II, vii. Perhaps it was Cino's profession that inclined him so much towards these exchanges.

53 Cino was exiled from Pistoia in 1307, and he did not return until 1333.

54 The text of this poem is taken with permission from G. Zaccagnini, *I Rimatori Bolognesi del Secolo XIII* (Milano 1933), p. 118. Dante says Onesto was one of those who departed from his native Bolognese dialect (*De Vulgari Eloquentia* I, xv), and Petrarch names him among the vernacular poets in *Triumphus Cupidinis* IV, 35. This poem condemns the narrow imagery of the stilnovisti and their practice of writing poems to eath other.

Select bibliography

There is an immense amount of secondary material on Courtly Love, and this bibliography, attempting to deal with literature in several different languages, makes only a few suggestions, some of them a matter of redirecting to more complete lists. I have confined the suggestions to the principal works in English, except for some French works which are the central discussions. Many works are referred to in the notes to the various sections of the book, and are not repeated here. This brief list is an attempt to note the most important works in chronological order, to give some indication of the developments in the criticism of courtly love writings since Gaston Paris. I have not included the editions of particular writers, which appear in the notes. The division is self-explanatory; the considerable literature about the troubadours warrants a section of its own because so much of the discussion of courtly love has applied to them in particular.

1. COURTLY LOVE IN GENERAL

Gaston Paris, 'Études sur les romans de la Table Ronde. Lancelot du Lac. II – La Conte de la Charrette' (*Romania* XII, 1883, pp. 459–534).

L. F. Mott, *The System of Courtly Love studied as an Introduction to the* Vita Nuova *of Dante* (Boston, Mass. 1896).

W. A. Neilson, *The Origins and Sources of 'the Court of Love'* (Boston, Mass. 1899).

W. G. Dodd, *Courtly Love in Chaucer and Gower* (Boston, Mass. 1913).

T. F. Crane, *Italian Social Customs of the Sixteenth Century* (New Haven, Conn. 1920), Chapter 1.

M. Lot-Borodine, 'Sur les origines et les fins du *service d'amour*', *Mélanges Alfred Jeanroy* (Paris 1928), pp. 223–42.

T. P. Cross and W. A. Nitze, *Lancelot and Guinevere* (Chicago, Ill. 1930).

C. S. Lewis, *The Allegory of Love* (Oxford 1936).

D. de Rougemont, *Passion and Society* (trans. London 1940, from French *L'Amour et L'Occident* (1939)).

T. A. Kirby, *Chaucer's Troilus: a Study in Courtly Love* (Louisiana State University Press 1940).

J. J. Parry, trans., *The Art of Courtly Love*, by Andreas Capellanus (New York 1941). Excellent introduction; short, but useful, bibliography, p. 3, note 3.

J. S. P. Tatlock, 'The People in Chaucer's *Troilus*' (PMLA 56, 1941, pp. 85–104).

A. J. Denomy, 'An inquiry into the origins of Courtly Love' (*Mediaeval Studies* 6, 1944, pp. 175–260).

——, 'The *De Amore* of Andreas Capellanus and the Condemnation of 1277' (*Mediaeval Studies* 8, 1946, pp. 107–49).

——, *The Heresy of Courtly Love* (New York 1947).

T. Silverstein, 'Andreas, Plato and the Arabs' (*Modern Philology* 47, 1949–50, pp. 117–26).

A. M. F. Gunn, *The Mirror of Love: a Reinterpretation of the Romance of the Rose* (Lubbock, Texas 1952). Short bibliography of courtly love criticism, p. 327.

M. Valency, *In Praise of Love* (New York 1958).

M. Lazar, *Armour Courtois et fin' amors dans la littérature du XIIe siècle* (Paris 1964).

P. Dronke, *Medieval Latin and the Rise of European Love-Lyric* (Oxford University Press 1968).

F. X. Newman, ed., *The Meaning of Courtly Love* (University of

New York Press 1968).

H. A. Kelly, *Love and Marriage in the Age of Chaucer* (Cornell University Press, New York 1975).

R. Boase, *The Origin and Meaning of Courtly Love* (Manchester University Press, New York 1977). Contains an exhaustive bibliography, pp. 140–66: 'A selected bibliography'.

2. THE TROUBADOURS

H. J. Chaytor, *Troubadours of Dante* (Oxford University Press 1902).

J. Anglade, *Les Troubadours* (Paris 1908).

A. Jeanroy, *La Poésie Lyrique des Troubadours* (Toulouse/Paris 1934).

Simone Weil, 'A Medieval Epic Poem', and 'The Romanesque Renaissance', in *Selected Essays 1934–1943* (English trans., Oxford University Press 1962).

L. Spitzer, *L'amour lointain de Jaufre Rudel et le sens de la poésie des troubadours* (Chapel Hill, N.C. 1944).

A. J. Denomy, 'Fin' Amors. The pure love of the troubadours, its amorality and possible source' (*Mediaeval Studies* 7, 1945, pp. 139–207).

A. R. Nykl, *Hispano–Arabic Poetry and its Relations with the Old Provençal Troubadours* (Baltimore, Ms. 1946).

A. J. Denomy, '*Jois* among the early troubadours: its meaning and possible source' (*Mediaeval Studies* 13, 1951, pp. 177–217).

——, 'Concerning the accessibility of Arabic influences to the earliest Provençal troubadours' (*Mediaeval Studies* 15, 1953, pp. 147–58).

H. Davenson (H.–I. Marrou), *Les Troubadours* (Paris 1961).

P. Dronke, 'William IX and courtoisie' (*Romanische Forschungen* LXXIII (1961), pp. 327–38).

R. Briffault, *The Troubadours* (trans., Bloomington, Ind. 1965).

A. R. Press, *Anthology of Troubadour Lyric Poetry* (Edinburgh 1971).

R. T. Hill and T. G. Bergin, *Anthology of the Provençal Troubadours* (2nd ed., Yale University Press, New Haven, Conn. 1973).

L. M. Paterson, *Troubadours and Eloquence* (Oxford University

Press 1975).

L. T. Topsfield, *Troubadours and Love* (Cambridge University Press 1975). Wide-ranging bibliography, pp. 275–82.

3. OTHER LITERATURES

K. Bartsch, *Romanzen und Pastourellen* (Leipzig 1870).

G. Azais, ed., *Breviari d'Amor* of Matfre Ermengaud (Beziers/Paris 1862–81).

G. Paris, Preface to L. Petit de Julleville, *Histoire de la langue et de la littérature Française* (Paris 1896), vol. 1.

A. Jeanroy, *ibid.*, pp. 366ff: 'Les Chansons'.

M. Lot-Borodine, *La femme et l'amour au XIIe siècle: Chrétien de Troyes et son oeuvre* (Paris 1909).

P. Aubry, *Trouvères et Troubadours* (Paris 1909).

J. Anglade, ed., *Las Leys d'amor* of G. Molinier (Toulouse/Paris 1919–20), 4 vols.

G. Cohen, *Un grand romancier d'amour: Chrétien de Troyes et son oeuvre* (Paris 1931), ii and vii.

S. Painter, *French Chivalry* (Baltimore, Ma. 1940).

T. Frings, *Minnesinger und Troubadours* (Berlin 1949).

L. Spitzer, 'The Mozarabic Lyric and Theodor Frings' Theories' (*Comparative Literature* IV, winter 1952, no. 1; pp. 1–22).

C. S. Singleton, *An Essay on the Vita Nuova* (Harvard University Press 1949).

S. M. Stern, *Hispano–Arabic Strophic Poetry*. Studies selected and edited by L. P. Harvey (Oxford University Press 1974): chapter 5, 'Literary Connections', pp. 204ff.

Glossary of terms

This glossary contains words in several languages: Provençal, French, German, Italian and Latin. Many of the words (those for dawn-song, for example) are cognate in several languages and accordingly begin with the same letter; in such cases, there is a single entry for them all (e.g. *alba, aube, aubade*). But when the corresponding word is not cognate, it receives a separate entry with a cross-reference in the definition to the corresponding terms in other languages (e.g. *tagelied*).

Adynata. The figure of 'the world upside-down', whereby things are shown behaving in a manner which is contrary to their nature.

Affinar, afinar. To refine, make perfect, usually through love.

Alba, aube, aubade. Dawn-song of the parting of lovers. Cf. German *tagelied*.

Amor, amore, amors, amars. Love, with various implications depending on the form of the word or the writer by whom it is used. *Amars* is used by Marcabru and followers of his to mean evil, sensual love, by contrast with elevating, refining *Amors*. Likewise *amor entiers* is used by the troubadours to mean elevated, whole love (sometimes corresponding to the religious love of the tradition from St Augustine), in contrast to *amor frait*. This distinction is also made in the terms *entier cuidar* and *frait cuidar*.

Amor de lonh. Love from afar.

Bel Acueil. The son of Cortoisie in the *Roman de la Rose* who encourages the lover's suit and brings the lovers together: lit. 'fair uniting'. (He is probably the original of the bawd Bella Cohen in Joyce's *Ulysses*, according to Mr Mark Holloway.)

Bon Saber. 'Good knowing'; i.e. insight into proper procedure in love. The late courtly society in Toulouse, the *Gai Saber*, took its title from this phrase.

Canso. A love-song, sometimes opposed to the more serious 'vers' and 'sirventes'.

Chaitius. A captive of love.

Congé. A poem of farewell, particularly common among the *trouvères*.

Connoissensa, conoissensa, canoscenza. The power of discriminating understanding in love.

Cortezia, cortoisie. The virtues of the lover and their systematisation as a code of procedure to be followed.

Dangier. The figure in the *Roman de la Rose* who represents the lady's disapproving resistance to the lover's suit.

Devinalh. A riddle poem, the meaning of which was usually expounded in another poem.

Dienst. Love-service in the *Minnesang*, a term almost as wide as 'cortezia'.

Doc Regart. Sweet looks: the figure of the lady's encouragement in the *Roman de la Rose*.

Dorfspoesie. 'Village poetry'; the vigorous and straightforward anti-courtly poetry principally associated with Neidhard von Reuental.

Fin amor. True love, as opposed to *fals amor*, impermanent or superficial love. It develops the sense 'refined' which is related to Latin *finire*, in spite of the fact that the adjective in *fin amor* is linked etymologically with Latin *fidus*, faithful.

Foudatz. Foolish and immoderate behaviour in love, not governed by *mesura* or *sen*.

Gai Saber. Knowledge of courtly *jois*; the title of a late courtly society in Toulouse.

Gardador, gardiador. Watchman; whether friendly or not, he is always represented as an opponent of the lover's fulfilment. Cf. Arabic *raqib*.

Gilos, jalous. The jealous guardian of the lady, whether husband, father or uncle. Cf. Arabic *hasid*.

Goliardic. As used in the poetry of the Latin Goliards or *vagantes* who wrote short poems, mostly satirical or parodic. It is derived from the name 'Golias', associated in twelfth- and thirteenth-century manuscripts with these poems, particularly the so-called 'Apocalypse of Golias'. The name is probably derived from Goliath, for obscure reasons.

Hohe Minne. Elevated love, corresponding to Provençal *Fin Amor*. Opposite *Niedere Minne*.

Hoher Mut. Elevated spirit, modelled perhaps on Provençal *Jois*. The opposite is *Niedere Mut*.

Jois. The condition of fulfilment in the lover when his objective is attained. In different Provençal poets, it can mean either religious or sexual bliss.

Jongleur, joglar. Performer of a song or poem, as distinct from the *troubadour* or *trouvère*, who was the composer. The troubadours could sometimes be *jongleurs* too.

Lausengier, losengeour, lauzenjadors, etc. Lit. 'lying flatterer'; but this figure is the great enemy of the courtly lover, and tells tales and speaks ill of him. The German correspondent is the *lugenaere* (liar) or *merkaere* (censurer). Cf. Arabic *wasi*.

Locus amoenus. A love garden.

Malebouche. The evil speaker and tale-bearer in the *Roman de la Rose*. Though his name means the opposite, his role is often the same as that of the *losengeour*.

Meistergesang. The later, decadent courtly poetry of thirteenth-century Germany.

Mesura. Moderation, without which *foudatz* results in the lover. It corresponds to the dictating love which Dante claims to follow faithfully in *Purgatorio* XXIV, 53–4.

Minne. Love, the German correspondent of *amor*. See 'Hohe Minne' above.

Not. The pain of love.

Partimen (or *tenso*). Troubadour debate poem, corresponding to German *Wechsel*.

Pastorela. Pastoral, related to the classical tradition of such poems. In Provençal it is specifically concerned with the seduction of a gullible shepherd-girl by flattery.

Planh. Lament.

Pretz, proeza (Latin *probitas*). The courtly reputation of someone, especially of the lady.

Razo, ragione (German *rede*). The meaning of a poem or song, expounding separately.

Saber. Knowledge about love, gained by the power of reason. Cf. *Bon Saber* and *Gai Saber* above.

Sen. Sense, understanding: opposite of *foudatz*, q.v. above.

Senhal. The pseudonym adopted by troubadour poets, usually in the *tornada* (q.v. below). It often remains obscure to modern readers. Sometimes the person disguised by it is not the poet himself.

Sestina. A poem of six-line stanzas in which the lines of each stanza end with the same six key-words, but in different order. See LIII here.

Sirventes. Provençal poems of contemporary comment, usually social, and more serious than the *canso* which was concerned only with love. Because of his excellence in the form, Guiraut de Borneil was regarded by Dante as the foremost of the troubadours in rectitude. Cf German *sprüche*.

Solace. The joyful comfort of love.

Sprüche. The German moralising poems, corresponding to Provençal *sirventes*.

Tagelied. The German dawn-song, corresponding to *alba* and *aubade*.

Tenso. A debate poem in Provençal (like the *partimen*), corresponding to the German *wechsel*.

Tornada. The *envoi* in one or two stanzas that troubadour poems sometimes ended with.

Trobar. In Provençal, the art of composing songs, both words and music. Divided into the *trobar clus* (obscure), *trobar ric* (ornamental), *trobar leu* (easy), *trobar clar* (clear), and so on. But the precise indication of the terms is often unclear.

Trouvère. The northern French poet, corresponding to the Provençal troubadour.

Trûtlied. Pre-courtly popular German lyric.

Valensa, valors. The courtly virtue which made the lover meritorious.

Vilania. Worthlessness and incomprehension, which make a man unfit for love.

Virtu. In Italian, the essential power or nature of something.

Wechsel. A German poem, corresponding to the Provençal *partimen* or *tenso*.